Mundelein Voices

Mundelein Voices

The Women's College Experience, 1930–1991

EDITED BY

ANN M. HARRINGTON

AND

PRUDENCE MOYLAN

LOYOLAPRESS.

3441 N. Ashland Avenue
Chicago, Illinois 60657

Cover design by Herman Adler Design
Interior design by Amy Evan McClure

Excerpt from "Burnt Norton" in *Four Quartets* by T. S. Eliot, copyright 1936 by Harcourt, Inc. and renewed 1964 by T. S. Eliot, reprinted by permission of the publisher. Excerpt from "East Coker" in *Four Quartets,* copyright 1940 by T. S. Eliot and renewed 1968 by Esme Valerie Eliot, reprinted by permission of Harcourt, Inc. Excerpt from "Little Gidding" in *Four Quartets,* copyright 1942 by T. S. Eliot and renewed 1970 by Esme Valerie Eliot, reprinted by permission of Harcourt, Inc.

All photos, unless otherwise indicated, are reprinted courtesy of the Mundelein College Archives, Gannon Center for Women and Leadership, Loyola University Chicago.

The photo at the bottom of p. 47 is reprinted courtesy of the Chicago Architectural Photographing Company, David R. Phillips.

The photos on pp. 77 and 88 are reprinted courtesy of Blanche M. Gallagher, B.V.M.

The photo on p. 127 is reprinted courtesy of the B.V.M. Archives, Mount Carmel, Dubuque, Iowa.

Library of Congress Cataloging-in-Publication Data
   Mundelein voices: the women's college experience (1930–1991) / edited by Ann M. Harrington, Prudence Moylan.
       p. cm.
Includes bibliographical references and index.
   ISBN 0-8294-1692-7
   1. Mundelein College—History. 2. Women—Education
(Higher)—Illinois—Chicago—History. 3. Catholic Church—Education
(Higher)—Illinois—Chicago—History. I. Harrington, Ann M. II. Moylan, Prudence Ann.
LD3571.M4 M86 2001
378.773'11—dc21

                                                                00-067862

Printed in the United States.
01 02 03 04 05 / 10 9 8 7 6 5 4 3 2 1

DEDICATION

*To all those who served at Mundelein College
through the years, and to those who studied at
the college and carried its values into the
circumstances of their lives.*

*We remember especially Mary Griffin,
our colleague in the development of this
volume, who died suddenly in 1998.*

CONTENTS

PREFACE

This book marks the realization of a dream often expressed to me in the early 1990s by Ann Harrington, B.V.M., and Prudence Moylan. As history faculty members formerly at Mundelein College, now at Loyola University Chicago, they longed to capture the sixty-year story of the women's college where they both studied and taught—a place they loved. They claimed it was a history, a memory, a story that needed to be written. I encouraged them to pursue their dream, and a committee was formed.

I arrived at Mundelein College in February 1991 as an interim president. I was not a Mundelein graduate nor had I ever studied there. From community contacts, I knew many of the B.V.M. sisters and a few of the lay faculty. For the previous two years, I had been a member of Mundelein's board of trustees and was aware of the challenges facing the college as it dealt with resource issues, enrollment, and finances. With the resignation of Mary Breslin, B.V.M., as president of Mundelein, the chairman of the board asked me to consider taking that position. It was a difficult decision. I was coordinator of the Women's Office of the Sisters of Charity of the Blessed Virgin Mary and was committed to women's concerns. I believed in the value of women's education; I appreciated the dedication of the religious and lay faculty to the college; I knew the integral part Mundelein held within B.V.M. history. For those reasons, I resigned from my position and came to Mundelein College.

The three options facing the Mundelein board were to restructure either as an adult college or a traditional-age college, to realign with another institution, or—worst-case scenario—to close. In the end, on June 12, 1991, Mundelein College signed a memorandum of agreement with Loyola University Chicago. It was a transfer of assets and liabilities; no money changed hands. Through the agreement, a percentage of faculty and staff members was incorporated into the Loyola system, some of Mundelein's programs were integrated into Loyola's curriculum, and other programs were placed on a five-year trial for possible adoption. Students received the financial aid promised them by Mundelein and were allowed to complete their Mundelein College degrees on a specific timeline. The final Mundelein graduation took place in 1993.

The memorandum of agreement required an oversight administrator for a five-year transition period, and I came to Loyola in that position. In the fall of 1991, a small group of women faculty and administrators joined with me as a committee to ponder the possibility of a Mundelein center at Loyola that would focus on women. The outcome two and one-half years later was the creation of the Ann Ida Gannon, B.V.M., Center for Women and Leadership. Today it is an academic center as well as a heritage space for Mundelein College. It houses the Women and Leadership Archives, provides offices and meeting space for Loyola University Chicago's Women's Studies Program, and maintains the Institute for Women and Leadership, which sponsors conferences and activities that focus on leadership and changing the environment for the common good.

The center is named to honor Ann Ida Gannon, B.V.M., president of Mundelein College, 1957–74. Its mission is to transmit, in a new way, the heritage of Mundelein's concern for women and education. The establishment of the Gannon Center for Women and Leadership provided the opportunity to sponsor a writing project that could tell the Mundelein story. Barbara Baynes Mahoney, class of '53, introduced me to the Rice Foundation, and in January 1998 the foundation awarded a grant to support the Mundelein College History Project—the beginning of a dream come true.

This book captures the Mundelein story through memoirs written by its graduates and faculty. As liaison to Mundelein graduates over these past ten years, it has been my experience that each woman has her own Mundelein story, her own memory of a college experience alive in her heart. This also may be true for men, who first attended Mundelein College as graduate students, and later were admitted to the Weekend College program. A small number of men matriculated as undergraduates in the 1970s and 1980s, but the college never altered its identity as a women's college. Men attended with that understanding. The decade may vary, the faculty may have been young or old, the programs innovative or tried-and-true—the remark is always "my Mundelein." There are many more stories yet to be told. But today the dream is fulfilled. The first book is written. These stories renew memories and strengthen values. And they carry the spirit of Mundelein into the twenty-first century.

Carolyn Farrell, B.V.M.
Associate Vice President
Loyola University Chicago

ACKNOWLEDGMENTS

This volume of essays has been a labor of love. After the affiliation with Loyola University Chicago in 1991, the lack of any substantial collection of works relating to Mundelein College became painfully evident. Hence, the essays that follow. While we, the editors, took on the overall coordinating of the volume, we were assisted at every turn by our steering committee: Joan Frances Crowley, B.V.M.; Mary DeCock, B.V.M.; Mary Griffin (until her sudden death in 1998); and Mary Alma Sullivan, B.V.M.. They shared the brainstorming, decision-making, and information-gathering functions and so much more.

We acknowledge especially the ever-present help of the archivists in the Women and Leadership Archives. Archivist Valerie Gerrard Browne eased our path at each and every visit and was particularly helpful in preparing photos for use. Ann Ida Gannon, B.V.M., president of Mundelein College, 1957–74, and now archivist for the Mundelein College collection, proved to be an invaluable source of knowledge as we attempted to reconstruct various eras of the college. Also working in the archives, Jeanelle Bergen, B.V.M., provided us with lists and little-known facts that helped bring the past to life. Finally, the archivist for the B.V.M. congregation, Anita Therese Hayes, B.V.M., searched out items we could not locate in the Mundelein archives. Each of them deserves much praise for their constant patience and good humor.

Because any undertaking such as this needs funding, we owe a big debt of gratitude to the Ann Ida Gannon Center for Women and Leadership, and especially to its director, Carolyn Farrell, B.V.M., for many support services. We benefited from a grant she received from the B.V.M. congregation as start-up money for this project. For this, we are grateful. The secretaries, Nancy Hirsch and her successor, Carol Coyne, always received us most graciously and provided space and supplies for our meetings. We wish to thank in a special way the Daniel F. and Ada L. Rice Foundation for a substantial grant that allowed us to prepare this volume of essays in presentable shape for submission to our publisher, Loyola Press. Along those lines, without the expertise of Janet Boyd, part-time data entry, and Lillian Hardison, secretary for the Loyola University Chicago history graduate program, who helped us format the manuscript, our submission to the press would have been greatly delayed. And the Loyola Center for Instructional Design, especially Monica Salinas-Liening, helped us with the photographs that appear in the book.

Mary Lauranne Lifka, B.V.M., professor of history at Lewis University, and Paula Pfeffer, professor of history at Loyola University Chicago, both former Mundelein College history faculty, gave the essays a first reading and helped us reach greater clarity and precision in our writing. Mary Nowesnick, executive director of marketing communications and university publications at Loyola University Chicago and a Mundelein College graduate, served as the final copy editor before submission. At Loyola Press, we were first assisted by Vinita Wright and then steered through the final process by Rebecca Johnson. How grateful we are. However, for the content of the volume, including any errors that may have slipped through, we take full responsibility.

Ann M. Harrington, B.V.M.
Prudence Moylan
Editors

INTRODUCTION

We invite you to remember Mundelein through the stories told in this collection. Images form as in a kaleidoscope. Individual memories are the fragmentary pieces that, when turned and seen through the prism of Mundelein, make interrelated patterns. You may recognize your own college experience in these patterns, or you may be inspired to tell your story. The story of women's colleges begins with the foundation of Mount Holyoke female seminary in 1837. Mundelein College, established in 1930, was a relatively late arrival in this story. Mundelein claimed fame in 1930 as the first skyscraper college for women; in 1957 as the largest women's college in Illinois; and in 1991 as the last women's college in Illinois when Mundelein affiliated with Loyola University Chicago. Today there are eighty women's colleges in twenty-six states and the District of Columbia; twenty-three of these are Catholic women's colleges.

The history of Catholic women's colleges has yet to be written. This collection is not a history in the traditional sense of the term, although the essays are arranged in roughly chronological order. The authors include graduates, faculty, and administrators whose collective memories provide insight into familiar characteristics of Mundelein College that persist through the years. All of the authors in this collection chose their own subject, and they are all participants in the stories they tell, except for Mary DeCock who writes about the origins of the college.

The importance of the Sisters of Charity of the Blessed Virgin Mary (B.V.M.'s) in the story recurs as a pattern in all of the essays. Their story begins with five Irish laywomen who ran a school in Dublin. They decided in 1833 to bring their work to the United States, and that same year, with the help of the Reverend Terence J. Donaghoe, they founded the congregation in Philadelphia. By 1843 they had moved to Dubuque, Iowa, where they continued in the work of education. Today the sisters are involved in a variety of works and can be found in twenty-six states, as well as in Central and South America and Africa. The Second Vatican Council (1962–65) in the Roman Catholic Church directed religious congregations to renew and adapt their lives and institutions in light of their original charism. One of many changes that resulted was the opportunity for sisters to choose to retain their religious names or to return to their baptismal names. Yet another change came after the 1960s when the use of titles in everyday encounters among colleagues and students declined. Name changes presented a challenge to authors and editors. It proved impossible to find a single consistent way to identify sisters. So after a first full citation of an individual's name, the authors use the form of the sister's name most appropriate to their own experience with that sister.

In addition to the central importance of the B.V.M.'s, several more patterns recur in the essays. The Mundelein connection with the Catholic Church in Chicago appears most clearly in the essays by Mary DeCock, B.V.M., and Carol Frances Jegen, B.V.M. Ecumenical collaboration as a matter of historical record between institutions and as a personal experience of hospitality and shared values appears in essays by Stephen Schmidt, Nancy Bartels, and Carol Frances Jegen, B.V.M. The men in this collection comment on their reevaluation of assumptions about women in general and sisters in particular as a result of their work at Mundelein. Perhaps the clearest pattern is simply the joy of learning and the pleasure of meeting challenges and overcoming obstacles with intelligence and practicality. All the authors describe relationships with the place and the people as a life-changing experience.

The guidelines for this project emphasized not only our desire to explain events in the context of their times but also our intent to consider feminist perspectives. This encouraged contributors to include both ordinary and extraordinary experiences and to explore complex relationships of difference. All were free to interpret their experience as they wished but were asked to provide source material and references for their stories when possible.

In addition to soliciting the historical narratives for the book, the Mundelein History Project sponsored the development of archival material in the form of oral interviews and questionnaires. All the materials of this project will become part of the Mundelein College archives and the Women and Leadership Archives of the Ann Ida Gannon Center for Women and Leadership. We hope that these stories will spur others to expand the history of Mundelein College using this rich collection of sources.

Prudence Moylan
Ann M. Harrington, B.V.M.
April 13, 2000

❦ *Part One* ❦

Creating a College: The Foundation of Mundelein, 1929–1931

Mary DeCock, B.V.M.

The date was June 3, 1931. At the corner of Granville and Sheridan, six hand-some Chicago policemen astride shiny new City of Chicago motorcycles re-directed Sheridan Road traffic westward as they waited to begin their task of formal escort.[1] Just past the Sheridan Road curve, 384 students and 54 faculty formed a guard of honor up to the front entrance of Mundelein College, where the unflappable Sister Mary Justitia Coffey, B.V.M., waited in smiling anticipation for the motorcade to arrive. Cardinal George Mundelein was coming to formally dedicate the new skyscraper college for women that bore his name. By tomorrow morning, Sister Mary Justitia knew, Chicago papers would once more detail another Mundelein College first—the completion of one breathless, astonishing, dramatic year of academic pursuit in a building of landmark proportions that in the teeth of the deepening economic depression flashed all the external symbols of its staggering $2-million (mortgaged to the hilt) price tag.

Led by the all-girl uniformed bands of the St. Mary's and Immaculata B.V.M. High Schools, together with a colorful contingent of uniformed Catholic laymen—the Knights of St. Gregory—the cardinal would enter the Mundelein auditorium. There, he would address one of his most devoted constituencies and hear a masterful recital on the Kilgen liturgical organ, which still bears a plaque identifying it as his gift to the college. From there, he would work his way up to the fourteenth floor, blessing each classroom and lab as well as the sisters' living quarters, before returning to the main-floor, red-leathered Cardinal's Room for a brief reception.

In all, it was a spectacular conclusion to nineteen months' labor of astonishing proportions on physical, psychological, intellectual, spiritual, and financial fronts. If this all sounds inflated and a bit self-congratulatory, I thought so, too, until I researched this article. Now, I believe that the appearance of Mundelein College on the Chicago educational scene was at least a small miracle given the financial constraints of the depression, the principled idealism of the largely self-educated foundresses, the seemingly inexhaustible energies of the first religious and lay faculty, and the amazing support of the

B.V.M. congregation and of the sisters, pastors, students, and parents of the twenty-eight B.V.M.–run schools in the Chicago area.

So, in this essay, I will attempt to tell the story of the foundation of Mundelein College with fresh detail and perhaps fewer adjectives than heretofore. This will include negotiations between the B.V.M. congregation and Cardinal Mundelein that preceded the opening of the college, the acquisition and financing of the land on which the college was built, a brief description of the skyscraper building that housed the college, the education of sisters to teach and administer the college, the response of the first student body, and the overall coordination of these events by two remarkable women, Sister Mary Justitia Coffey and Mother Mary Isabella Kane, who saw their labors primarily as fulfilling the will of God and of Cardinal Mundelein.

Whether you call it a dream deferred or a series of false starts, the foundation of Mundelein College was a long time coming. The dream had to do with satisfying the need of the rapidly growing order of B.V.M. sisters to provide college educations for its members. The false starts represent the several times different B.V.M. leaders attempted to negotiate such an educational site in Chicago or Milwaukee. In some ways, the problem was the fruit of the sisterhood's own success. For the late nineteenth and early twentieth centuries brought the congregation an annual rush of new members—graduates of the many parish elementary schools in Chicago or of St. Mary's High School on the city's West Side. The sheer number of applicants quickly outpaced the ability of Mt. St. Joseph, the B.V.M. college in Dubuque, to accommodate them for summer study—the sisters' standard time for taking courses leading to a college degree.

But the real problem was traditional church law that hampered all orders of women religious. Women could not enroll in Catholic colleges run by and for men. Male members of religious orders could not teach members of the opposite sex in their classrooms. Sisters could not take classes from Catholic laymen. But—catch-22—pastors were advised to see that their parish schools were staffed by qualified teachers, and religious orders who staffed parish schools were obliged to establish teacher-training programs or normal schools that would ensure adequate preparation of sisters and brothers who taught the children. The sisters' solution to this problem was to set up their own institutes or houses of studies and engage qualified teachers to bring the classes to them.[2] Meanwhile, state certification boards tightened accreditation laws for public school teachers and threatened to extend their reach into parochial schools.

Between 1903 and 1929, three mothers general attempted to open houses of studies in Chicago, but their plans collapsed for various economic and political reasons: the money was urgently needed elsewhere, the Dubuque archbishop demanded their investments in Mt. St. Joseph, the opening of a sisters' college in connection with DePaul or Marquette looked promising but met with various types of resistance, the different geographical interests represented by voting members of the Mother General's Council outnumbered those from Chicago and put expansion plans there on hold. Meanwhile, sisters created their own alternative ways of self-education. They honed their teaching skills under master teachers, created their own workshops and extension courses, and sometimes enrolled at state universities and land-grant colleges to get the necessary degrees.[3]

It was against this background that three B.V.M.'s, Mother Mary Cecilia Dougherty (superior general of the order), Sister Mary Isabella Kane (provincial superior for the Chicago area), and Sister Mary Lambertina Doran (principal of St. Pius Elementary School on Chicago's West Side), arranged a "courtesy call" to the newly appointed prelate of Chicago, George William Mundelein.[4]

The date was February 22, 1916, a mere two weeks after his inauguration as the archbishop of Chicago. Behind their courtesy was a very practical matter. At the suggestion of the bishop of Dubuque, they wished to solicit Mundelein's assistance in obtaining from Rome permission to sell a piece of property in Chicago. The proceeds would give them funds to open a long-desired house of studies where sisters could make retreats and live while taking summer-school classes through DePaul and Loyola. To make the enterprise self-supporting, they hoped to use it during the year for educating some fourth-year high school students and perhaps a few college students—a small and affordable beginning for serving their many missions in the diocese.

The new archbishop's enthusiastic response broadened their modest horizons. Not only would he grant the permission, his agent in Rome would assist in obtaining it. Then he unveiled to them his cherished plan of creating a Catholic University of the West, a coalition of existing Chicago-area universities and colleges, supplemented by three colleges for women—one each on the north, west, and south sides of the city. The heart of this joint enterprise would be the diocesan seminary Mundelein planned to develop. He would authorize the sisters to borrow money to finance one of these colleges, visit the site that they selected for the building, and send priests from the seminary to assist them with lectures and classes. Because he liked a bit of competition among religious orders, he planned to recruit other orders of sisters for the other women's colleges.

According to Sister Mary Isabella's notes on the meeting, the discussion then turned to the advantages of not "thinking small" and of the need for much work and prepublicity to recruit students for a venture of such magnitude. The meeting ended with Mother Cecilia's agreement to return to Dubuque, where she would communicate the new opportunity to her councilors for their approval before she wrote to Rome for the permission to sell. The letter to Rome was drafted, but Mother Cecilia's efforts to solicit cooperation from her councilors did not succeed. On May 15 she wrote to Archbishop Mundelein expressing regret that the congregation was not able to finance a college in Chicago at that time. His response also expressed regret as well as hope for future funding by a wealthy benefactor.

The B.V.M. board of directors was only the first of many obstacles Archbishop Mundelein met in attempting to create his Catholic University of the West. The Jesuits at Loyola University and the Vincentians at DePaul University refused to yield their autonomy to Mundelein's new diocesan

Mother Mary Isabella Kane, B.V.M., superior general of Sisters of Charity of the Blessed Virgin Mary, Dubuque, Iowa.

seminary, St. Mary of the Lake. The Dominican Sisters of Sinsinawa agreed to build a women's college, but it ended up in suburban River Forest, not on the West Side of Chicago. DePaul University provoked Mundelein's rage by announcing intentions to open a division for women with B.V.M. Sister Mary Lambertina Doran as its dean.[5] His response was another letter to Mother Cecilia requesting her to open a central high school for girls on the North Side of Chicago. The answer to that request was the creation of Immaculata High School, but not until Mother Mary Isabella Kane was elected superior general. With Sister Mary Justitia Coffey as principal, the school opened in 1922 at Irving Park and the lake, and soon became a center for extension courses through Loyola University.

By 1928 the B.V.M.'s dire need for a women's college to educate their sisters in Chicago had subsided. Loyola, DePaul, and Marquette universities had opened their summer sessions to women. Catholic University of America had opened a summer extension program at Loras, the Catholic men's college in Dubuque. Nevertheless, Chicago's Cardinal Mundelein continued to pursue Mother Mary Isabella about opening a college for women on the North Side of Chicago. The time was hardly ripe for such an investment. A fund-raising drive had just been completed to provide an endowment for Mt. St. Joseph—now rechristened Clarke College. The opening of a college division at Immaculate Conception Academy in Davenport was under discussion. But Mother's seven pages of notes, dated "The Feast of St. Leo, April 11, 1928," summarize a conversation between the cardinal and some sisters that opened with "What is your Mother doing about the College?" and closed with an admonition to "carry the message to Mother and her Council and let them think about it." Some Chicago sisters had the now-Cardinal Mundelein's ear! Her notes describe a building to be.

> 75 ft. frontage. Run up into the air. Cafeteria and Gym below (swimming pool) the Classrooms above & the Sisters' quarters above the classrooms. Roof garden on top screened in for Sisters—terraces round top Near elevated station easy of access—not necessarily far from Immaculata. If you keep to the center of the city you will attract the girls in number of a 1000. Later on put up a dormitory building for out of town girls. Decidedly a day school. It is the first women's college in the city. The time is ripe now for a progressive Community like ours to make it the leading College in the city. It is a novel idea that will attract girls—It is the modern way of living. Why not have the expanse go up instead of spreading.

His Eminence wanted Rosary College to be strictly a day school and his idea had been to get the big people of the city to contribute scholarships about forty a year so as to attract and attract [*sic*] the crowd. The planning of the crowd. The planning of the staff and thought toward the college should begin now. I told the Sisters it must not be a part of the Immaculata. What difference if there should be street cars and elevated below if you are above it.[6]

There follow several pages of notes on zoning restrictions, property values, the thoughts of Chicago businessmen on the comparative costs of building in the suburbs, and of the competition with Loyola and DePaul should the enterprise be downtown. Her notes end with "The cost of ground and building would doubtless reach over a million dollars. And it would be more than a year until it would be ready."

On April 23 Mother Isabella updated her board of directors on educational problems that were on her agenda: "The matter of establishing a women's college in Chicago <u>as the Cardinal requests it</u>" and the decision "that a Junior College be opened in Davenport in September."[7] Then, armed with her councilors' support and the details gleaned by the Chicago sisters, Mother Isabella visited the cardinal and summarized her own interview with him on "April 25, 1928, Wednesday, Patronage of St. Joseph." Those seven pages in her black notebook record their sort of handshake agreement that she would discuss with her council plans that the proposed college should go forward "on the North Side near Loyola," although, she reminded herself, "if he could, he would like to have us in the Loop for transportation <u>facilities</u>." She offered her own interpretation of the interview. "The cardinal is a very rapid talker and it was difficult for me to get in all the points I had in mind—through effort I succeeded in representing to him conditions which made it difficult for us to undertake this gigantic work at this time."

Cardinal George Mundelein.

She then reminded him of the low salaries of sisters in the grade schools, the need for meeting the requirements for modern education, as well as the cost of preparing sisters for the faculty through studies at Catholic University and elsewhere. She also spoke realistically of the increased cost of property since the opening of Immaculata and agreed with his plan for a building, which by that time was referred to as "a skyscraper" (for which the cardinal's architect was already making sketches!). In closing, she reminded herself, almost as an afterthought, "Chicago is our recruiting ground for our Novitiate."

On April 27, 1928, Mother Isabella reported the above conversation with the cardinal to her board of directors. No action was taken at that time.

Her own decision having been made, Mother Isabella's thoughts now turned to property and finance. Her land searches on Chicago's North Shore had extended from Rogers Park to Evanston and Wilmette, and now real-estate queries in Rogers Park proved what she had suspected: few lots were available and they were very expensive. A lot at the corner of Sheridan and Thorndale, just five blocks south of Loyola, was available at the cost of $600,000—"more than was paid for Immaculata with two buildings included." A lot available on Loyola and Albion Avenues already was mortgaged for $225,000. By October 29 she was ready to travel to Chicago, where with Sister Mary Justitia, now a provincial, as her companion,[8] she met with the cardinal to discuss her options. Apparently, the discussion began with finances.

Mundelein presented his suggestion for financing the property in Rogers Park: issue bonds through "the Halsey Stuart Bond House" at the rate of 5 ½ percent, secured through a mortgage on the yet-to-be-built skyscraper; then use money from other congregational sources to buy back the bonds $1,000 at a time and accumulate the interest from the bonds. In effect her answer to his suggestion was: I think we could do better at the Continental Bank; we can take out a loan in the usual way and secure it with a mortgage on other properties we own. In light of the impending financial disasters that would soon shake the American economy, the impact of this decision was doubtless one of her most far-reaching for the B.V.M.'s and for the future of the college.

With Mundelein's blessing on that procedure, Mother Isabella proceeded to secure the vote of her board of directors, and on November 1, she applied for a loan of $500,000 from Continental Bank with mortgages on Immaculata and St. Mary's High Schools as collateral. After the building is completed, a Mr. Lewis of Continental assured her, she could refinance the loan at a lower rate of interest through an insurance or commercial loan company. Then (lest he be guilty of indiscretion), he would double-check his arrangements with the cardinal.

Mother Isabella's conversation with the cardinal on the difficulty of acquiring property had proved to be most useful. He expressed no interest in the land packages her agent had been pursuing, but offered to intervene actively in the acquisition of land. He suggested that she not mention the use of the property they were investigating until the first deed was acquired— property values would decline when residents discovered that their new neighbors would be college students. Mundelein's style of leadership was to investigate situations quietly, then act quickly.[9]

Mother Isabella's notes reveal that less than two weeks later, on November 12, Mundelein's agent, Frank Mulholland, entered negotiations with one Eugene McVoy for the purchase of a lot, 110 by 348 feet, at the corner of Sheridan Road and Devon Avenue on property adjoining the campus of Loyola University.[10] On that same day, she transferred to the cardinal the sum of $5,000 earnest money to secure the exchange. Twelve days later, Mother Isabella reported to her councilors that she had collected from B.V.M. houses $125,443.70 to pay for the land: $10,000 from St. Mary's High School; $5,000 from Immaculata; $20,000 from Our Lady of Angels Academy in Clinton, Iowa; $196.28 interest on the above deposits; $267.42 from Motherhouse funds; and $90,000 borrowed at 5 ½ percent interest from the Continental Bank, where she had opened a checking account. Then on December 4, 1928, the congregational treasurer, Sister Mary Realmo, with Sister Mary Justitia, visited the cardinal to deliver $120,000 to complete payment for the Sheridan Road property. In turn, he conveyed to them the deed of land ownership for 40 feet of land fronting on Sheridan Road in Linn's North Edgewater addition to Chicago.[11]

Only then, on December 14, 1928, with deed in hand, did Mother Mary Isabella inform the congregation of the cardinal's request to open a college in Chicago. But the announcement was no surprise to the sisters teaching there. The immediate response of students at St. Mary's and at Immaculata was a cooperative spiritual bouquet to the cardinal as a Christmas greeting. He registered his surprise in a post-Christmas letter to Mother Isabella, noting the significance of this rare act of cooperation between these two usually competitive student bodies.

By May 2, 1929, another of the cardinal's delegates had succeeded in securing 150 more feet of land on Sheridan Road adjoining the property already acquired. His negotiator for these transactions was his friend Jerome Kerwin; the price for the lots was $207,000, and the purchase included one house.[12] The cardinal's men had delivered a better deal than the sisters could have managed on their own. Mother Isabella's notes on the purchase seem rather wistful: $332,616.50 for property measuring 254 by 253 feet as compared to Mount Carmel's 120 acres on the Mississippi, plus the 320 acres on the Motherhouse farm. But, of course, the latter had been purchased at approximately $2 per acre!

With the land properly secured, plans already made for other aspects of the college began to surface. The cardinal's architect, Joseph McCarthy, submitted to Mother Isabella his first design for the skyscraper. It described a modern, steel, fireproof structure supporting brick facing with limestone trim. The first ten floors designated for classrooms covered 3,350,000 square feet and carried a price tag of $1,646,200. Floors eleven to fifteen were designated for convent living; they would cost only $449,999.34. Mother Isabella promptly informed McCarthy that the $2,098,199.34 sketch submitted was "beyond our means" and asked for a revision of the same with reduced costs. Versions two (submitted on July 23) and three (arriving on September 27) met the same fate. Somewhere during that period of time, Mother Isabella's own architect, Nairne Fisher of Dubuque, joined McCarthy as an associate architect for the building.[13]

Sister Mary Justitia's role in the college emerged quietly. On June 26, 1929, she submitted her resignation as provincial, but not before she had identified among the senior novices at Mount Carmel five college graduates to be sent on for further study. In recent interviews, three of those former novices, Sisters Mary John Michael Dee, Francine Gould, and Irma Corcoran recounted their substantially identical first encounters with this woman who was to be their first superior. Sister Mary Irma's account reads this way:

> On the day after profession, when Sister Mary Sylvester emerged from the room in which a provincial superior was giving directions to newly professed Sisters, I stepped into the place she had vacated and, I suppose, knelt—I believe that was the custom in those pre–Vatican II days—then rose and faced the serious but not severe face of the very large but well-put-together woman on whom in many ways my future would hang. Now, she greeted me by name and said, "Sister, you will go to Presentation [Convent] in Chicago and await further orders. Sister Mary

Albertona will be your superior while there, and you will live the regular community life. You will write to your parents once a month but to no one else." She smiled and extended her hand. "God bless you, Sister," she said. I said, "Thank you, Sister," and departed.[14]

While Sister Irma sweated out her undecided future at Presentation convent, Sisters Mary Francine and Sylvester (Geisler) struggled through their silence at Annunciation convent, while Sisters Mary John Michael Dee and Columba (Kriebs) pondered privately at Holy Family. When later in the summer Mother Mary Isabella came to the city, they learned directly from her that they would immediately begin full-time studies for master of arts degrees to prepare themselves for the opening of the new college in fall 1930. Sister Mary Irma, with undergraduate majors in history and French from Mt. St. Joseph, quaked at the thought of her assignment to Columbia University for a master's in English literature, with further directions to take at least one history course from the popular Catholic historian Carleton Hayes. Sister Mary Francine, who had majored in Latin at Mt. St. Joseph, accepted with resignation her assignment to St. Louis University for a degree in education, while her partner, Sister Mary Sylvester, was glad to pursue further studies in math and science. Sisters Mary Columba and John Michael discovered that their degrees from "secular universities" in Iowa and Kansas merited them the "trustworthy" distinction of continuing their studies for master's degrees in educational psychology and economics at another "secular" institution, the University of Michigan.

Then, on August 26, 1929, the whole congregation learned that Sister Mary Justitia had been appointed to "take charge of matters connected with the establishment of Mundelein College," an assignment ambiguous enough to encompass many roles. We now know that taking charge meant oversight of every detail of the erection of the Skyscraper, dealing with on-the-spot problems of architects, contractors, electricians, plumbers, deliverymen, and solicitors of all sorts. It also meant to furnish the Skyscraper, devise a curriculum, organize a faculty, and recruit a student body. So, on September 8, Sister Justitia and four youthful sister companions took up residence in the newly purchased house at 6367 Sheridan Road, which, according to Sister Mary John Michael, sometimes was grandly referred to as "the west campus," or at other times less grandly, according to Sister Mary Irma, as "the little green house."[15] Here she would demonstrate that—like the cardinal whose style of operation she had observed over her twenty-six years at St. Mary's and Immaculata—she could think big and go first class all the way![16]

Sister Mary Justitia was uniquely prepared for her job. The daughter of immigrant parents, she had discovered the B.V.M.'s while teaching in small parochial schools in western Iowa and entered the order in 1900.[17] After a year as directress of a fledgling community boarding school in Holden, Missouri, she became a Chicagoan. Plunged into the immigrant influx of the West Side as a teacher at St. Mary's High School, she made a reputation for herself in the public sector through the remarkable success of her senior students in passing the teacher's exams at Chicago Normal School. When the board of examiners threatened to put an annual quota on the number of St. Mary's students who could take certification tests each year, they encountered the resistance of Chicago's Archbishop James E. Quigley and opted once again for open competition.

Sister Mary Justitia Coffey, B.V.M., first president of Mundelein College.

In the early part of the century, when St. Mary's High School had doubled as a house of studies and as a summer center, Sister Justitia began her college education there with the Jesuits of nearby St. Ignatius College as "lecturers." During a one-year leave of absence from St. Mary's, she studied at Catholic University of America in Washington, D.C., taking courses and tutorials offered by laymen in a convent parlor because women still were not admitted to the campus of the bishops' university, where classes were taught by and for men. Returning to her teaching post at St. Mary's, she completed her course work through more extension and summer courses and earned her B.A. in philosophy in 1914. She began to study for her master's degree in 1916 through Jesuit Father Frederic Siedenburg's downtown school of sociology, the only Loyola University program that could admit women to its graduate courses. In 1922, one year after she built, organized, and opened Immaculata High School, she finally completed her master's degree in education. Experience left no doubt in her mind that young Catholic women needed strong Catholic women's colleges if they were to enter as equals into the competitive, male-dominated world.

Naming her new high school "The Immaculata," Sister Justitia kept the tuition low but adapted her style and the culture of the institution to the daughters of rising middle-class Catholics, careful at the same time not to offend the sensitivities of Irving Park's largely Protestant community.[18] Inspired by a cadre of youthful B.V.M. teachers, which Sister Mary Justitia exacted of Mother Isabella as a quid pro quo for accepting the demanding assignment, Immaculata's girls made their presence known to Archbishop Mundelein through their dramatic participation in Chicago's Eucharistic Congress, and to the Catholic Church at large by their enthusiastic work as sodalists in Jesuit Martin Carrabine's Chicago Interscholastic Student Catholic Action (CISCA). If St. Mary's had set out to Americanize Catholic education for the daughters of European immigrants, Immaculata introduced its young women to experiences of an energetic social Catholicism that directed their attention to soup kitchens, houses of hospitality, and the ugly facts of racial inequality.

So when the need for an experienced and qualified founder for a North Side Catholic college for women arose, both Mother Mary Isabella and Cardinal Mundelein knew who could do it. Sister Mary Justitia's academic preparation for the job may have been minimal in the eyes of accrediting agencies, but she had a wealth of experience and plenty of sheer drive. She tackled an assignment that would have daunted many a more cautious and credentialed educator. And she gave herself a year to launch the project.

Despite all the frantic activity in the little green house on the west campus during that initial year, life for the sisters was amazingly regular.[19] Bells were answered, meals and prayers occurred regularly and on time, and each day

Sister Mary Justitia, accompanied by one of the young sisters, took her morning walk around the neighborhood. En route, they finished their joint rosary, noted the progress of the new building at the Convent of the Sacred Heart at Rosemont and Sheridan, pondered Lake Michigan's deep blue waters, and inspected the overall progress of work on the Skyscraper. Thus (in the language of the religious tradition) the "superior" got to know her "subjects." The stories that gave birth to the myths of Mundelein College have survived that first year as though they were hard facts. Justitia the building supervisor had a sharp eye for detail, an instinct for flattery when needed, and an authoritative manner that demanded and got results. When she told workmen to take off their shoes before they entered the Skyscraper, did they really reach for their shoelaces? It is not impossible. Sister Mary John Michael vividly remembers that when Sister Mary Justitia called in the fire department to borrow long ladders for hanging drapes in the new auditorium, the firemen stayed and executed the hanging!

A practiced sense of public relations guided Sister Mary Justitia in her planning. She knew that the tuition must be low ($75 a semester), but the quality of education must be high. The cardinal may call it a "commuter college" and stress availability of transportation, but it must appeal to girls of all classes and be distinctive in every way from Immaculata. The academic curriculum must be strong and traditional, but—in true B.V.M. tradition—it must be practical, so business courses, home economics, and education should also be available. And all must be attractively presented. Good relations with the priests next door must be maintained, and she herself would keep an eye on "the wily Jesuits."[20] And the college, though new, must open with all the trappings of tradition. While unpaid bills waited for a less rainy day, she carried on a lively correspondence with a professor at Harvard whom she had hired to design the new Mundelein College coat of arms, flag, and shield, as well as a coat of arms for the B.V.M. congregation, which had never had one.[21] Most important, the unfolding story of Mundelein College must be told to the people of Chicago. For this, Sister Justitia's chosen assistant was Sister Mary Madelena Thornton—talented, charming, and disarmingly aggressive. A graduate of Mt. St. Joseph College with one whole year of experience as a teacher, Sister Madelena was eager to test her skills against the big-city press.

On October 21, 1929, the board of directors in Dubuque finally committed the congregation by vote to open the college in Chicago.[22] Groundbreaking day was set for November 1, the ninety-sixth anniversary of the founding of the B.V.M. congregation. The press kits were ready and the construction crew alerted.

Then, on October 29th, headlines informed the American nation that the stock market had crashed. Business came to a standstill.

But not at 6363 Sheridan Road. Even had the sisters foreseen the long-term consequences of that economic tragedy (and I assume they did not), it was too late to turn back. Work on the building had already reached the fourth floor. Madelena's first media event did indeed capture *Chicago Tribune* space for pictures of the rising structure on Sheridan Road. It also captured the imagination of the city. As the story was told later, "LaSalle Street trembled" at the brash undertaking by a handful of nuns on Chicago's North Side.[23] Because of that undaunted courage, the little community in "the new Sheridan Road convent" pinched their pennies mercilessly and sat down to Thanksgiving dinner—and many meals after that—nourished by a shower of food from Chicago's B.V.M. convents. The year 1929 was not a good year for B.V.M.'s to be without a steady income.

As the reality of financial disaster impressed itself deeply upon the world, Mother Mary Isabella took steps to rally the support of the congregation and marshall resources wherever she could. Chicago pastors received a courteous letter asking for whatever financial help they could give. B.V.M. schools from Seattle to Cicero were offered two ways to support the cause of the new college—with money or with books.[24] They could organize a competition among the schoolchildren to contribute pennies or nickels to a self-denial fund and so raise money for furnishing the new Mundelein College chapel. Sister Mary Ann Margaret Geary, then a first grader at St. Gertrude's elementary school, remembers how she begged her father for pennies to contribute and how he, in turn, would take her hand and walk with her to the lake where they watched the progress of "our new college."[25] To help stock the new library, which needed a collection of at least ten thousand volumes by opening day, the sisters could send books directly to Sister Mary Justitia. The most dramatic response to this request came from the Rev. John Rothensteiner of St. Louis. Informed of the collection by Sister Mary Callista Campion, who was at that time a University of Illinois student writing a dissertation on the life of this renowned German scholar, he sent two thousand books within the first year and eventually bequeathed his entire twenty-thousand-volume library, which became the heart of Mundelein's rare-book collection.[26]

Assembling an adequate faculty had been one of Sister Mary Justitia's long-term projects, one which benefitted greatly by her three-year stint as provincial. The five young women sent off to study were by no means the only ones prepared for teaching at the new college. The 1930–31 faculty roster lists at least fifteen sisters who earned master of arts degrees between 1928 and 1930, and four who were enrolled in Ph.D. programs. A few sisters brought distinguished records of teaching performance or scholarship from other B.V.M. institutions, and several of the "young sisters" Justitia had bargained for to open Immaculata followed her as teachers to Rogers Park. Positions the sisters couldn't fill were held by six laywomen, four of them specializing in physical education. Five laymen and seven priests (six of them Jesuits) staffed the departments of philosophy, religion, and political science. Loyola University generously accepted Sister Justitia's offer of five dollars per hour for the Jesuits' services instead of the usual ten.[27]

On August 15, 1930, Mother Mary Isabella appointed Sister Mary Justitia superior and president of Mundelein College.[28] The opening of the college was just six weeks away. Acting in her newer role as chairman of the board of trustees of Mundelein College, Mother Mary Isabella obtained authorization from her board of directors to take out yet another loan, this time secured by a mortgage on Mt. Carmel itself.[29] She also informed her councilors that she had granted permission to student sisters to stay out after dark while studying for a degree.[30]

On September 1, 1930, the sisters moved into the almost finished Skyscraper.[31] Two weeks later, on September 15, the school officially opened with registration. Where the three hundred young women who signed up before noon came from is not recorded. The plan had been to enroll only freshmen, but—apparently because of pressure from pastors—sophomores and juniors were admitted, too. According to Sister Mary John Michael, "Registration day was difficult. Yes, I said *difficult.*" Sister Mary Francine's recollection was more dramatic: "Registration day was a disaster."[32] To reorganize course offerings for the unexpectedly large student body, classes were postponed until October 3, the Feast of St. Michael. By that time, Sister Mary Justitia had held her first "administrative faculty" meeting and announced the library open for use. Housed in room 401 of the Skyscraper, the library's collection was classified, cataloged, and shelved in thirty days![33]

What exactly was meant by an "administrative faculty" is not clear, but end-of-year records do show that there were eleven standing faculty committees, each chaired by an experienced teacher, with regularly scheduled monthly meeting dates. Each of the nineteen departments offering a major was headed by a seasoned B.V.M. instructor, and by June of 1931 there were seventeen departmental clubs as well as eight interdepartmental "production" groups sponsoring all-college activities: a monthly newspaper, *The Skyscraper;* a college magazine, *Clepsydra;* a drama group, the Laetare Players; the Glee Club; the College Orchestra; the debate teams; the Sodality; and a college yearbook, *The Tower.*

The creation of the *real* college began in earnest with the arrival of the students.[34] By January, Sister Mary (Assisium) Cramer (then a freshman) remembers, "Some of the courses were very tough. But by the end of the first semester, we had rated the teachers on the length of assignments and on interest as lecturers."[35] Even without that assistance, 45 of the 384 students managed to make the first honor roll.[36]

In October they experienced the first of a lavish enrichment of such nonclassroom opportunities as celebrating the bicentennial of Virgil's birth (at a lecture by W. A. Oldfather, Sister Mary Donald McNeil's classics professor from the University of Illinois); meeting Father Daniel Lord, S.J., editor of a sodality magazine, *The Queen's Work;* and participating in the first Mass of the Holy Spirit. By May the young women had created their own extracurricular agenda, including a junior prom at the Drake Hotel, a boat ride on Lake Michigan, and a water carnival sponsored by the Terrapins, who had already captured second prize in a national swim meet. The elegant Social Room had been used for socials—bridge parties, receptions, gatherings with the Loyolans—and the tearoom had been used, among other things, for teas, some of them complete with hats and gloves. The college newspaper reported on them all.

The "Mundeleiners" joined with other Catholic-college students to mark the anniversary of Père Marquette's discovery of the Mississippi River, sponsored a CISCA convention for Chicago-area sodalists, attended an intercollegiate Calvert Club breakfast at the Blackstone Hotel, joined DePaul coeds for a sports play day, and participated in a model League of Nations assembly at the University of Chicago. But none of the above caused more stir than the decision that the debate team won over Loyola University's men who had "Resolved: That the Emergence of Women into Public Life Is to Be Deplored." Lest anyone suspect that the decision was a gentlemen's agreement, the Mundelein debaters also defeated Northwestern and Purdue, and lost their only match of the year to Yale.

In December the college offered its first public dramatic presentation, a Christmas play *The House of Life*. Sponsored by the drama department's Laetare Players as a "Special Benefit Performance with proceeds for Furnishings of the New Auditorium," it provided choruses and walk-on appearances for 250 students, and the program listed some 150 sponsors as well as two pages of "Facts You Ought to Know about Mundelein College." The play ran for three nights. Fox Movietone news shot drama-department scenes in advance and showed them in downtown theaters on Saturday night to encourage an audience. The proceeds of the play are not recorded, but the outcome of the event was priceless. The media had discovered Sister Mary Leola Oliver, the dynamic chair of the drama department. In the years to come, Chicagoans would know her student stars through their appearances in newspapers, on radio, in the theater, and in the movies.

The Christmas holidays opened with a candlelight ceremony that became one of Mundelein's most cherished traditions.[37] With the building in total darkness, candles gleaming in the windows formed a fourteen-story cross of lights. Sheridan Road traffic slowed to savor the richness, students huddled outside in the cold to view their own creation, and the next morning over breakfast, Chicagoans read about it in their newspapers. By the time the cardinal arrived in June for the formal dedication, Mundelein College was a household name in Chicago.[38]

To answer my original question, in what sense of the word can we call the foundation of Mundelein "a miracle"? Catholic scholar Richard McBrien gives as one definition of miracle "a special manifestation of God's presence."[39] Assuming that "doing God's will" is an aspect of manifesting God's presence on earth, let us look at the opening of Mundelein College and its three founders from the perspectives of religious and feminist studies.

In the academic jargon of today, the context of the foundation of Mundelein College was patriarchy, an organization of society in which power, property, and other resources, including gender roles, are controlled either directly or indirectly by an elite group of men. The three key figures in the foundation of the college were immersed in and handed on that tradition in different ways. Cardinal George Mundelein represented and operated in the world of the "fathers," where power speaks and those who use it wisely give glory to God by building the church. Appointed archbishop of America's second city, he envisioned creating the Catholic University of the West, and he needed the cooperation of the religious orders to achieve it. The men's orders simply refused to fit into his blueprint, but the women's orders were more vulnerable. Mundelein's contemporaries tell us he was not comfortable working with women, but in the era of woman suffrage, he needed an order of sisters to help him break new ground. The B.V.M.'s were that order.[40]

Mother Mary Isabella gave as her reason for opening the college George Cardinal Mundelein's "agitating." Mundelein's biographer, Edward R. Kantowicz, attributes Mother Isabella's decision to her frail health, the cardinal's flattery, and the desire to complete plans her predecessor had postponed.[41] Probably all of those factors swayed her decision. But in 1928 Mother Isabella had good reasons to decline the cardinal's demands. By that time, Chicago sisters had many opportunities to complete their education without opening another college. Mother Isabella was seventy-four years old, was halfway through her second term of office, and had completed eight major building projects, some of them still to be paid for. During Mundelein's tenure, she already had opened four elementary schools and a central high school in the archdiocese. A firm, decisive, and energetic woman, she had served the sisters and the cardinal's interests well, and no one knew that better than Mundelein himself. The provincials of her order now presided over their own power base in Chicago—a "separate sovereignty" of three hundred sisters, staffing two large central high schools and twenty-eight parish schools, seven of them on the North Side.[42] Good sister that she was, she undoubtedly heard the will of God speaking to her through the cardinal's wishes—she should cooperate in rescuing young women from the godlessness of Northwestern University and the University of Chicago.[43] But she was also an artist and a builder. What better capstone to a long and challenging career than a skyscraper that she helped create from the ground up?

Sister Mary Justitia shared the cardinal's educational vision as well as some of his characteristics. She recognized his power and flattered him by honoring it. Her dealings with him were surrounded by pomp and ritual. It was she who named the college Mundelein, organized the motorcycle escort, and prompted the students to present him with an American flag to fly over one of his pet projects, the College of the Propaganda in Rome where North American seminarians studied.[44] Her reward was a blessing of the college from the Holy Father and visits from Cardinal Mundelein's friends from the Vatican who willingly exclaimed to the press about his college by the lake.

Sister Mary Justitia also signed her letters to her mother superior as "your loving child," a recognition of her niche in the hierarchy of the religious order.

In turn, she expected obedience from her sisters. Tradition tells us that failure to conform to her orders (or perhaps even her expectations) sometimes could meet calculated reprisals—a cold shoulder, a humiliating reprimand. Those who measured up to her expectations got the dubious reward of more and more difficult tasks, as well as a gesture of support or encouragement.

As in all Catholic colleges of the time, the structures of hierarchy were built into the procedures. Hands-on superiors were expected. Within their own realms of expertise and authority, faculty were "free" to the extent that they recognized the boundaries of Catholic orthodoxy and the criteria of good taste, which were expected of all. Students were expected to study and encouraged to create and excel. Education for the B.V.M.'s was not mere "women's work," but a mission to be accomplished, a career to be proud of.

Within their shared patriarchal world, the three founders of Mundelein College saw Catholic education as a means of Americanization.[45] Within that context, their particular leadership styles developed and made their imprint upon the women they educated. What imprint might we expect?

As a fifth-generation American educated in Rome, Cardinal Mundelein had as his goal the development of a church in Chicago that was 100 percent American but also 100 percent devoted to the doctrine of the Catholic Church. As prelate in Chicago, he correctly identified the B.V.M.'s as women who shared his admiration for Americanization.[46] As a Catholic, he preached the dignity of women, and as an American, he asserted the equality of women and promoted their education, but he struggled to understand the unsettling fact of woman suffrage.[47] The mixed message of that struggle appears in striking clarity in his address to the graduates of Mundelein College in 1934.

> You are the pioneers of that group of Catholic women who combine within themselves the training they have received from a Catholic day college together with the influence of a good Christian home. We need you to be leaders of a great army of Catholic women. A great privilege has been given to you. First, that of equal suffrage with men. We are going to call on you to use it for the protection of the home, the church, and the country in the struggle against those loud-mouthed busy-bodies of women who so often sponsor vicious and destructive legislation, arrogating to themselves the right to represent and to talk for their sex. When such a danger threatens, then, wherever you are, listen to the warning voice of your church. We look to you then to think, to speak, and to act for Catholic womanhood—to worthily represent us.[48]

Equality was limited to suffrage; public policy was the realm of the hierarchy.

The two women who cooperated closely with Cardinal Mundelein in the foundation of the college were also 100 percent American and Catholic, and they were longtime good friends. Mother Isabella arrived in the United States at age ten, an Irish immigrant like her parents. For four years she lived in Holy Family Parish in the heart of Chicago's West Side melting pot before joining the B.V.M.'s, an American order founded in Philadelphia in 1833. Sister Mary Justitia, the American-born daughter of immigrant Irish parents, joined the B.V.M.'s as a young adult and three years later began an eighteen-year teaching stint at St. Mary's High School near Holy Family Parish, the school that first attracted Mundelein's attention to the B.V.M.'s.

As spiritual followers of Mary Frances Clarke, the Irish immigrant founder of the order, who was herself committed to Americanizing young women,[49] both Mother Isabella and Sister Mary Justitia regarded themselves as "fit instruments in God's hands for the salvation of souls," a community prayer adapted from St. Ignatius Loyola, founder of the Jesuits. These two exceptional women were talented, creative, tireless, and committed to mission. And they were Americanizers.

Mother Isabella (baptized Mary Veronica Kane) grew to adulthood and obtained her education as a teacher of art and music in a world of women— the Iowa high school boarding schools conducted by the B.V.M.'s. She learned to exercise power in a variety of situations during the fifteen years she served as a local superior and principal. She was committed to educating young women. As mother general she gained recognition in the world of men as an outstanding builder of high schools and institutions for women.

Sister Mary Justitia received her early education in the public schools of North Hadley, Massachusetts, and her early teaching experience in the schools of rural Iowa. Her competitive sensibilities were nurtured through preparing young women to achieve success in the Chicago public school system, which at that time did not welcome Catholic teachers. She was a perfectionist. Her attitude toward women was to educate them to be leaders, to be the best they could be, and above all to be loyal daughters of the church. Her philosophies of education and womanhood were Catholic in outlook, and they were hammered out in the patriarchal world of experience.

At first glance, a coalition of these three leaders seems unlikely. But from 1916 (the year of Mundelein's arrival in Chicago) to 1929, they worked together toward a common goal and grew to understand each other's styles of leadership. It was no surprise to anyone when, at one of their several meetings preceding the decision to build a North Side women's college, Sister Mary Justitia initiated a conversation that went something like this: "And you agree, your Excellency, that we name the college after you?" To which the Cardinal laughingly responded: "As I mentioned to one of the Jesuits at Loyola this morning, I suppose I will have to allow you to do this for commercial purposes." And Sister's response: "Not at all, your Excellency. The inspiration in the project is yours, and we recognize your great interest and kindness toward our community. We would be honored if the college could bear your name."[50]

**Cardinal George Mundelein with his niece Rita Eppig
at graduation, June 1934.**

Mother Isabella was the first member to drop out of the team. In January of 1930, with the Skyscraper completed and the college incorporated in the State of Illinois, she secured the future of Mundelein College by refinancing the debt on the building. The new loan ($1,500,000) through the Mercantile National Bank in St. Louis, was backed by mortgages on six B.V.M. schools in Illinois, Iowa, and Kansas.[51] Shortly thereafter she completed her second term as mother general. Then, in 1933 she received her first college degree, an honorary doctor of laws from Loyola University. It mentioned her tact, courtesy, and kindness and her "beneficent influence on the spiritual and intellectual well-being of her religious congregation." It did not mention that, after a lifetime of accumulating courses while serving in various positions of community leadership, she had finally acquired—at the age of sixty—a high school diploma from St. Mary's High School, while serving there as provincial.[52] When Mother Isabella died in 1935 at the age of eighty, Sister Mary Justitia lost her best friend.

On October 2, 1939, a stunned Chicago learned of the sudden death of Cardinal Mundelein, whom a *Chicago Tribune* columnist described as "the most influential Catholic in the world . . . next to the pope."[53] His last act had been to draft a speech to be delivered the next day on national radio, supporting the war plans of President Franklin D. Roosevelt, who had come to regard the cardinal as a friend and political advisor. Mundelein's funeral was peopled with cardinals, bishops, politicians, priests, sisters, and laity. And as her last act of homage, Sister Mary Justitia arranged to have his funeral cortege to Calvary Cemetery move solemnly up Sheridan Road past the college he had learned to call his "God-child."[54] She had lost a reliable partner. The future of the college was in her hands.

Sister Mary Justitia served as president of Mundelein College for twelve years, with a three-year interval off from 1936 to 1939 to meet the demands of canon law.[55] In 1945 she turned over to her successor, Sister Mary Josephine Malone, a nationally known, fully accredited college with a highly qualified faculty and an enthusiastic student body of more than nine hundred. Within a few years it would become the largest Catholic college for women in the United States. The basic academic and administrative structures then in place would serve the college until the 1960s. The education it offered combined the classical arts and sciences and the practical arts of business and home economics, and the college recognized the value of experience-based learning, which depression-era students acquired of necessity. The culture of the college was woman-oriented; it honored family and motherhood, combined with a distinct career orientation and a bent toward involvement in the life of the church and society. It was 100 percent Catholic, stressing traditional respect for the clergy, individual piety, and concern for social action. And it was 100 percent American—during World War II, Mundelein College promptly became a training center for women recruits to military service.

Sister Mary Justitia, with the long-suffering support of her overworked faculty, had completed her presidency with distinction. Kantowicz aptly describes her as a "shrewd and able administrator." Those who knew her well describe her as "competent and nervy, with an instinctive know-how in what had to be done NOW, and how it could be done quickly and most economically without sacrificing quality"; "interested in her teachers . . . open, kind, fair, and persuasive . . . a large woman with a heart as big as her person"; "one great, good woman and religious."[56] She had measured up to her assignment. Under her direction, the college had survived and flourished. Survival was the small miracle.

Endnotes

1. Program of dedication, O.1.2.1, Mundelein College Archives (MCA), Gannon Center for Women and Leadership, Loyola University Chicago. In an interview on June 12, 1999, Sister Mary John Michael Dee, a faculty member when the college opened, recalled that Sister Mary Justitia had requested of the chief of police in Chicago "six of your most handsome police officers on six handsome horses." The chief promised the officers but could not spare the horses. The arrival of the men on brand-new motorcycles was a pleasant surprise. The six chosen policemen reported years later that their colleagues never let them forget their chosen status as "most handsome."

2. Decree 205 of the *Acta* and *Decreta* of the Third Council of Baltimore in 1884 ordered all bishops—"if need be, invoking the authority of the Sacred Congregation"—to confer with superiors of congregations dedicated to teaching about establishing normal schools for teacher preparation. See J. A. Burns, *The Growth and Development of the Catholic School System in the United States* (New York: Benziger Brothers, 1912), 110. Quoted in Jane Coogan, *The Price of Our Heritage II* (Dubuque, Iowa: Mount Carmel Press, 1978), 458. Both *house of studies* and *sisters college* as used in B.V.M. documents refer to houses owned by religious orders where sisters could live while taking college courses taught by university professors or other qualified instructors brought in for that purpose, or eventually as places for sisters to reside while studying at a nearby university.

3. The restrictions imposed by the Third Council of Baltimore in 1884 eroded slowly. In 1893 Mother Gertrude Regan purchased land in Chicago for a house of studies, which never materialized. In 1894 Mother Cecilia Dougherty organized an academic "curriculum" for new members, as well as institutes conducted by B.V.M. "master teachers" for those already teaching. In Chicago, sessions were held on three Saturdays every month, and sisters traveled from all over the city to the parish

schools where the classes happened to be held. With the opening of St. Mary's High School in 1899, sessions were held there and lectures were given by the Jesuits from nearby St. Ignatius College. Then in 1905 the bishops' own Catholic University of America initiated correspondence courses for sisters and traveling summer lectures and institutes given by laymen from their Department of Education. Two years later, when Marquette College in Milwaukee gained university status, the Jesuits petitioned their father general for permission to admit women to study; three years later that permission was granted over the objection of some of Marquette's own Jesuit stalwarts! By 1911 Mother Mary Cecilia was negotiating unsuccessfully to open a sisters college at DePaul and/or Marquette. Then in 1912 she negotiated successfully with Catholic University to admit six B.V.M.'s as students in degree programs with classes taught by laymen in the living room of a Benedictine convent in Washington, D.C. In 1913 Father Frederic Siedenburg, S.J., opened a school of sociology affiliated with Loyola University Chicago, but "off campus" in the Loop, and admitted women to summer, evening, and Saturday classes; by 1915 the Jesuits were traveling to convents to offer sisters classes which would count toward a degree at Loyola. By 1914 Catholic University established an extension for sisters at Dubuque (Loras) College. Before the opening of degree programs to sisters, individuals earned credits from various places, and Mother Mary Cecilia negotiated individually for their degrees from Catholic universities, or sisters attended secular institutions, particularly land-grant colleges, which offered specialized programs such as home economics that were not available at Catholic universities.

4. Mother Mary Isabella Kane's small black notebook, Sisters of Charity of the Blessed Virgin Mary (B.V.M.) Archives, Mount Carmel, Dubuque, Iowa (B.V.M. Archives). Unless otherwise stated, all references to Mother Mary Isabella's activities are from this source.

5. Coogan, 416. The April 17, 1917, issue of the *DePaul Minerva* carried the story. This cooperative venture had been encouraged by Archbishop Quigley before Mundelein's arrival. After Mundelein's refusal, the coed venture became DePaul High School for Girls with Sister Mary Lambertina as its principal. The school closed when Immaculata opened five years later.

6. Mother Mary Isabella Kane's small black notebook.

7. Minutes of the Board of Directors, B.V.M. Archives. All underlines are M.M.I.'s.

8. When Sister Mary Justitia's term as superior/principal at Immaculata ended in 1927, Mother Mary Isabella named her provincial of Holy Family province. This appointment endowed her with the power to negotiate faculty appointments to the various schools under her aegis.

9. Edward R. Kantowicz, *Corporation Sole: Cardinal Mundelein and Chicago Catholicism* (Notre Dame: University of Notre Dame Press, 1983), 11.

10. Deeds and titles for all land purchases for Mundelein College are in the Mundelein College Archives, A.1.2.c.

11. Lot 7 and east 30 feet of lot 6; west 10 feet of lot 8.

12. Lot 4 and west $\frac{1}{4}$ of lot 5 in Linn's North Edgewater addition, from John Jacobson

and Kate Jacobson for $90,000. East 45 feet of lot 5 and west 30 feet of lot 6 in Linn's North Edgewater addition, from Lillian R. and Frank H. Johnson, for $117,000.

13. Fisher had worked with Mother Isabella on the remodeling of the motherhouse and on several high school building projects, the most recent having been Holy Angels Academy in Milwaukee, erected in 1928.

14. Irma Corcoran, B.V.M., "A Life with Sister Mary Justitia Coffey, 16 August 1929– 5 November 1947," MCA.

15. Eventually, the little community in the green house numbered fifteen. The hilarity of recurring chaos that marked their struggle for survival there is recounted with wit and detail by another of the young sisters, Sister Madelena Thornton, author of *The Chronicles of Mundelein College for the Years 1930–1957,* vol. 1, 1930–1936, MCA.

16. Kantowicz, *Corporation Sole,* 3.

17. Sister Mary Justitia Coffey Papers, E.1.4, MCA.

18. The school's unblushing adoption of symbols of such middle-class culture, especially naming the school The Immaculata, raised the eyebrows of some faculty and students of St. Mary's, who stressed instead their school's egalitarian and democratic traditions. Remnants of competition between the two institutions are still alive in the two alumnae associations.

19. Corcoran, "A Life with Sister Mary Justitia Coffey."

20. Sister Mary John Michael recalls that, initially, the Loyola University administrators were less than enchanted at having a new women's college next door and with the cardinal's request that they provide faculty for the departments of religion and philosophy. Sister Mary Justitia's correspondence with the Loyola Jesuits reveals that she dealt with them respectfully, but that she also presented herself successfully as an administrative equal.

21. Pierre de Chaignon la Rose, a specialist in medieval heraldry, was on the faculty at Harvard. He designed a coat of arms, college shield, flag, seal, and banner for Mundelein College, combining a book, a star, the B.V.M. symbol, and the phoenix with its reference to Chicago rising from the ashes of the Chicago fire. Asked about the appropriateness of the phoenix, Mother Mary Isabella approved of it as "better than the wolf" on the Loyola banner!

22. Minutes of the Board of Directors, B.V.M. Archives.

23. Scrapbooks, 1929–30, MCA.

24. Correspondence of Mother Mary Isabella, B.V.M. Archives.

25. By June, seventy-five parish elementary schools had collected $14,489.42 for the chapel. St. Charles on Chicago's West Side topped the list with $1,745; schools in Tigard, Washington, and in Fort Dodge and Marcus, Iowa, turned in $5 each.

26. Rothensteiner Collection, G.9.I.a., MCA.

27. Sister Mary Justitia Letters, E.3.A, MCA.

28. To have done so earlier would have shortened her time as president after the school opened. According to canon law at that time, a superior could serve only six continuous years, and the B.V.M.'s did not see fit to separate the two offices until 1955.

29. Minutes of the Board of Directors, 30 August 1930, B.V.M. Archives.

30. Minutes of the Board of Directors, 9 September 1930, B.V.M. Archives.

31. Because of the depression, labor was plentiful and the building was completed in approximately sixteen months.

32. Sister Mary John Michael Dee and Sister Mary Francine Gould interviews by author; tape recordings, June 12 and 19, 1999, MCA.

33. *The Chronicles of Mundelein College for the Years 1930–1957,* Vol. 1, 1930–1936, MCA.

34. Final registration was 384 young women—250 freshmen and 134 sophomores and juniors.

35. Conversation with the author, June 18, 1999.

36. *Skyscraper,* January 1931, MCA. Student events are recorded in the *Mundelein Chronicle* and elaborated in the student newspaper, *The Skyscraper,* which began monthly publication in January 1931.

37. When Mundelein College merged with Loyola University Chicago in 1991, a revised version of the candle-lighting ceremony became the first transplanted Mundelein tradition.

38. Scrapbook, 1930–31. During its first year of operation, Mundelein was featured in at least fifteen major stories in the *Chicago Tribune* and the *Chicago Daily News.* MCA.

39. *Catholicism,* study edition (Minneapolis, MN: Winston Press, 1981), 1249.

40. Kantowicz, *Corporation Sole,* 94.

41. Ibid., 96.

42. *Separate sovereignties* is the phrase Kantowicz uses in describing the power bases pastors of ethnic parishes created through their schools, organizations, colleges, etc. B.V.M.'s shared those ethnic power bases through their schools in Irish, Italian, and Czech parishes, but their real power base was in the sheer numbers of schools and teachers in the Archdiocese of Chicago.

43. This is one of the arguments Cardinal Mundelein used for opening women's colleges.

44. *The Skyscraper,* Vol. 1, 4,1.

45. Adaptation of immigrants to the language, structures, and procedures of life in the United States.

46. "When I came here, I found St. Mary's High School, a school where girls of all classes meet on an equal footing, where the only aristocracy is the aristocracy of brains. The methods of this institution are marked by briskness of attack. The girls are prepared for active service in the school, in commerical life, and in the home." Archbishop Mundelein's address at the St. Mary's High School commencement

shortly after the opening of Immaculata in 1922. Cited in Coogan, *The Price of Our Heritage*, 272–3.

47. Most members of the American Catholic hierarchy had opposed the suffrage movement as contrary to women's nature. When the Nineteenth Amendment passed in 1920, Mundelein, then archbishop of Chicago, attempted to reconcile that fact with his 100 percent American and 100 percent Catholic formula.

48. Papers of Cardinal Mundelein, MCA. A.6.1.a.

49. Mary Frances Clarke, an early proponent of the Iowa boarding schools for girls, drew no distinctions in teaching students of any class, religion, or ethnic background and accepted young women of any nationality into the order.

50. Mother Isabella to her councillors, 24 November 1928. B.V.M. Archives.

51. Minutes of the Board of Directors, 2 January 1931, B.V.M. Archives. The schools were St. Mary's and The Immaculata in Chicago; Immaculate Conception and St. Joseph Academies in Davenport and Des Moines, Iowa; and Mount Carmel Academy in Wichita, Kansas.

52. In 1915 St. Mary's validated the credits she had received from various B.V.M. high schools. Her resume also lists some forty courses in art, languages, and music from private tutors, from the Art Institute in Chicago, the Kansas City Academy of Music, as well as several taken through Catholic University when she was provincial.

53. Gerald P. Fogarty, *The Vatican and the American Hierarchy from 1870 to 1965* (Wilmington, Del.: Michael Glazier, Inc, 1985), 203.

54. Mundelein College Commencement Address, 1934, Cardinal Mundelein Papers, A.6.1.a. MCA.

55. During that three-year interval, Sister Mary Consuela Martin, B.V.M., was president of Mundelein College.

56. Comments from interviews with Sisters Irma Corcoran and John Michael Dee and the correspondence of Angela Fitzgerald, D.1.1.a.5, Mother Mary Isabella Correspondence, MCA.

The Mundelein Skyscraper: Building Space for Women

Prudence A. Moylan

In October 1928 Virginia Woolf explored the importance of *A Room of One's Own* with women at Newnham and Girton Colleges in Cambridge, England.[1] In October 1929 the Sisters of Charity of the Blessed Virgin Mary (B.V.M.), led by Mother Mary Isabella Kane, began construction on a skyscraper college. The B.V.M.'s were building many rooms that women could call their own. The Skyscraper, Mundelein College, still stands as a public landmark to the work of the Sisters of Charity, B.V.M., in educating women. In 1991 Loyola University Chicago acquired the Skyscraper in an affiliation agreement that ended Mundelein College's existence as a women's college. This essay explores the many meanings attached to the Skyscraper: Mundelein College for Women, 1930–91, through an examination of the building in its urban context, of the varied uses of its interior space, and of the memories of those who called it their own.

The study of women's spaces has achieved historical significance in recent decades thanks to the innovative work of scholars in public history, urban history, and women's history.[2] The National Park Service has committed itself to identifying buildings that reveal women's historical place and influence in the landscape.[3] On December 8, 1980, Congress authorized the Seneca Falls site of the first women's rights convention as a national park.[4] In the same year, the Skyscraper was listed on the National Register of Historic Places in celebration of its golden jubilee.[5]

These new approaches to history enabled me to develop new insights into the significance of the Skyscraper as a building and a college. This task has become not only an intriguing research project but also a way of theorizing my experience of forty years working and briefly living in this space as a student and as a faculty member. After the affiliation of Mundelein with Loyola in 1991 I began to see the Skyscraper as a keeper of my memories, a memorial for much of my life's work. Historic preservationists have always recognized that places are keepers of our cultural memory. When Ann Harrington, B.V.M., and I initiated the Mundelein History Project in 1997, I came to see the Skyscraper as more than the keeper of my memories. It was a public landmark and memorial of the history of the women who lived and worked in it. I hope the results of my research and reflection on the importance of this building will renew memories and develop understandings on how the Skyscraper expressed Mundelein's relationship to Chicago, its urban environment. The analysis and appreciation of exterior form and interior space may illuminate for us the vision of the women who created and used it. It has been my pleasure to deepen memories of Mundelein College through research and reflection on the Skyscraper. The historic preservation of the Skyscraper as a site of cultural memory honors both women's learning and women's leadership.

Mundelein College and the City of Chicago

The architecture of the Skyscraper connected it with the dynamic developments of the city of Chicago in 1929. Modern style, the dominant style in the period 1923–32, reached its peak of popularity in 1929. In that year, while the Skyscraper was rising at Sheridan Road and the lake in Rogers Park, the Palmolive Building and the Board of Trade were both built in downtown Chicago. Art historians credited Eliel Saarinen's second-prize entry in the 1922 competition for the Chicago Tribune Tower with providing the design inspiration for the skyscraper of the 1920s. Soaring vertical lines with "rhythmic piers and corner accents flowered into admirably proportioned setbacks at the top" described not only Saarinen's design but also most modern buildings.[6] Kenneth Frampton explained the style, which did not correspond to any historical precedent, as having "arisen out of a spontaneous desire to celebrate the triumph of democracy and capitalism in the New World." Frampton identified it as "an exclusively urban style . . . reserved for the worldly realm of offices, banks, department stores."[7] The B.V.M.'s, however, confidently claimed this urban style for their college.

Mother Isabella Kane decided in consultation with Cardinal Mundelein in 1928 that the sisters would build a skyscraper. Land was so expensive that a skyscraper college would "save time for students as well as save on property investment."[8] As an artist and builder, Mother Isabella realized that while steel and concrete were the necessary technical elements of the skyscraper, style was a matter of choice. Architect and client had to agree on the design of the building, so she needed to find an architect who had a compatible vision.

Cardinal Mundelein recommended his architect, Joseph W. McCarthy, for the project. McCarthy had designed St. Mary of the Lake Seminary in a colonial style. His original design for Mundelein College submitted in June 1929 specified a brick exterior with limestone trim.[9] Mother Isabella rejected these plans as too expensive and asked Nairne Fisher, an architect who had just opened an office in Dubuque, to review the plans for her.[10] Mother Isabella and Fisher shared a vision for the skyscraper college, which was documented in their correspondence. After his service in World War I, Fisher spent a short time studying at the Ecole des Beaux-Arts in Paris, where he no doubt was influenced by the new ideas for buildings that became the modern style of the 1920s. Fisher also worked with Mother Isabella on buildings for Clarke College, the B.V.M. college in Dubuque.[11]

In early August Mother Isabella had Fisher review McCarthy's revised plans.[12] By the end of August she had worked out an arrangement whereby Fisher would draw up the design and plans, and McCarthy would be the supervising architect.[13] In September Fisher wrote to her saying he would bring her some ideas to consider for the skyscraper college.[14] By the end of September Fisher was listed as associate architect on the project, and the plans for the building were approved. The final plan exemplified modern style with vertical lines, geometric ornament in low relief on spandrels, and ziggurat setbacks.

Creating the angel guardians at the main entrance—Uriel, "the light of God," on the east and Jophiel, "the beauty of God," on the west—provided the most detailed evidence of the collaboration of Kane and Fisher. The angels were not in Fisher's approved sketch of the building in September 1929 but were added in a later version. When recalling the work in a letter of January 4, 1978, Fisher wrote that Mother Isabella requested a design for angels on either side of the main entrance. He sent her an "original sketch of the entrance feature" on February 12, 1930.[15] At the end of March, when Fisher inspected the models, he found them unacceptable. When he wrote to Mother Isabella explaining the need to redo the models, he assured her that "when the new models are ready, I will see that you have an opportunity for criticism and suggestions."[16]

Charles Fisher, the architect's brother, who did the drawings for the cut stonework on the Skyscraper, wrote to Mother Isabella on April 18. He reported that he had completed the drawings "with the exception of the front-entrance figures, which we are arranging to take care of just as soon as the models are completed, which we presume will be some time next week."[17] Charles Fisher explained that he would complete the drawings in Chicago "so that there will be no delay in ordering out the proper sizes for the stone blocks and delivering them to the building."[18] In his 1978 letter, Nairne Fisher identified Axel C. Carlson, head of the design section of his firm, as influential in "developing the angel forms, as well as in carving throughout the structure."[19] Fisher recalled "full-size details were drawn in our office. Many were seen and final-ized by Sister Mary Isabella, B.V.M., before being sent to the contractor for exe-cution by his stone subcontractor."[20] The final "carving was done at the building site by expert stone carvers."[21] Charles Fisher praised the North Shore Stone Company, the cut-stone contractor, for putting "the work into the mill in the shortest possible time" and for the quality of workmanship.[22]

The arrangement of McCarthy as supervising architect and Fisher as asso-ciate architect created an effective partnership. McCarthy was the cardinal's architect. The cardinal had an interest in the project and the sisters were very aware of the need to maintain the cardinal's interest. McCarthy also knew contractors and suppliers in the Chicago area and could negotiate the best price for work and materials. Mother Isabella Kane, however, wanted a close relationship with the architect in the design process. Fisher had an office in Dubuque and was very receptive to full consultation on the project. With this arrangement, Mother Isabella could work with the architect of her choice without disregarding the cardinal's interest or the advantage of having an architect who was well connected in Chicago.

While Mother Isabella kept in close contact with Fisher on all aspects of the design, Sister Mary Justitia Coffey, B.V.M., the superior of Mundelein College, was in daily contact with the general contractor, William Lynch, at the building site. The sisters, who appreciated the cardinal's interest and assistance, actually directed the work themselves. They also arranged their own financing. Cardinal Mundelein suggested ways the sisters might get financing, but they explained to him that they could make more advanta-geous arrangements with Continental Bank.[23] The financing of Mundelein College continued to be negotiated between the B.V.M.'s and Continental Bank right up to the affiliation agreement with Loyola in 1991. The B.V.M. sis-ters, especially those in Chicago, also collected money that helped to furnish the Skyscraper and purchase books for the library. The leadership skill of Mother Isabella Kane and Sister Justitia Coffey in directing their building proj-ect demonstrated a mastery of the diplomacy and courage required to manage the collaboration of architects, contractors, bankers, and clerics.

Every building project is a communal effort, and the success of Mundelein College in Chicago required the support of the Catholics of Chicago. The skyscraper college was linked to the Roman Catholic archdiocese by being named for the cardinal and by the reputation of the founding community of sisters, the B.V.M.'s, whose work as teachers in parish elementary schools and B.V.M. high schools across the city was well respected. The B.V.M. crest and motto, *Sicut lilias inter spinas* ("Find the lily among thorns") appears above the main entrance. Cardinal Mundelein's crest appears on the main stairway. The exterior and interior ornamentation of the building proclaimed its Catholic heritage. The east façade has a stone cross in bas-relief, three stories high. The north façade has a smaller cross in relief. The angels at the main doors point upward to a cross atop the south façade and draw the eye to the two bas-relief figures of the Blessed Virgin Mary, patron of the Sisters of Charity. The exterior art-deco design of chamfered corners and arches repeats in the marble altar niches, the windows, the communion rail, and the pews in the Stella Maris Chapel on the second floor. The chandelier that includes the initials B.V.M. in its design, reputed to be Mother Isabella's, echoes the sunburst motif on the main elevator doors.

The style for the architecture of the Skyscraper, art deco, or modern, took its name from the 1925 exposition in Paris, Exposition Internationale des Arts Décoratifs et Industriels Modernes. This style created a new urban design that combined new materials and technologies with the tradition of expert crafting. It emphasized rectilinear, geometric form, combining glass and steel to produce a hard-edged look that was both uncompromising and unsentimental. The streamlining parallel lines and rounded corners gave an aerodynamic look, fitting for the new age of speed. Industrial technology created a new aesthetic.

The steel and concrete Skyscraper rose 198 feet to the maximum height allowed by zoning regulations in 1929. The setbacks at the fourth, eighth, and eleventh floors, also required by zoning ordinance, produced the ziggurat shape characteristic of this style. Although massive in size, the setbacks created a proportioned shape. The silver-gray Indiana limestone that sheathed the building enhanced the strength, power, and dignity of the structural form. A hipped roof topped the central tower.

Exterior design elements repeated within give the building a sense of rhythm and harmony. The three setbacks, the primary example of the tripartite repetitions in the building, are outlined in the radiator grills, doorplates, and light fixtures. The exterior grillwork on windows and porches and the interior stair railings all have a tripartite design. Chamfered arches and corners on the exterior are mirrored in the stacks of the music library on the seventh floor and in the furniture design for the tables and chairs in the fourth-floor library. The geometric and botanical patterns in the limestone and metal reveals and friezes on the exterior are repeated in wainscots and cornices and on elevator doors within. The Allegheny metal screens for the recessed radiators on the first floor recreate the Skyscraper outline with schematized precision.

The first floor provides a good illustration of the varied materials used in art-deco style and the interest in technology: Allegheny white-metal radiator screens and stair railings; wood in doorframes and doors; mahogany bookend parquetry on wall panels in the East Room and the Cardinal's Room; varied marbles on walls, floors, stairs, and lavatories; brass light fixtures in the main hall; and stucco on the walls of the auditorium. In the north corridor, three sets of double doors give access to the student dining room. The swimming pool at the north end of the first floor gleamed with green and white tiles, and the adjacent locker room provided hot-air tubes at two heights so that students could dry their hair while standing or sitting. The kitchen had the equipment required to serve one thousand students and seventy-five sisters, indicators of the grand expectations of the founders. The auditorium seated 1,100 and had a projection booth that met commercial standards.

Mother Isabella Kane and Sister Mary Justitia Coffey were women attuned to the tempo of their times. Art deco and modern style harmonized technology and tradition. Geometric severity was softened by natural elements in ornamentation and made interesting by surprising juxtapositions of varied materials. Seventy years later, the Skyscraper still engages both the intellect and the emotions as an example of unity in diversity.

Building a modern skyscraper in Chicago was only one of the indicators of the B.V.M. connection to the dynamics of the city. Kevin Lynch's classic study, *The Image of the City,* identified five elements as components of a city's image: paths, edges, districts, nodes, and landmarks.[24] Examining the Skyscraper in Lynch's terms demonstrates very specific elements that link it to the image of the city of Chicago. The various plans and building permits locate the Skyscraper on Devon Avenue and Sheridan Road. Sheridan Road, a major path, linked Chicago with Fort Sheridan to the north of the city. It was lined with residential mansions along the lakeshore. Devon and Sheridan intersect at 6300 north where Sheridan Road turns west, forced by the westward shift of the lakeshore. This turn was the last major directional shift westward on Sheridan in the city of Chicago. Lynch commented that an abrupt shift in direction provided "prominent sites for distinctive structures."[25] Sister Justitia Coffey specified 6363 North Sheridan Road as the address in the Commonwealth Edison permit requested in March 1930, thus establishing what became the permanent address of Mundelein College. The Skyscraper was the distinctive structure at this corner, making its contribution to the developing urban landscape of Rogers Park, the Chicago neighborhood where it was located.

Paths in a city are also major transportation routes. The B.V.M.'s considered the convenience of public transportation in the site choice. The Sheridan Road bus stopped at the west door of the college. In Rogers Park the first stop on the elevated train that ran between the Loop and Howard Street was Loyola, for the street name that derived from the Jesuit presence at St. Ignatius Parish and Loyola University. When Mundelein opened, the station was signposted as the stop for both Mundelein and Loyola. The college, located on an important street and dependent on the public transportation system to bring students to and from the campus, became a node in Chicago, a central destination for women from the North, South, and West Sides of the city.

Chicago has, in its lakeshore, one of the most dramatic edges of any city in the world. The Burnham Plan preserved the lakeshore for public use, and images of Chicago almost always include the skyscrapers and the lakeshore as its distinctive features. From the outset, Mundelein College announced its location at Sheridan and the lake, claiming a powerful connection with the city's image.

The Skyscraper was a landmark in its urban neighborhood because of the structure's size and location. Though the college faced the street and the Edgewater community area to the south, it was actually located on the north side of Devon Avenue in the Rogers Park community area. Rogers Park defined itself as the "gateway" to Chicago or to the North Shore towns. The Skyscraper greeted northbound travelers as they reached Rogers Park. (By contrast, Loyola University buildings all faced Lake Michigan or faced away from the urban streetscape.) The Skyscraper was the first such building in Rogers Park and remained the tallest building in the area for decades.

The annual Christmas candle-lighting ritual emphasized the college's sense of communication with Chicago. On the evening before the students began the Christmas recess, they celebrated a ceremony of carols, which included hanging wreaths on the front doors and processing with candles through the building until they formed a candlelit cross in the south-facing windows of the Skyscraper. The ritual was reported to stop traffic on Sheridan Road, where the cross was visible for more than a mile. The faculty and students of Mundelein College shared with the city their celebration of the light and the beauty of God coming in the dark of winter.

The Skyscraper maintained its appellation even as high-rise apartment buildings rose to much greater heights, replacing the mansions on Sheridan Road. Although the building was no longer a visible landmark in the urban landscape of Edgewater and Rogers Park, it acquired an official landmark status when placed on the National Register of Historic Places in 1980, a celebration of its golden jubilee. Mundelein College was an urban institution decisively linked to the image of Chicago.

Skyscraper as Symbol

For both faculty and students, right from the start, the Skyscraper was synonymous with Mundelein College. Sister Mary Justitia Coffey expressed the symbolic importance of the building when she asserted that "it is the aim of those in charge of this institution that the quality of the instruction shall be in keeping with the exterior of the college—modern, complete, efficient."[26]

Sister Mary Rafael Bird, B.V.M., was reputed to be the author of a thirty-two-stanza verse that welcomed B.V.M. visitors to Mundelein in its first year.[27] An outline drawing of the Skyscraper introduced the stanzas. The visitors "get off the bus" at "sixty-three," indicating the address chosen by Sister Justitia. Stanza two identified "hidden radiation," referring to the decorative metal screens that covered the first-floor radiators. Stanza four announced the auditorium and the paging system installed in the switchboard office. Stanzas five through twelve pointed out the marble tile in the Social Room and the swimming pool, where "we don't swim"; the equipment in the gymnasium and the classrooms; the library books; and the stove hood in the kitchen of the model apartment. More stanzas directed the visitor to notice the folding wall in the community room on the fourth floor and the laundry on the ninth floor and reported on the arbitrariness of the Otis elevator. The sisters' rooms were described as "quite bare" but with " a view [and] fresh air." The view and fresh air were also mentioned in conjunction with the solarium and the music library on the seventh floor and the exercise roof on the fourth floor. The last stanza suggested a visit to the chapel and asked a prayer "For this newest new venture,/This tremendous adventure." It is obvious from the detail in this verse tour that the sisters took great pride and delight in the building with all its new technology. The excitement of the "tremendous adventure" also inspired the students.

Agnes Griffin, class of 1939, wrote the college song that gives a student perspective on the symbolic identification of the Skyscraper and Mundelein College.[28] In the song, "Mundelein, Alma Mater" has "blue skies above, . . . sunlight to gown, . . . blue lake beside, . . . angels to guide." Clearly, the Mundelein for which the students would stand and cheer, and for which they would pledge their "living love" and loyalty was the Skyscraper at Sheridan Road and the lake.

The building was pictured in most literature about the college; it was described in detail in the newspaper coverage of the opening of the college. In the first year, the students named their newspaper *The Skyscraper*. A logo, designed in 1985 for the college stationery, showed the outline of the building enclosing a lily, symbol of the Sisters of Charity of the Blessed Virgin Mary. The stationery designed for the Ann Ida Gannon Center for Women and Leadership, established in 1994, uses the geometric border design from the elevator doors. The Gannon Center was established to demonstrate within Loyola University Chicago a continuing commitment to the education of women, the central mission of Mundelein College.

An association of art-deco architecture with images of women was expressed in fashion metaphors. Anne Hollander in a 1979 retrospective description of art-deco style in 1930s women's clothing said it "lent itself very well to the new cool, self-sufficient female image."[29] Mundelein was the first self-contained skyscraper college for women. The sisters' habits did not reflect 1930s fashion, but their building definitely expressed an attitude of confidence in their position as women, as Americans, and as Roman Catholics. In the 1950s Mundelein students used the fashion metaphor with a different emphasis. The Skyscraper was repainted, tuck-pointed, and reroofed in 1954. The student newspaper characterized the changes as a face-lift and a new fall outfit. "As she primps before a vast audience traveling up Sheridan Road, the years fall away. She blooms like a youthful building of sixteen, instead of an almost matronly twenty-five."[30] Even in this stereotypical feminine image, the Skyscraper's urban relationship is prominent. Coverage of Mundelein students in the Chicago newspapers also reflected a feminine stereotype. The features always first mentioned the "beauty" of the students, no matter what accomplishments were being reported.

Early descriptions of the skyscraper college present contrasting, if not conflicting, images. In the first publicity brochure, September 1930, the sisters described Mundelein as "a temple of classic beauty in the midst of a great city. A home of academic culture amidst the hurry and confusion of modern life."[31] Newspaper coverage of the new endeavor stated that "the college . . . in its commanding position on Sheridan Road is a triumph of modern architectural skill," and continued with the comment that the sisters had established a "household of learning."[32] The combination and juxtaposition of images—temple, home, triumph of architecture, household of learning—name it as both public and private space.

Interior Space

The distinctions between public and private space and ceremonial and utilitarian space that Thomas Schlereth suggested for studying historic houses also may be applied to a study of the Skyscraper.[33] As a self-contained college and residence, the building integrated a variety of spaces. In addition to classrooms, offices, dining rooms, and sleeping rooms, it included a chapel, a swimming pool, a gymnasium, an exercise roof, a solarium, and porches on the eighth and eleventh floors, as well as an institutionally equipped kitchen and laundry and a boiler room to heat the building. In the design of the Skyscraper, the first and second floors were primarily public and ceremonial spaces.

The first-floor reception room, the Cardinal's Room, the guest dining room, and the college offices were considered off-limits to students. The guest dining room was also known as the president's dining room and the priest's dining room, indicating its privileged users. Until the 1960s students only used the center staircase for the candle-lighting ceremony, and the main entrance was used only for commencement. Even when the first floor was open to daily use, the front doors opened only on graduation day.

The sisters' space was a combination of public and private space. In their work, the sisters met students in classrooms and offices. The first community room for the sisters was a classroom shared with the home economics department. Sisters also recalled gathering in room 206, the Social Room, for square dancing and in room 405 for an hour of sewing and conversation each evening. In the 1960s after the Coffey Hall residence was built, the fourteenth floor of the Skyscraper was opened up to provide a "penthouse" community room for the sisters. They had a separate dining room on the north side of the central kitchen. In the late 1960s the sisters' dining room was opened to faculty and staff at lunchtime. The B.V.M. congregation revised its constitutions in 1968 and the rule against eating with family or colleagues was eliminated, so a separate dining room was no longer required.

The sisters gathered both morning and evening in the Stella Maris Chapel on the second floor for meditation, participation in the Mass, and communal prayer. Resident students also attended Mass and used the chapel for private prayer. Sisters had private rooms on the ninth to the fourteenth floors, although at various times resident students occupied some of these floors. A separate semiautomatic elevator, restricted to use by the sisters and later the faculty, with an exception for residents who lived on the upper floors, ran from the basement to the fourteenth floor. This "little elevator" door was in an alcove on each floor so one had to know where to find it. Although the sisters' residence was above the academic area of the Skyscraper, they considered the entire building their home because in the functions of their daily lives—prayer, meals, work, community recreation, sleep—they moved throughout the structure.

The sisters were also accessible throughout the building. At the switchboard, there was a list of bell codes, similar to Morse code, that linked the sisters by sound even when they were far from one another. A sister learned to listen for her own bell, but she also heard the bells that called others to take a phone call or respond to a request. This system, which made them available to outsiders, was also used by the sisters to save time in finding one another within the building.

The resident students shared a part of what it meant to be "at home" in the Skyscraper as they lived their daily lives within it. The majority of students, however, were commuters who connected to the interior space in a more limited way. Students generally entered by the west door and went downstairs to their lockers. The south end of the basement was functional student space where everyone had a locker, and the bookstore provided not only texts and notebooks for class but also candy and small gift items. The student lounge was comfortable but not large. Many students worked while attending college and had little leisure time to spend on campus.

The college academic departments were housed on specific floors with the intention that this would reduce the need for students to move around for their classes. Extracurricular projects drew students to work together in the appropriate locations for the newspaper, the literary magazine, and the synchronized swimming team. Students in a particular major spent time together on academic projects in the laboratories, the art studios, the music practice rooms, or the little theater.

Access to the academic floors was by elevator or stairs. For students, there were two manually operated elevators and three stairways that linked the floors of the building. The elevators were in the core of the central tower, and the stairways zigzagged up the outer edges of the building on the west, east, and north sides. The window at all the stairway landings provided not only light but also spectacular views for the breathless climbers. A fourth stairway linked the tenth and fifteenth floors, using the space above the manual elevators that ended on the ninth floor. This central stair was artificially lighted and always seemed to me like a secret passage through the cloister. The plumbing and incinerator chute also occupied space in the central core. The bodily metaphors for these mechanisms come easily to mind in the image of the veins, arteries, and intestines essential to keep life flowing through the structure.

The elevators and stairs appeared frequently in student comments over the course of history. The stairs were used because the elevators were too crowded, too slow, or not working. When young B.V.M.'s arrived as college students in 1957, they were told to use the stairs rather than add to congestion on the elevators. The stairways were an important feature of the building design. Nairne Fisher took pride in the fact that the interior stairs satisfied the requirements for fire safety and eliminated the need for unsightly external fire escapes.

The auditorium was common ground for faculty and students since attendance at a weekly assembly was mandatory. It might be an occasion for the president or dean to address the students, or it might be a guest speaker or performer. The auditorium stage linked students to the world of public issues as well as to the world of fine arts. Required assemblies ended in the 1960s along with many other performances or ceremonies.

By the 1970s all of the boundaries on interior space in the college were dissolving. The guest dining room became known as room 100, a gathering place for lunch or for department meetings. When the president's office moved from the first floor of the Skyscraper to the Learning Resource Center in 1983, the campus minister moved into the space. The reception rooms were still generally reserved for official functions, but they could be used by faculty and student groups. The Cardinal's Room became the formal dining room.

The contrasting memories of the first floor from the 1930s and the 1970s illustrated changing usage. Students in the early years remembered the first floor as cold, both because it was not well heated and because it was formal space that excluded them. By the 1970s and 1980s, faculty and students had conversations on the main staircase, and student organizations held bake sales, solicited memberships, and celebrated festivals in the front corridor. After 1974, weekend students arriving early on Saturday or Sunday mornings at the start of a new term found coffee and doughnuts there to welcome them.

Gender and Space

Scholars have defined college campuses as "liminal space" or a "middle landscape" because they are not clearly identified as masculine or feminine, public or private.[34] In the case of Mundelein College, what did it mean to be a liminal space designated for women? The history of scholarship on gender and space beginning in the 1960s has used several theoretical perspectives. Women's history used the rhetoric of separate spheres for men and women and mapped this concept onto physical space. Most of these early studies of public-male and private-female space allocations used the history of women's exclusion from public-male spaces as evidence of female subordination and male control. Another theme in the scholarship of separate spheres, however, explored women's use of "female space" to create networks and exert power and influence. We have already noted these gendered aspects of Mundelein College. The college, as a separate sphere, was necessary because women were generally excluded from Catholic colleges for men. This enforced separation often proved to be an advantage for women by allowing them to develop their own talents and abilities.

More recent scholars reject the idea of statically defined separate spheres and examine the way in which spaces influence the behavior and power of men and women within them and then take on these associated masculine or feminine meanings. The Skyscraper building for Mundelein College created complex gender associations. The building has masculine characteristics, as the skyscraper was a preeminent phallic symbol in modern culture, and its architectural style was the preference of the male American corporate leaders who built the Board of Trade and the Palmolive Building. Yet women who determined that their educational enterprise shared the values of modern efficiency and technological innovation, which the skyscraper also represented, built Mundelein. These women claimed the right to assert their presence in the urban landscape as equal to the presence of businessmen. Women who entered this space learned their claim to equal status and in the process renegotiated the meaning of space and gender.

Jeanne Halgren Kilde, in her study of Chautauqua, rejected earlier static definitions of gender and proposed to study the process by which spaces become identified with gender categories and the way gender itself changed as new behaviors and actions of men and women challenged social understandings of male and female selves. Mundelein's women students engaged in behaviors that challenged gender understanding by taking public transportation across the city in order to attend. The college was designed as an urban institution with a clear sense of the importance of public transportation access. Entrance into the space was controlled, nonetheless, by the process of admission to the college, except for performances and ceremonies that were open to the public. These entrance regulations created a secure environment in which women could explore their interests.

Until the 1960s men had only limited access to the college. They were invited and welcomed to ceremonial and social events on the first or second floors. The only men's lavatory was on the first floor. A few men, usually priests, taught courses. A priest came daily to say Mass. The Cardinal's Room on the first floor provided a small but distinctive space that signified his unique relationship to the college. Only the name was unusual, however, since all institutions built by religious communities of women had to provide a space for visiting clergy. Men came to the college only at the invitation of the women students or administrators. Women in the college experienced a world in which they determined the time and place of association with men.

There were definite boundaries of public and private space in the Skyscraper, but they were established and controlled by women. The leaders of the college had easy and daily access across these boundaries even as they regulated the access of other women and men. The world of women in the college environment provided for informal associations and serendipitous encounters among faculty and students. This single-sex, but celibate, world affected the understanding of gender. Women were free from the cultural preoccupation with their bodies and able to enjoy their minds. Friendships among women were encouraged and assumed to be both natural and beneficial.

Women's colleges, historically, were always aware of the need to demonstrate high academic standards and intellectual rigor. Sister Mary Justitia's emphasis on meeting nationally established accrediting criteria and on educating the faculty indicated a determination to achieve excellence. Research on the success of women's-college graduates, which includes Mundelein alumnae, has demonstrated the quality of the education provided.[35] Students and faculty commented with pride on the comparative quality of the intellectual environment. This was testimony not only to the high academic standards of the college but also to the persistence of cultural assumptions that women's intellectual achievements are second-rate.

Recent work by Judith Butler on gender as performance may add to previous explanations of why women's college graduates are counted among society's leaders in numbers that far exceed their actual percentage among all college graduates.[36] Women learned in the skyscraper college that self-assertion and a claim to equal space and place are normal behaviors, and once this performance was learned, it was transferred to other environments in which it was not the norm. Women's-college graduates had the confidence to act on their own gender understanding rather than to retreat into more limited cultural definitions of the feminine.

Conclusion

Thomas Schlereth concluded his list of strategies for studying a historic house with the topic of historical interpretation. The question of how to interpret Mundelein's past for current and future students through the structure of the Skyscraper presents a formidable challenge. A feature in the *Loyola Phoenix* on March 3, 1999, has shown the need.[37]

Peter Gianopoulos set out with two companions to explore the "Hidden Secrets of Loyola." A sketch of the Skyscraper, identified as Mundelein College, formed the centerpiece of the two-page feature, but the reason for the choice of this sketch was never provided. The explorers visited the "Sky basement," where they found a "large abandoned room filled with old-fashioned lockers, the doors hanging loosely from their hinges." Their next stop was the seventh floor and the "abandoned greenhouse . . . [with] a decrepit fountain, now overgrown with brown weeds." In my view the picture of the greenhouse showing the lighted white framing against the dark night sky was quite beautiful despite the brown weeds, perhaps only evidence that it was winter. Next, the "legend of the fourteenth floor" drew the explorers upward. The legend named the fourteenth floor as the "rendezvous for an illicit affair between a priest and a nun. . . . The floor has been haunted by the nun, who threw herself out a window when the affair turned sour." The voyeurs had to leave before they found any evidence for the legend. The students found in the Skyscraper only evidence of a polluted environment of decay and illicit sexuality. By contrast, the explorers' response to the final secret, the crypt of Loyola's Madonna Della Strada Chapel, was amazement at "the beauty and religious ancestry of the shrine." The Skyscraper deserves a better interpretation than that provided by student sleuths.

Loyola University Chicago, the owner of the Skyscraper, has invested in its physical preservation. The exterior underwent two years of extensive renovation from 1994 to 1996, which was longer than it took to erect the structure. Classrooms also have been renovated. The Ann Ida Gannon Center for Women and Leadership, established at Loyola in 1994, carries on the work of the original Mundelein College to educate women and to develop their leadership skills. The Gannon Center, the Women and Leadership Archives, and the Women's Studies Program share an attractive space with a lake view in the Loyola Science Library, formerly the Mundelein College Learning Resource Center, built in 1969. The name Mundelein College has been continued as the name for the Loyola school of part-time and continuing adult education formerly known as University College. This part-time division of Loyola was the first to admit women students at the downtown campus in 1914.

The task of making the Skyscraper a true memorial that communicates the cultural heritage of women's leadership remains to be done. The ceremonial, social, and residence spaces in the Skyscraper all await renovation and a determination of their future use. The kitchen has been taken out. The swimming pool and the gymnasium are no longer used because Loyola has a separate sports facility, the Halas Center. The upper floors remain empty until resources are available to enlarge the elevator access to meet current city codes. The self-sufficient, multipurpose integrity of the Skyscraper will not be restored, but how can its history be remembered in this space?

Because the Skyscraper is on the National Register of Historic Places, the National Park Service's work identifying and interpreting buildings as sites of women's history may provide guidance. Making the Skyscraper a continuing tribute to the history of the women of Mundelein College will, no doubt, demand the same courage, diplomatic skill, and tenacity that characterized the women who built it. They are mentors worthy of emulation.

Entering the front doors of the Skyscraper, which was
done only on special occasions, provided a lovely view of
the marble staircases leading to the second floor.

The outline of the Skyscraper building is echoed in
many of the architectural elements in the building,
including a doorknob and a radiator grill covering.

Visiting dignitaries were often entertained in the Cardinal's Room on the first floor of the Skyscraper.

Students, parents, and dignitaries attend the dedication of Mundelein College, June 1931.

A nighttime view of the Skyscraper building,
looking northwest across Sheridan Road.

Endnotes

1. Virginia Woolf, *A Room of One's Own* (New York: Harcourt Brace Jovanovich, Inc., 1929).

2. Dolores Hayden, *The Grand Domestic Revolution: A History of Feminist Designs for American Homes, Neighborhoods, and Cities* (Cambridge, Mass.: MIT Press, 1981) and *The Power of Place: Urban Landscapes as Public History* (Cambridge, Mass.: MIT Press, 1995); Page Putnam Miller, *Reclaiming the Past: Landmarks of Women's History* (Bloomington: Indiana University Press, 1992); Kevin Lynch, *The Image of the City* (Cambridge, Mass.: Harvard University Press, 1960); Larry R. Ford, *Cities and Buildings: Skyscrapers, Skid Rows, and Suburbs* (Baltimore: Johns Hopkins University Press, 1994); Thomas J. Schlereth, *Artifacts and the American Past* (Nashville: American Association for State and Local History, 1980); Estelle Freedman, "Separatism as a Strategy: Female Institution Building and American Feminism, 1870–1930," *Feminist Studies* 5:3 (fall 1979): 512–29; Linda K. Kerber, "Separate Spheres, Female Worlds, Woman's Place: The Rhetoric of Women's History," *Journal of American History* 75:1 (1988): 9–39.

3. Polly Welts Kaufman, *National Parks and the Woman's Voice: A History* (Albuquerque: University of New Mexico Press, 1998). The Third Annual Conference on Women and Historic Preservation was sponsored by the Preservation Planning and Design Program, University of Washington, and the Regional Director, Northeast Region, National Park Service, May 2000.

4. Women's Rights National Park, http://www.nps.gov/wori/

5. Sister Mary Lauranne Lifka, B.V.M., prepared the successful application for listing on the national register. The official notice is given in a letter, 16 June 1980, Mundelein College Archives (MCA), Gannon Center for Women and Leadership, Loyola University Chicago, B.1.2. Congress authorized the National Register of Historic Places in 1966. It is the nation's official list of cultural resources worthy of preservation. The register was created as "part of a national program to coordinate and support public and private efforts to identify, evaluate, and protect our historic and archeological resources." http://www.cr.nps.gov/nr/

6. Everard M. Upjohn, Paul S. Wingert, and Jane Gaston Mahler, *History of World Art* 2nd ed. (New York: Oxford University Press, 1958), 590; Marcus Whiffen, *American Architecture Since 1700: A Guide to the Styles* (Cambridge, Mass.: MIT Press, 1992), 239.

7. Kenneth Frampton, *Modern Architecture: A Critical History,* 3rd ed. (London: Thames and Hudson, 1992), 219–22.

8. Sisters of Charity of the Blessed Virgin Mary (B.V.M.) Archives, Mount Carmel, Dubuque, Iowa, Mother Isabella Kane's notebook, 11 and 25 April 1928.

9. Letter from McCarthy to Kane, 1 June 1929, MCA, Folder B1.1. Mother Isabella Kane note, 1 May–23 July 1930[sic], MCA, Folder D1.2.

10. Letter Fisher to Kane, 12 June 1929, MCA, Folder B1.1.

11. Board of Architectural Examiners, Iowa. Architects in Iowa listing.

12. Letter Fisher to Kane, 6 August 1929, MCA Folder B1.1.

13. Letter Fisher to Kane, 27 August 1929, and Fisher to McCarthy, 5 September 1929, MCA Folder B1.1.

14. Letter Fisher to Kane, 4 September 1929, B.V.M. Archives, Correspondence 1916–35.

15. Letter Fisher to Kane, 12 February 1930, MCA B1.1.

16. Letter Fisher to Kane, 29 March 1930, MCA, A4.1b. Mother Isabella Kane's hand-written notes on the back of the photograph of the approved models for the angels, MCA, A4.1b.

17. Letter Charles Fisher to Kane, 18 April 1930, MCA, A4.1b.

18. Ibid.

19. Letter Nairne Fisher to Sister Ann Ida Gannon, B.V.M., 4 January 1978, MCA A4.1b. Letter Fisher to Kane, 1 May 1931, MCA Folder B1.2.

20. Letter Nairne Fisher to Sister Ann Ida Gannon, B.V.M, 4 January 1978, MCA A4.1b.

21. Ibid.

22. Letter Charles Fisher to Kane, 18 April 1930. MCA, A4.1b.

23. Mother Isabella Kane's notebook, 1 November 1928, B.V.M. Archives.

24. Kevin Lynch, "The City and Its Elements," in *The Image of the City* (Cambridge, Mass.: Harvard University Press, 1960), 46–90.

25. Ibid., 56.

26. Newspaper clipping, 21 September 1930, MCA Scrapbook, 1930–33.

27. B.V.M. Archives, Folder, Mundelein History.

28. Agnes Griffin (aka Sister Mary Ignatia and Mary Griffin) joined the B.V.M.'s and later returned to work at Mundelein as a faculty member and academic dean. The words for the college song were written by Gertrude Feeny, Mundelein class of 1942.

29. Anne Hollander, "Art Deco's Back and New York's Got It," photocopy, MCA, B1.4e.

30. *Skyscraper,* XXV:1 (4 October 1954): 2, MCA.

31. September 1930 announcement, MCA, Scrapbook 1930–33.

32. Newspaper clippings, 8 August 1930 and *Chicago Tribune,* Sunday, 27 September 1931, p.1, MCA Scrapbook, 1930–33.

33. Thomas Schlereth, "Historic House Museums: Seven Teaching Strategies," in *Artifacts and the American Past* (Nashville: American Association for State and Local History, 1980), 91–119.

34. Jeanne Halgren Kilde, "The 'Predominance for the Feminine' at Chautauqua: Rethinking the Gender-Space Relationship in Victorian America," *Signs: Journal of Women in Culture and Society* 24:2 (1999): 449–486. Kilde provides a summary of scholarship on gender and space, which I used to organize this segment of the essay.

35. M. Elizabeth Tidball, "Perspectives on Academic Women and Affirmative Action," *Educational Record* (spring 1973): 130–35; "Women's Colleges and Women Achievers Revisited," *Signs: Journal of Women in Culture and Society* 5 (1980): 504–17; Mary J. Oates and Susan Williamson, "Women's Colleges and Women Achievers," *Signs: Journal of Women in Culture and Society* 3 (1978): 795–806; Cornelius Riordan, "The Value of Attending a Women's College: Education, Occupation, and Income Benefits," *Journal of Higher Education* 65 (1994): 486–521.

36. Judith Butler, *Gender Trouble: Feminism and the Subversion of Identity* (New York: Routledge, 1990) and *Bodies That Matter: On the Discursive Limits of "Sex"* (New York: Routledge, 1993).

37. Peter Gianopoulos, "Hidden Secrets of Loyola," *The Loyola Phoenix*, 3 March 1991, 14–15.

Part Two

Memories of Mundelein, 1933–1937

Jane Malkemus Goodnow

The response to the question, "What was the happiest day of your life?" is often "the day of my marriage" or "the birth of my child." For me, it was a day in the summer of 1933. I had just graduated from Immaculata High School. My mother, my two brothers, and I were living on West Jackson Boulevard, where we had moved from Rogers Park so that my mother would be close to Our Lady of Sorrows Basilica. She was the weekday organist, playing five or six Requiem Masses a day. Divorced, receiving minimal child support, she struggled to support and educate her three children. Even the low tuition at Immaculata had been hard to come by (was it $60 a semester or a year? I had been humiliated that spring by not being allowed to take final examinations because of unpaid tuition).

After graduation I wondered what I was to do. Take a job in a dime store? Wait tables? Devote myself to cooking and keeping the apartment in order?

That midsummer morning I went down to the vestibule for the mail. A long envelope was addressed to me. Tearing it open, I read that I had been awarded a two-year scholarship to Mundelein College as a result of competitive exams. Calling the news to my mother I raced up the stairs. We shared a wonderful glow of pride and happiness. I was particularly pleased to think that I had caught up with my brother who was on a scholarship in science at DePaul University.

Mother, with unwonted courage and independence for that time, had left Louisville, Kentucky, for Chicago in 1928 to further her own career as a musician and to give us children the educational and cultural advantages of the big city. We diligently visited the Field Museum, the newly opened planetarium, and the Art Institute. My brothers and I became members of the Jack and Jill Players, performing in *The Taming of the Shrew, Aladdin, Rip Van Winkle,* and other dramas suited for children. It was taken for granted that we would go to college, which neither of our parents nor our uncles and aunts had done.

Then came the Great Depression and the divorce. Mother gave music lessons at her pupils' homes as well as fulfilled the demanding post of assistant organist at Our Lady of Sorrows. My unbounded happiness that summer day was in sharing her relief at my having secured two years of college at the newly opened skyscraper college.

It had been a depressing move from Rogers Park, where we were a block from the beach, to West Side Jackson Boulevard, where not even a grassy strip separated our stolid apartment house from the street. Now, as a student, I would be returning lakeside to the gleaming limestone building where two angels sternly guarded the central door. No student, however, must enter through those portals. The student entrance was the west door, which led directly down a flight of steps to the lockers.

To enter that skyscraper of learning, I would have to leave home early, cross Jackson Boulevard, walk a miserable half mile through a depressed neighborhood to the elevated train, transfer in the Loop, descend at Loyola station, cross Sheridan Road, pass the Granada Theater, then trudge a long block to the west door. It was a bitter journey in winter, especially when bucking a stiff wind. I had to struggle to open the door with one hand while the other was laden with books. (No backpacks in those days.)

Freshman registration was in the gym. As electives I chose Greek and astronomy. I had enjoyed four years of Latin and had helped my brother build a six-inch reflector telescope. As I was looking about for a familiar face from Immaculata, a tall intensely alert nun swooped down on me.

"You are Jane Malkemus?" I nodded. "Then you must enroll in the drama department."

This exchange was my meeting with Sister Mary Leola Oliver, B.V.M., a forceful mentor who was to shape my years at Mundelein. She had seen me in A. A. Milne's *The Ivory Door,* the senior play at Immaculata.

I protested that we could not afford the extra fees. Sister dismissed this objection, so Greek and astronomy were dropped for Interpretive Dancing and Voice and Diction. Sister Mary Leola was an inspiring drama coach and director. As a producer, she oversaw details of scenery, lighting, and costumes with professional skill and exactitude. She could have succeeded on Broadway.

Ascending by elevator to the drama department on the eighth floor, I always felt elated, as though I were rising above the regular classes with a pre-scribed agenda. On the eighth floor, we could express ourselves and develop our talents. Miss Anne Larkin, capable and traditional in her methods, taught Voice and Diction. We breathed from our diaphragms and recited tongue twisters, such as "Round and round the rugged rock, the ragged rascal ran." Interpretive dancing was taught by a layperson. Wearing loose, modest shifts, we circled about waving scarves to the "Waltz of the Flowers" from the *Nutcracker Suite.*

At a tea for the senior drama students, we freshmen dressed in colonial costumes and danced to the Minuet in G by Beethoven. This ceremony took place in February on the mezzanine of the auditorium by candlelight. Dainty sandwiches and cakes were served. Though we grumbled and fussed at having to serve the seniors, we rather enjoyed the exercise as part of our training in poise and graciousness.

The first play I was in was a stylized sketch in which the characters represented face cards. I remember it only because I incurred the wrath of Sister Mary Leola. I was paired with another girl of the same short stature to represent the knaves of hearts. We had to introduce the piece by walking across the stage in a simple costume of a tunic and red knee britches. There had been a picture-taking session at an outside studio the day before the performance. That morning we realized that we had left the britches at home. We solved the problem by a frantic dash to the nearby dime store on Devon Avenue to buy red tissue paper. Cut out, hastily basted together, our paper britches almost resembled the cloth ones; however, as we goose-stepped across the stage there was a great rustling and crackling. Sister Mary Leola was waiting in the wings. "What is that noise?" she demanded. We confessed and bore the storm of her dramatic displeasure, "trembling with fear at her frown."

There was another dereliction on my part that first year. The major production, chosen for its all female cast, was *Nine to Five,* and first-year students were the technical crew. I was property mistress. One of the properties in my charge was a vase in which the lead character would arrange a significant bouquet of flowers in the second act. Just before the curtain was to rise after the intermission, Sister checked the stage. "Where is the frog that belongs in the bottom of this vase?" she asked. Where indeed? At the dress rehearsal I had emptied the water from the vase with the frog into the swimming pool near the stage—a short cut, closer than the designated utility sink. Sister's annoyance at my failings did not lead her to cast me out of the drama department, however.

Because of similar schedules and interests, we drama students formed a clique. There was Margaret Cleary, a willowy blonde of classic beauty, and Mary Rose Brown whose rich resonant voice gave significance to whatever she read. Fortunately for me, in our sophomore year, a new member joined the drama class. She was the granddaughter of our landlord and lived in the apartment below us. She had a car, so we drove together to the college, thus freeing me from the long El ride.

Another new student enrolled in the fall of 1934, a slender, dark-haired girl whom Sister Mary Leola had recruited from Rosary College. Shakespeare's *Twelfth Night* was to be the major production, a play crammed with good parts. Our first reading was in the classroom on the eighth floor. The newcomer read the part of Viola. After all these years, I can still hear her reading Viola's reply to Olivia's question, "Why, what would you?"

Make me a willow cabin at your gate,
And call upon my soul within the house;
Write loyal cantons of contemned love
And sing them loud even in the dead of night;
Halloo your name to the reverberate hills,
And make the babbling gossip of the air
Cry out "Olivia!"

A thrill ran up my spine on hearing that violin voice interpret those lines so movingly, with perfect timing and enunciation. Having heard good readers at the Jack and Jill Theater and at radio auditions, I could recognize the exceptional quality of the voice and the reading. It was the voice of Mercedes McCambridge. She became the undisputed star of our drama department. She was perfect in the role of Viola—witty, lithe, and spontaneous. Margaret Cleary was the lugubrious Malvolio, Mary Rose Brown was Sir Toby, and I, the feisty clown, Feste.

The role required that I sing several songs alone—the delightful "Oh Mistress Mine," "Hey, Ho, the Wind and the Rain," and "Come Away Death." I was terrified; I had never sung before, not even in a chorus. However, Sister expected that I would sing. I loved the role, so I sang out loud and clear, and probably off key.

The summer between my freshman and sophomore years, I had the good fortune to secure supporting roles in the radio serial *Jack Armstrong, the All-American Boy.* The pay was generous for those days, and I was able to buy myself some suitable clothes. I am sure that I must have been one of the most poorly dressed at the college. Certainly I had few changes. There were many students from affluent families, such as Mayor Kelly's niece, as well as the daughters of the harpist with the Chicago Symphony. Yet I never felt looked down upon. I was busy scrambling for grades, writing for the college publications, and doing my bit in the drama department.

In the fall of 1935, my junior year, our major production was *The Comedian,* by Henri Gheon, a play about a real Roman actor who converted to Christianity and became the patron saint of actors. Margaret Cleary was convincing as the actor, Mercedes was his patrician lover, and I was his Christian brother, the instrument of Genesius's conversion to Christianity. Though performed by an all-female cast, the play was credible.

In 1936 Sister had the novel and bold idea to form a verse-speaking choir after the manner of the ancient Greeks. Divided into light and dark voices, the choir recited narrative and descriptive passages while individuals spoke solos when appropriate. For public appearances, a lay teacher, Catherine Denny Phelps, directed us. With incredible insistence and assertiveness, Sister secured an audition for us at NBC. As a veteran of many auditions, I thought the blasé producers would dismiss us as a well-intentioned group of females from a religious college. Among ourselves, we complained that Mercedes had all the solos for the audition.

Unimagined success! The Verse-Speaking Choir was signed with Mercedes McCambridge by NBC to appear in a variety show with an orchestra. The show also featured the well-known comedy team of Fibber McGee and Molly.

In addition, the exciting news was that Mercedes McCambridge had been awarded a five-year contract with NBC as a dramatic actress. Thus, she was launched on a career that began with Arch Obler's weekly *Lights Out* in Chicago, then Orson Wells' Mercury Theater in New York, and on to Hollywood where she won an Oscar in 1949 for best supporting actress in *All the King's Men*. Later, she was nominated for best supporting actress in *Giant*. Mercedes' success was a tribute to Sister Mary Leola's acuity as a talent scout.

As for me, I had to admit that after all my years of auditioning, I had only minor success. My dramatic talent was adequate. I decided to concentrate on developing my skills as a writer.

I had always had a certain facility with words, so when it was suggested that I write a piece for the Verse-Speaking Choir, I wrote a piece called "Knitting Needles." It told the story of the same pair of knitting needles, handed down through generations from a southern belle, to a farmer's wife, to a sweatshop worker, and finally to a mother knitting for her World War I soldier son. The solo parts were interspersed with narration and description by the chorus who intoned the refrain "knit one, purl one." It was embarrassingly sentimental, but works for radio were often intentionally obvious. I was pleased that my work was on the same program as Alfred Noyes's "Highway Man."

I had never knitted. The idea was given to me by Sister Mary Irma Corcoran, B.V.M., the adviser for the college magazine, *Clepsydra,* and the poetry book, *Quest.* Ideas for many poems, stories, and essays were planted by

Sister Mary Irma so subtly that the student took the idea, let it germinate, and then developed the concept as her own.

Whereas Sister Mary Leola was awesome, Sister Mary Irma was *sympathetique* in the French sense of the word. Like an understanding aunt or blood sister, she welcomed us into the publications office on the fifth floor. The "pub" became a haven where we fledgling writers could go to complain, cry, laugh, and write. The fifth-floor publications room became my refuge. There I ate my lunch, an apple and a piece of cheese hurriedly grabbed from home. I never had enough money for the cafeteria. Sister was our confidant and our friend. We speculated that she was not much older than we were. We enjoyed the story she told of her reception at the convent in Dubuque when she presented herself for admission, wearing a short dress, high heels, and makeup. The portress mistook the friend accompanying her for the would-be postulant.

After regular classes, afternoons were passed in talking over new ideas, revising works, and discussing personal problems. Suddenly at 5:00 P.M., Sister would exclaim, "Oh, time for the Office. . . . Well I just can't make it to the chapel. I'll say it later." When we had finished our work, we would crowd into the small elevator (reserved for faculty) to descend in shared intimacy to the deserted first floor.

The original name for our magazine, *Clepsydra*, seemed fitting. It was the name for a water clock, or "water stealer" from the Greek, for its measurement of the stealthy flow of hours. Indeed I spent hours gazing on the waters of the lake, ever changing from bright blue to dull slate or deep gray with fiercely foaming surf. An epiphany of my childhood had been my first glimpse of Lake Michigan at Oak Street Beach on a day when the surf ran high. I had seen only the muddy Ohio, and I was exhilarated at the thought of those waters extending to the horizon. As an adult, I would cross the Atlantic and Pacific Oceans, cruise the Indian Ocean, the Baltic, Mediterranean, and China Seas. But none of those bodies of water thrilled me more than the fresh inland sea of Lake Michigan.

When I told Sister of a summer spent sailing with my brother and his friends, she suggested I write about my experiences, calling the essay "I Saw a Ship a-Sailing." I described our adventures learning to sail on a small home-made boat, which was moored in Montrose Harbor. There we met the owners of the large beautiful sloops and racing boats. They often recruited us as crew on their cruises and races. It was a thrill to sail across the then unpolluted waters of the lake to Michigan City or to take part in weekend regattas. I tried to express the excitement of being riskily heeled until the water rushed over the gunwales, the sound of canvas flapping as the boat came about, the feel of the ropes at which my brother and I tugged with callused hands. We dared to go out in rough weather, but loved the moonlit nights when we dreamed of circling the globe under sail.

This essay on sailing was the first of my writings to win honors in a national contest for Catholic publications. Also written from ideas suggested by Sister Mary Irma were stories set in the Kentucky of my childhood and another set in Ireland with the magical title "The Music of the Sidhe." These also won first prize. I was pleased with official recognition but was most gratified when students told me they had enjoyed my work.

The Skyscraper, the school newspaper, under the able direction of Sister Mary Madelena Thornton, B.V.M., published essays that I wrote as features. One of these was a humorous account of my inexpert duplication of required experiments in the chemistry lab. Fortunately, no permanent harm was done to fellow students, the physical plant, or myself.

Besides the three annual issues of the college review, Sister Mary Irma also supervised the publication of a volume of poetry that appeared just before Christmas. It included poems from the general student body as well as the "pub" regulars. To open the slender blue book with *Quest* lettered in gold on the cover and to see one's most cherished and personal thoughts set out in clear print was like opening a treasure. As a joint project of the art department, many of the poems were aptly illustrated. One of the most accomplished artists was Virginia Gaertner, who was to have a distinguished career as an artist and designer of stained-glass windows.

One of our more naturally gifted poets was my close friend Joanne Dimmick. I remember the lines:

> What led you to dance so windily,
> By moonlight, Fawn,
> Dappled as if some snow maiden
> Had laid her melting fingertips against your side?

Our appreciation was enhanced by Sister Mary Irma's poetry class. A few seconds after the bell, she would rush in with a stack of books from whose edges fluttered strips of paper marking the place of some beloved poem. She would read to us in her soft breathy voice from Francis Thompson's "The Hound of Heaven" or Gerard Manley Hopkins's "Glory Be to God for Dappled Things." Many times for environmental causes I have pleaded as Hopkins did in "Inversnaid."

What would the world be, once bereft
Of wet and of wildness? Let them be left
O let them be left, wildness and wet;
Long live the weeds and the wilderness yet.

We were certainly tested on the lexicon of poetry, meter, imagery, and so forth, but it was Sister's infectious enthusiasm that made us love poetry and want to write it. Considering her teaching duties as well as her role as adviser for the *Clepsydra* and *Quest,* it is no wonder she seldom made it to the recitation of the communal Office. Sometimes she shared one of her own poems with us and revealed herself as a true poet. Her ability was recognized years later by the critic Louis Untermeyer with whom she had studied a summer in New York. He encouraged her to publish, but alas, the book of her collected poems never appeared.

Sister Mary of the Cross McFarland taught a survey of English literature. It was the first period of the day, when our minds were uncluttered and receptive. Perched on the edge of the desk (an unconventional posture for a B.V.M. in those days), she would regularly challenge us with thought-provoking questions or quote passages from memory. I particularly remember her reciting Chaucer in the original Middle English. Her influence lingered. Years later, when I visited England, I went out of my scheduled way to visit Canterbury. The drama students in her class reveled in reading Shakespeare aloud. As deftly as Kenneth Clark, Sister led us through the movements of classicism, romanticism, realism, and naturalism, illustrating how each era reflected the culture of their times. She had a gift for synthesis and explanation of text.

The dynamic and straightforward Sister Mary Liguori Brophy, B.V.M., taught sociology. She encouraged us to confront problems of poverty, prejudice, and economic injustice, and to evaluate the organizations that attempted to correct them. After reading Jane Addams's biography, I felt compelled to follow her example. If my destiny was not to be a great actress or writer, perhaps I could be a social worker. When I spoke about my new calling to Sister Mary Liguori, she looked at me and said, "You're not tough enough." A just evaluation, as I realized when I volunteered at a settlement house on Halsted Street.

Our philosophy class was a survey rather than a direct reading of original writings. Our principal study was Jacques Maritain's exposition of Scholasticism. We were quite in step with the University of Chicago, where Mortimer J. Adler had introduced neo-scholasticism and included the works of St. Thomas Aquinas. At Mundelein, courses in apologetics and logic showed us the reasonable foundation of our Catholic faith.

On days of recollection, we listened to talks by guest priests. On the third Sunday of Lent, Laetare Sunday, members of the drama club, the Laetare Players, would assemble in Sunday finery for Mass in the chapel on the second floor. At the breakfast that followed, the senior who had given most service to the club would be awarded a golden rose.

Another impressive ceremony marked the last day before the Christmas holiday. In the darkness of the late winter afternoon, all lights in the building would be extinguished, and we would place a candle in designated windows so that the lights formed a great cross, as seen from the exterior. Leaving the college, we would linger in the cold, craning our necks to see the lights flickering in the dark silhouette of the building.

These religious rituals supported the practice of our faith. Like other well-brought-up young women of the time, we were expected to guard our virginity until marriage. Sex was not the obsession it is today. Nevertheless, our religious mentors felt some obligation to give us some sexual education before graduation. We seniors assembled in the sixth-floor lecture room to hear a Catholic physician speak to us about sex. Unintentionally, the advice on natural birth control was inaccurate, as subsequent research determined the time of human female ovulation more precisely. Whether "Vatican roulette" was practiced or not, many of my friends had large families. I had six children.

Our Midwestern horizons were broadened by distinguished visitors from abroad who were invited to our assemblies. Among these were Shane Leslie, the English essayist, and Padriac Colum, the Irish poet. Padriac Colum wrote an introduction for *Quest* in which he commented on one of my poems. We also had a preview of *The Sound of Music* when the Trapp family, recently exiled from Austria, sang for us a cappella.

The dauntless Sister Mary Leola also penetrated the literary and journalism world of our city. Her contacts, particularly with John P. Lally of the *Chicago Daily News*, opened doors and opportunities for us. Feature stories, photo spreads, and comments in informal "gossip" columns publicized the drama department. WCFL, the local labor radio station, allotted us a weekly half hour of broadcast time. Louise Litten, a producer on their staff, was engaged to teach a course in script writing at Mundelein. Our chief assignment was to write scripts for the weekly serial drama produced by the drama department. Characters were created to fit the voices and talents of our drama students.

As I had had experience in radio with the Jack and Jill Players, I became the principal scriptwriter, a task I truly enjoyed. I was immensely pleased

Students of the radio script-writing course wrap up class activities.

when the director compared one of my scripts to *One Man's Family,* a popular radio serial that aired for years on NBC.

My scholarship ended after two years, so I needed other funds for tuition. Fortunately, Roosevelt's New Deal provided help for needy students under the NYA (National Youth Administration), a subsidiary of the WPA (Works Progress Administration). A student was paid for working a fixed number of hours a week for the college or university. When I registered for my junior year, I was assigned to Sister Mary Francis Xavier Baldwin, B.V.M., in the music department. My duties were to dust her studio on the seventh floor each day. I was pleased with the solitary mindless task of sliding the dust mop around, keeping the grand piano shining, while I paused frequently to stare at the lake. I felt humbled, a little like Cinderella.

After a week or so, Sister Mary Leola intervened. She wanted me assigned to the drama department. Sister Mary Xavier was disappointed, and I was reluctant to leave the music department, where I enjoyed hearing scales run on a flute and Chopin preludes or Bach fugues from the piano practice rooms. "Why couldn't I work half-time there and half-time in the drama department?" I asked. Sister Leola was upset and exasperated with me.

"Very well," she said. "If you would rather dust than write scripts."

It was for no more than a couple of weeks that I divided my time between the seventh and eighth floors, for I was soon spending all my working hours in the drama department. Script writing, rehearsing, and spending time in the studio for the Verse-Speaking Choir or the serial drama all counted as class credit as well as NYA hours. In this respect, Mundelein was in the vanguard in allowing credit for actual life experience.

The summer of 1936, between my junior and senior years, my mother became ill. She had always had a heart problem, which she ignored, taking cold baths and adhering to a vegetarian diet. In addition to playing and singing five Requiem Masses a day, she continued to give piano lessons. She directed a girls' choir at the church and a women's chorus at Niles Center. The latter duty required a long trip by elevated to the suburb. My dear friend, Agnes Griffin (who was to become Sister Mary Ignatia), was the accompanist for this group. As Mother's health failed, Agnes relieved her of some of her duties as an organist.

Yet mother grew weaker. She had sought alternative cures from nutritionists and masseurs but finally consulted a doctor. When she could no longer work, she chose to lie on a daybed in the front alcove of our apartment because it was brighter than the courtyard bedroom. I prepared eggnogs and whatever would tempt her. Finally I wrote Mundelein saying I would not be able to return to school that fall because of my mother's illness.

Sister Mary Leola, with a companion, then made an unprecedented trip across town to visit mother and to see what could be done. There was little the sisters could do to help the situation.

September passed. On October 3, my mother's birthday, our downstairs neighbor told me that my mother would not recover. For the first time, I had to confront the fact of her death. Finally, after a brief hospitalization, she was moved to a sanatorium in Indiana. My brother David and I broke up the apartment. He moved to the Northwestern University campus to pursue his fellowship in chemistry, my younger brother moved in with a neighbor so as to attend a local high school, and I was welcomed as a resident student in Philomena Hall by the lake. Mother's grand piano went with me and was installed in the parlor; an antique secretary with various mementos and books was stored in the college basement.

Who arranged all this? Undoubtedly, Sister Mary Leola. I remember Sister Mary Consuela Martin, B.V.M., calling me into her office to assure me that I should not hesitate to ask for anything that I needed—even toothpaste. My father, from whom I had been estranged since the divorce, was to supply some financial aid, but it was not enough to cover my tuition and board.

As I had entered a month late, I had to study hard to catch up with my classes, though my thoughts were continually with my mother. On weekends I made the trip to the sanatorium by bus. Each time I left her with great reluctance. On Friday, November 13, an early morning phone call from a priest friend of ours informed me that my mother had died. I called my brothers. Then, on that cold gray November morning, with a heavy heart, I took the elevated to the bus, and the bus to the mortuary in the Indiana town to arrange for my mother's removal to Chicago. After all these years, I can still recall the terrible sadness of that journey.

After the funeral at Our Lady of Sorrows, where my mother had played for so many similar services, I returned to Mundelein. That evening, Sister Mary John Michael Dee, B.V.M., the stern mistress of Philomena Hall, mounted the stairs to the third-floor dormitory to give me a sleeping pill. After Mass the next morning, I rushed back to the dorm to sob out my grief.

Some cynic has said that the bitter truth is not that we do not recover from grief, but that we do. So the comfort of my friends and teachers, the routine of classes helped me to adjust to the loss of my adored mother.

My three roommates and I were quite compatible in our "garret." A toaster and a percolator, salvaged from my household goods, supplied us with the making of nighttime snacks. Occasional cigarettes were sneaked in the lavatory with the skylight propped open for smoke to escape. These smokes were sneaked more for the excitement of the risk than from actual craving.

Thanksgiving was passed at the home of one of my mother's friends. Christmas, my brothers and I took the train to Louisville, Kentucky, to be with relatives. Before I left, Sister Mary Consuela called me into her office to offer me an enormous box of fine chocolates, surely someone's gift to her.

The major drama presentation that winter was a program by the Verse-Speaking Choir. I was assigned one of the solos. However, at rehearsal my mind went blank. Sister Mary Leola gently attributed it to strain and relieved me of the part. I didn't mind much.

The second semester of my senior year passed quickly. My favorite course was aesthetics. One of the readings was Henry Adams's *Mont St. Michel and Chartres*. After class, gazing at the lake, Agnes Griffin and I shared our longing to visit those historic wonders. Twenty-three years later, in 1960, we would do so.

I had recently arrived in France to begin a three-year residency with my husband and children while Agnes was in Europe on a Fulbright fellowship.

We met in Paris and motored to Chartres, picnicking on wine and cheese on the way. We thrilled to see the disparate towers of Chartres rising out of the plain. Entering the cathedral, we were awed by the stained-glass-lit interior and moved to hear a band of student pilgrims singing a hymn to the Virgin. While Agnes, then wearing the traditional B.V.M. habit, searched for the window known as "La Belle Dame de la Verrière," I was drawn to a side chapel ablaze with lights. On the altar was the blackened statue of the Madonna that had survived the twelfth-century fire. Women were lighting votive candles, then devoutly kissing a pillar. I observed the same ritual, lit a candle, and embraced the pillar, petitioning Our Lady for a suitable home or apartment to rent for our family of four children. A few months later, I was to learn that I was pregnant at the age of forty-five.

The black Virgin of Chartres, I learned, was the patroness of barren women! That bit of pious tradition had not been included in our study of Chartres.

However, in the spring of 1937, France was still a dream. Besides aesthetics, I participated in the script-writing course taught by Louise Litten. This resulted in my being offered a job, after graduation, as a continuity writer at WCFL. This was fortunate since I had no special training as a stenographer or teacher, positions that provided a constant income. The country was in the slough of the depression and opportunities for employment were few. Occasional parts in radio serials would not have guaranteed a steady salary.

I graduated cum laude in the spring of 1937. I received honors for a story in the National Catholic Publications contest. The subject of the story was a woman artisan who lived in Cremona, Italy, in the seventeenth century. She defied tradition in creating a masterpiece of a violin. The inspiration for this character was my mother's determination and devotion to music. I was commissioned to write the class poem, a framed copy of which was given to each graduate. The sonnet was an expression of gratitude for the years spent in the classrooms by the lake, regret at leaving, and anticipation of the future.

In later years, I was to appreciate the intellectual training I had received at Mundelein. In postgraduate courses at other universities and in Great Books discussion groups, I was able to compete favorably with graduates of prestigious secular institutions.

On reflection, I realize that I was sustained in many of life's crises by the elegant example of poise, discipline, and spirituality given to me by the wonderful women of Mundelein.

O This Learning,
What a Thing It Is! Remembering
Sister Mary Leola Oliver, B.V.M.

Mercedes McCambridge

I have been asked to set down some of my recollections of Sister Mary Leola Oliver, B.V.M. It's difficult for me for several reasons. First of all, Sister was probably *the* most influential person in my life. One does not talk lightly about such things. Emotionally, I will probably have a little trouble recounting some of the things. And being Irish, I may elaborate on some of the things that I say about Sister and about me. I make no apologies for that; it's inevitable if you're Irish. You must decorate the truth because the truth is rather tacky, taken on its own terms. But for whatever the reason, it is with my admiration and love for a truly great woman, Sister Mary Leola Oliver. After I became acquainted with her, I made up a story about how she was a great star in the British theater and, when she came to this country, was converted to Catholicism and entered the B.V.M. order. That's why she was so brilliant in the theatre. Actually, I know nothing of Sister Mary Leola's background. I only knew her after her emergence in full flower on the eighth floor of Mundelein College. That's where it all began.

In my senior year in high school at St. Thomas Apostle School on the South Side of Chicago, my teachers were Dominican sisters. And I was devoted to them. Well, not all of them, but almost all of them. There was a scholarship exam being conducted at Mundelein College up in the frozen north of the city, and I was entered into it by my elocution teacher. I entered it and won the second prize. The first prize went to Mary Rose Brown. I will never forget it, because at sixteen it's hard to admit that somebody is a better actress than you are. It's a scar I carried with me all my life. Darn you, Mary Rose Brown!

Anyhow, as I say, I was devoted to the Dominican Sisters, so they kept telling me that it would be fine if I went to Rosary College (their college in River Forest, Illinois), where they had a wonderful dramatic-arts teacher. So I did that for my freshman year. But from time to time, during those long journeys out to River Forest, I would think about that dynamic little nun who was in charge of the scholarship examinations at Mundelein that day. She haunted me. If ever I were to become a nun, I thought, that's the kind I'd like to be.

Sister Mary Leola had fire in her heart and in her eyes. She was dynamic to the nth degree. So after my freshman year at Rosary, I transferred to Mundelein and the college honored the scholarship that I passed up a year earlier. It wasn't all that much financially, but every little bit helped in those days. And so began my association with Sister Mary Leola.

She . . . how do you begin to talk about this woman? She was very petite and her eyes were the most outstanding feature. They sparkled constantly, and they probed incessantly. She wore a black veil, a long black skirt, and a short black cape under which was a black blouse—her religious habit—and she always had little notes pinned to her blouse. Probably my fate was written on those notes more times than I care to imagine. She would call me to account for whatever I had done that day, or the day before, which had so displeased her—times when she felt I was selling myself short and not living up to what *she* felt were not only my possibilities but my inevitabilities.

Sister was—for me—a very hard teacher, a taskmaster. But I think my best teachers have always been the ones who have been hardest on me. The ones who kept insisting that I had more to give than I wanted to give. The ones who really believed that it wasn't so important that I would make a fool of myself by overdoing something. They would insist that the important thing was to go ahead—do it! "Show me what you can do, not what you are afraid to do because you don't want to have anybody notice your lacks. If you lack something, let's see what we can do to overcome it." This is Sister talking.

She felt that way particularly about diction. Oh, my goodness! And she has certainly handed that to me because I . . . I don't know why I have any friends at all. I cannot stand anyone who says "ninedy" or "ninedy-nine." No! Or anyone who says "strenth" or anyone who says "nucular." Oh, my goodness! And I can't bite my tongue. I find myself saying again and again, "Don't do that."

There's a *g* in *length*. And there's no such thing as "nucular" and there's no word that is pronounced "ninedy." "They're not pronounced the way you do it. You pronounce a *d*. That's wrong! Don't do that." That's how Sister used to talk to me. And, God help me, that's how I talk to my friends. It's not very nice. It was all right for Sister; she was my teacher. But who the heck do I think I am? Well, partly that's her fault, too. Sister made me think that I was really something. So if I'm overblown in my self-estimation, it's not my fault. Sister did it. Oh, I wish I could talk to her right now. She would enjoy this. She'd reprimand me for it, scold me. But then, she'd enjoy it.

Ah, let me see. Diction. Body movement. She made us, all of us in the drama department who were that much interested, she made us stride and limp and cower and kneel and stretch and bend. Every possible thing that you could think of a body doing while it was in motion. It was a wonderful game.

Mercedes McCambridge, class of '37, shows her Oscar to Sister Mary Leola Oliver, B.V.M., her mentor in the Mundelein drama department. Photo circa 1950.

She knew everything about stage design. I remember how impressed I was with her miniature stages that we would set up in her office on the eighth floor of the Skyscraper. She would map out the scenes with her own miniature sets and with all of the furniture in the set. In her notebook she would record how she had moved the actors around and how she had changed the scenery and how long it took. Then she would estimate all of those things for the big stage downstairs in the auditorium. It was very difficult to stage things in the auditorium because that's what it was. It wasn't an honest-to-God theater. Still isn't. But I loved that place. When I've been there lately—which hasn't been all that often, but as often as I can—I always genuflect before I go into the auditorium. For me, it's church. And that's due to this little woman, this tiny woman.

She made me do an entrance in *Twelfth Night* from stage right. That middle entry onto the stage. There's one on the other side of the stage, too. It's not actually where the big proscenium is, where the big curtain is, but it's kind of a little side entrance. And all I had to do was to come out—this is rehearsal now—come out and deliver my speech. It is the one where Viola reflects that Olivia has made the mistake of thinking Viola is a fellow. And the speech begins, "I left no ring with her. What means this lady? Fortune forbid, my outside hath not charmed her. She made good view on me, indeed so much me thought her eyes had lost her tongue." Anyhow, that was that speech.

I was to enter, pause for a moment, gather my wits about me—rather, Viola's wits about her—and spout. Sister Mary Leola made me do it twenty-nine times. She was sitting out there in that auditorium all by herself. Every time I'd come out, she'd say, "Go back. Come in again." And finally, she started calling me "Miss McCambridge." Oh, boy, then I knew. What was I doing that was so terribly wrong? Well, she finally made me see that I had to find the problem for myself. She didn't tell me. She wouldn't do that. She would stay there until hell freezes over, until you got it yourself. Or sometimes she would say, "You're just not going to be able to do it." So what did I discover about my entrance? When I came out, I didn't plant my feet and then stand there. What I did was shift from one foot to the other. No. Viola's mood and temper at that particular time in Shakespeare's play would not have wavered. Since she was dressed in her suit, she would have stood there with her legs slightly apart in her knickers or her trousers, she would have put her hands on her hips, and she would have said her lines.

After this encounter, I considered going home and telling my mother that I could not go back to Mundelein anymore. "That woman is trying to kill me," I'd explain. "She has a *really* mean satanic streak. And she's just trying to kill me. That's exactly what she's trying to do." Well, when you're just eighteen, such interpretations are ready at hand.

Fortunately, my mother never heard my complaint, because it couldn't have been farther from the truth. Sister believed in so many of us—not just me. The first Verse-Speaking Choir was her brainchild. I think it was one of the finest expressions of college work that I've ever heard. Eight light voices, eight darker voices, and a solo voice in the middle. And guess who was the solo voice? You bet your life I was.

I am convinced that Sister Mary Leola was indeed my guardian angel. Of course, I was taught when I was small that women couldn't be guardian angels, only fellows could be. I resented that from the first day I heard it.

I *didn't* and *don't* want some unseen angel of the masculine variety following me around all the time, standing at my side. I don't like that. It just doesn't appeal to me. I think Sister Leola was my guardian angel for a while, and then even she had the good taste and the good sense to step out of the picture when my life went on to other realms. But I'm awfully grateful that she was there when I needed her.

I have said before that, usually in her productions, Sister would have her eyes set on one of the roles in the play that might have gone to her, had she been a student instead of the teacher. Heaven help the girl who was enacting the role that Sister might have wanted for herself. Sooner or later during rehearsal time, Sister would gather her outer skirts around her with a great safety pin, and tuck them through the cincture around her waist so that she wouldn't trip over herself. She would get up on stage while the poor student actor was asked to sit in the auditorium and watch Sister go through the student's part. I tell you it was fantastic to watch.

She did that to me a couple of times. But I remember most vividly in Ari Guyon's play *The Comedian,* in which I played Paupier. Sister would have liked that part. One day in rehearsal, she got it. And she was wonderful in it. And I don't know that I ever came up to her performance. But at least she was satisfied. She played it once that afternoon in rehearsal. And she was very, very good. She had quite a range. Her voice was wonderful. And her body language, even in her habit, was graceful and spontaneous and fresh. Sister was an actress. And she knew it, too. And she knew how to use diction, body movement, all the skills needed to engage the character with the audience. Oh, boy! Some of us in the drama department used to say, "Don't bring your father to meet Sister Mary Leola because he'll never go home to your mother." We didn't mean it irreverently. It was really an appreciation of a very charming and determined little person.

Sister had such pride in Mundelein. She believed it was Nirvana as far as an educational institution was concerned. And she knew how to get newspaper space in *The Chicago Daily News* and the *Chicago Tribune* to promote the drama department. I remember when the Verse-Speaking Choir was asked to come down to NBC to record one of our poems into the microphones. None of us had ever seen a microphone before. And Sister was there with us. The executives of NBC were very impressed with these seventeen young women—with crosses around their necks and halos of innocence over their heads there in the evil confines on the nineteenth floor of the Merchandise Mart. We did our thing into the microphones, and half an hour later, Sister

Mary Leola's Verse-Speaking Choir from Mundelein College was signed to a year's contract for an appearance weekly with the Chicago Symphony Orchestra, reading their Verse-Speaking Choir stuff. And yours truly was signed to a five-year contract with NBC, which, of course, changed my whole life. Sister Mary Leola did that.

She was, in a sense, a very wise entrepreneur. She was a politician. She had ambition—not for herself, but for her school. Well, maybe for herself. I don't think self-esteem or self-ambition is a bad thing, no matter what St. Augustine says! But Sister was actively engaged in helping Mundelein College make its mark. And, indeed, it did. Indeed, it did.

When the *Chicago Tribune* critic wrote about my performance in something or other—that I was the best nonprofessional interpreter of Shakespeare that he'd seen in a long time—I say honestly that wasn't me. That was Sister, through me. So much of my work at Mundelein and since has been Sister through me. She believed that interpretation is vital. She learned this from Sarah Siddon, and so say I: You mustn't play a part unless you can fall in love with the character; in other words, become a defense attorney for the character.

I used that philosophy, an admonition of hers, to the degree that, even interpreting Lucifer in *The Exorcist,* I found a sense of compassion for Lucifer. I think that Lucifer is the *true* prodigal son, and I believe that he will come back and ask forgiveness of his father. I believe if his father does not grant that forgiveness, that his father is not my God. So I found a way not to justify Lucifer in his headstrong actions, but to understand how unhappy he was and is. Sister taught me that empathy. I guess the greatest attribute for anybody, not merely an actor or a writer or a poet or a painter or a musician, but for any breathing thing, including dogs and cats and everything else, is compassion. I believe that's the important thing.

Sister and I used to have long talks about things. I'm sure she was guiding me, but I liked to think at times that I was teaching her everything she knew. She was proud of her school. She was proud of her order. She was proud of her department. She was proud of Chicago! Oh, my goodness! Sister appreciated things.

The night that I won the Academy Award for the first picture I was ever in—*All the King's Men*—I, who came to the role knowing nothing about screen acting, knew I had been taught by a brilliant teacher. Her instruction served me well. I sent my Oscar to Sister Leola, then living at Holy Angels Convent in Milwaukee. I told her it wasn't a permanent gift, but I wanted her to enjoy it with me for a while. And what did she do? This humble woman of

Christ and Sister of Charity of the Blessed Virgin Mary took the Academy Award down to the local theater and said, "Put a display case around this and show it to everybody." Ahhhhhh! How about that?

I hope these memories will have helped to bring alive this remarkable woman. Remembering has been an emotional exercise for me in appreciation of a woman who not only changed my life but also practically made my life. I thank Sister. I thank Mundelein. I thank God.

Life Flows through the Dream

Blanche Marie Gallagher, B.V.M.

The Chicago taxi stopped in front of the imposing skyscraper building that housed Mundelein College at "Sheridan Road at the lake," the illusory address on the college catalog. The building looked familiar from the cover of the catalog; it fascinated me, for it was the only college contained under one roof in the world.

Mother and I moved away from the cab toward the front steps, my mind whirling in fantasies woven around the possibilities of my new life in Chicago. I'd formed these fabrications about city life by viewing most of the movies of the thirties and forties. I had grown up in the last row of the movie theatre in Waverly, Iowa, because my father's best friend owned it and we received a yearly family pass.

That July day in 1942 was humid and our dresses were wrinkled for we'd been traveling to Chicago from Waverly, Iowa, on the Illinois Central train *Land of Corn* since 5:45 A.M. and now it was midafternoon. We ascended the imposing granite front steps and rang the doorbell. A nun appeared behind the glass doors. She waved her black-clad arm toward the west, and we finally understood from the gestures that we were not allowed to enter through the front door. We found the side entrance; my fantasy wavered.

Sister Mary Madelena Thornton, B.V.M., was all smiles as she greeted us. I was astonished, for I had overlooked one piece of research in my excitement with the cover picture of the building and the dream of living in Chicago. She was clad in the same black habit worn by the Sisters of Charity of the Blessed Virgin Mary at Clarke College in Dubuque, Iowa. I had felt dissatisfied with my first two years of college there, and I was determined to transfer. Another fantasy diminished.

My story did not please Sister Mary Madelena. She informed us that Clarke College was the boarding school conducted by the B.V.M.'s; Mundelein College was a commuter college founded to educate the working women of Chicago. Recently a concession had been made because of World War II; sixty young women who lived in Chicago's suburbs were now housed during the week on the campus, but there was no weekend housing at Mundelein College. Did I have relatives in Chicago who would offer me hospitality for weekends? No.

Sister Mary Josine Brabec, dean of residence, was called to confirm these residence regulations for us. We sat on white wicker porch furniture in the second-floor hallway and listened to her. Would we like a tour of the campus? Of course. The postage-stamp sized campus was fully reclaimed by the vastness of Lake Michigan to the east. We were awed by the marble mansion at the lake that was used as the college library. My large garden hat didn't fit between the stacks on the second floor. We were given lemonade. Sister Mary Josine was mellowing; perhaps some arrangement could be made. Patricia Rocap from Indianapolis had also asked for weekend housing. The staff would confer to consider weekend housing and to discuss my application.

A few weeks later I was informed of my acceptance. Gasoline had been rationed because of the war, and weekend housing was now considered part of the war effort of the college. I was assigned to the thirteenth floor of the Skyscraper building that I had so admired from the catalog cover, and I was to live inside this work of art. My roommate in room 1309 would be Marian Stoffel, a chemistry major from Cicero, Illinois. I was also one of a small number of weekend residents permitted to live in the Skyscraper on weekends. We would take meals in the tearoom on the first floor with Sister Mary Pierre Flynn, chair of the home economics department, as hostess; and we would explore the city during the weekends.

So September 1942 came, Mother and Dad drove me to Chicago, and I moved into the Skyscraper building. My dream had become reality. I reveled in my escape from Clarke, where we wore uniforms, navy dresses with white collars. Public school had not required uniforms, and clothes were important to me. Mundelein required no dress code other than fashionable sweaters, skirts, and dresses. We wore pants for outdoor sports only.

My parents lugged my belongings to the elevator, and I was stuffed into half of a room on the thirteenth floor, built to be a nun's cell. But room 1309 on the east side of the thirteenth floor enjoyed a lake view which expanded its space to the horizon. And it was all mine on weekends when my roommate, Marian, returned to her home in Cicero.

Mundelein College was only twelve years old when I arrived in September 1942. Enrollment was 620; our tuition, $150 per year. Mundelein's resident regulations seemed most generous. Sister Mary John Michael Dee, the other hall moderator, gathered about sixty resident women and described these directives: We had the freedom of the campus and the city each day until 7:30 P.M.; then study time of three hours on weeknights was quietly enforced. At 10:30 P.M., the nun in charge stopped at each door to say a prayer with us

before we went to bed. Because of the distances in the city, our weekend curfew was extended to 1:00 A.M. When we returned on Friday and Saturday
nights, a very sleepy sister opened the large doors and politely inquired about
our adventures.

My major at Clarke College had been art (interior design), so Sister Mary
Janet Staples, chair of the art department, and Sister Mary Carmelyn McMahon
welcomed me. Students tended to cluster around major departments, and an
art department is naturally a place of much activity and long hours of work
together in the studios. Two other art majors, Mary Jane Harvey and Margie
Ann Schaller, and I became lifelong friends.

Since Mundelein was the first college housed under one roof, academic
departments occupied specific floors of the building. The top two floors of the
Skyscraper, thirteen and fourteen, were used for student residence, and floors
nine through twelve were convent. The small elevator that provided access to
floors nine through fourteen carried only ten occupants, so we residents spent
much time waiting for this elevator and chatting with the nuns.

As an art major I spent
most of my time on the eighth
floor, which also housed the
drama department. I played
bassoon in the college orchestra,
which was rehearsed weekly by
Sister Mary Severina Stratton on
the seventh floor in the music
department. Although she
directed rehearsals of the
orchestra very capably, she was
never allowed to direct live concerts. Nuns did not appear in
public; Mr. Joseph Grill directed
the public performances.

**Sister Blanche Marie Gallagher,
B.V.M., in the art department
workshop at Catholic
University of America.**

I attended Mundelein at a very tense time; after the Japanese attacked the United States at Pearl Harbor on December 7, 1941, the nation was deeply involved in World War II. In Europe, France had fallen to the Vichy government, and England was under the German bombing blitz. The news that we received by radio, movie newsreels, and newspapers about Europe and Asia was very disturbing.

In September of 1942 Loyola's campus housed a boys' academy and a very sparsely attended university. College-age men were in military service. Loyola's Lake Shore Campus enrollment totaled 660 male students that September. Mundelein College had enrolled 602 women students. Mundelein women were welcomed on Loyola's campus only by formal invitation; we were not allowed to walk across the campus. This regulation posed a hardship for us because their campus provided a shortcut to the elevated train, our chief form of transportation.

Loyola men were invited to our campus for academic and social events. Tea dances were held in the gym in the late afternoons and early evenings for which we wore high heels, hats with veils, and white gloves. Many of the men attended our social affairs in military uniform, for most were in some kind of war training program.

Our other social activities took place at Fort Sheridan, Great Lakes Naval Academy, or at the various USO localities for soldiers and sailors in the city. We traveled in buses to dance with them and listen to their stories. These young men in service, many our own age, were being trained for a whole new lifestyle of sacrifice and discipline, and would soon be shipped overseas.

Most of the campus social activities were limited to very formal high teas given at every possible provocation by departments or clubs. We were being educated in all the niceties of hostessing these elegant events, for we were being groomed to become wives of men of consequence.

We were always formally addressed as "Miss" with our surname in classes, but art studios were more relaxed and faculty called us by our first names; so I was Patricia, my baptismal name, or Pat, instead of Miss Gallagher, in those relaxed environments. We worked long hours together on many of the service projects that art departments are called upon to provide, such as hand silkscreening 750 program covers for the Christmas candlelighting ceremony. The college newspaper warned that Christmas 1942 might be the last candlelighting cross in the windows of the Skyscraper building because of the enforcement of blackout regulations.

I was majoring in art with a philosophy minor. I knew that philosophy was important, especially in the war effort, for an article in the college newspaper, *The Skyscraper* pointed out that "at the root of victory one will always find Aristotle."[1]

Our Christian marriage class with Father William Clark did little to correct a skewed vision of my fantasy marriage-to-be, which was formed from the movies of the 1930s and 1940s. I wrote to my mother every class day when my attention wavered because one or another of my brothers had been attending college since I was five years old, and I knew how hopefully she went to the mailbox each day for a letter. She wrote to me every day, and my father called frequently.

Classes were unremarkable, but I received an exceptional education during my two years at Mundelein. The city offered the richness of the Art Institute, ballet performances, the music performances of the Chicago Symphony Orchestra, and a wide variety of theater. We sat in the gallery of the Auditorium Theatre for performances of the Ballet Russe for a 25¢ admission fee. The Friday afternoon performances of the Chicago Symphony Orchestra were equally inexpensive. The life-drawing classes with nude models at the Art Institute of Chicago challenged my drawing skills.

My small social group, made up of a few students from the art department and some resident students, rarely missed our TGIF (Thank God It's Friday) ritual at the Yacht Club of the Edgewater Beach Hotel, a few blocks south of the college. As we entered the Yacht Club, we walked across a swaying gangplank into a bar decorated to resemble the prow of a boat. We usually ordered Brandy Alexanders or Pink Ladies (made of gin and grenadine, which is red pomegranate juice syrup) because they looked pretty as we drank them. We could only afford one, so we drank elegantly and very temperately.

And we smoked cigarettes; I had smoked Menthol Kools since I was fifteen, at my mother's insistence. She was a chain smoker and maintained that if I could get a driver's license at age fifteen, I could smoke with her. Smoking was not allowed on the Mundelein campus, but the small dry cleaner's shop across the west alley welcomed us. We sat inside on the steps and gossiped with the owners, whom we called Ma and Pa.

Marian, my roommate, was trained as a model. She worked on Saturdays at Hrusseks, a dress shop on Michigan Avenue, and she volunteered to get me a job there. I had never been allowed to work in my little Iowa town, so I felt very urbane. Later, I found a Saturday job at Marshall Fields on State Street; a group of us worked on Saturdays at Fields and spent our small paycheck for dinner at Stouffers restaurant across the street. I dreamed about working full time as an interior designer after graduation and living in my own apartment on the near North Side of Chicago.

The worsening war roiled around us and completely riveted our attention. We learned first aid, gave blood, and tried to comfort each other as more relatives and friends enlisted or were drafted. I waited to hear that my two married brothers had been drafted. We knotted strings into rosaries for the men at the front as we rode the double-decker buses to the Loop. My classmate June Murphy wrote the Christmas Cantata of 1944 as a tribute to her twin brother who was a prisoner of war in Germany.[2]

Representatives of the new women's divisions of the Army and Navy, the WAACs and the WAVES, occupied tables outside our locker rooms in the basement and encouraged us to enlist. Editorials in *The Skyscraper,* the college newspaper, exhorted, "Each Mundelein student must share in the burden of the war and the destiny of the world."[3] I registered for my physical-education course in Riflery 101 at Northwestern University and learned to shoot prone and standing. We were being prepared for the worst.

The college chapel was flooded with students kneeling with arms outstretched during class breaks, praying for loved ones in battle or in training. We were encouraged to give up two Cokes a week to buy a jeep for Uncle Sam. For the first time, prom queens were elected by votes bought by students with war-bond stamps; the Sophomore Cotillion was postponed in 1943 because the leader of the orchestra had been drafted. Alumnae who had been commissioned in the WAACs and WAVES overshadowed celebrations of engagements and weddings in our college newspaper.

Rationing was a reality. Sugar came first, then gas, coffee, meat, and canned goods. Nylon stockings were scarce, so we bought leg makeup similar to liquid face makeup to rub on our legs for color; and for special occasions, we recruited someone to draw a "seam" down the back of our legs with an eyebrow pencil. We were threatened with the disappearance of girdles because of the shortage of rubber, but Eleanor Roosevelt pleaded that cause for women in Washington, and we were allowed to keep our stiff girdles, which were needed for the tight-fitting styles of the time.[4]

During the last month of junior year we reserved our living space for our senior year. Marjorie Schaller had also transferred from Clarke and was an art major. Marian, Margie, and I moved into Philomena Hall, a red-brick house between the Skyscraper and the library that accommodated thirty-five resident students.

The dearth of male students at Loyola worsened. The 1943 enrollment at Loyola's Lake Shore Campus dropped to 240, a two-thirds decrease from the previous year. The war constantly came closer to us; notifications came of brothers, fiances, and uncles who were wounded, missing, or killed in action. I avoided the women's lavatory near the art department on the eighth floor because it was the hiding place for students who had received bitter news and were crying. Life seemed very precious.

My senior status brought uncertainty into my life. All of a sudden, life was all very real and precious, and I was going to be out there in that reality. Still, college was great fun, Chicago was sparkling, and work went well at Fields. An editorial in *The Skyscraper* challenged: "With our eyes on the boys in service, we will see the imperative need for doing thoroughly the work at hand."[5]

Christmas of 1943 felt bleak. My brothers, both married with children, spoke of enlisting before they were drafted. My mother and dad, who had buried a five-year-old son and another who died at seventeen, were somber. My Christmas gift that year was four complete place settings of sterling silver, a nonverbal announcement of my future.

Our required senior retreat, always given by a Jesuit, took place February 1–3. During the night of February 2, I awakened to a Presence. I knew that I was invited to an espousal relationship with this Presence. I just knew; I didn't know how I knew. It was a voice, a knowing, nothing that I could doubt. I suggested to that voice that it had come to the wrong bed, for my roommate, Margie Ann Schaller, often said the rosary at night, kneeling by the side of her bed. I was not at all "holy," and I surely had other plans. This experience absolutely was not The Dream, and it couldn't have come at a more bewildering time.

The remainder of senior year was a disconsolate blur. Classes became unimportant. I had no choice of congregations because I only knew the B.V.M.'s. They were a teaching congregation, and I deliberately had not taken one class in education so that I would never have to teach. I returned home in April to inform my parents that I was entering the convent. My Norwegian-Methodist-Catholic mother greeted the news with disbelief (after all, they were just trying to keep me in a Catholic college), then forlorn acceptance. My Irish-Catholic father accepted my decision in great faith.

Mother and Dad, my two brothers and their wives, gathered to celebrate my graduation as I received my diploma from Cardinal Stritch. My two brothers had enlisted in the Navy and would leave in August. We didn't talk about my plans to enter the convent.

I entered the B.V.M.'s on September 8, 1944. After completing the novitiate, I taught in grade schools and high schools in Milwaukee, Wichita, and St. Louis. In August of 1955 I was assigned to the art department of Mundelein College. Sister Mary Janet had asked that I be appointed to teach with her. I was finishing a master of fine arts degree at Catholic University of America in Washington, D.C.

I felt great resistance to this assignment, for I enjoyed working with high school students, and I did not want to live in such a large community of seventy-two B.V.M.'s in that huge Skyscraper building. Some of the college students whom I was assigned to teach were ten years younger than me, and I felt very unprepared.

Obedience overrode personal preference, and I arrived in Chicago in August 1955 as Sister Mary Blanche Marie to begin my teaching career at Mundelein College. Our names were changed when we were received as members of the congregation. The changed name was considered a symbol of the death of the person we had been and the beginning of the new religious person. My forlorn mother, Blanche Jacobson Gallagher, felt gratified that I had been given her name, Blanche; Marie was Sister Mary Josine's baptismal name. Every B.V.M. was "Sister Mary" even though it seemed repetitive in my case.

Sister Mary John Michael Dee was now president, as well as religious superior of the seventy-two nuns assigned to the college, when I was welcomed into the Mundelein community. Sister Mary Janet, still chair of the art department, assigned the classes that I would teach: Art Structure, a beginning visual vocabulary for artists; Design I and II; and Introduction to the Arts, a liberal-arts requirement for all students with sometimes as many as 120 in one class. I also taught first-year religion and acted as college adviser for the students in my religion class. By 1955 students were addressed in classes by their baptismal names.

Loyola University Chicago, adjacent to Mundelein College, did not admit women to its Lake Shore Campus until 1966. In addition Loyola had no art department, so our enrollment continued to expand. Tuition in 1955 was $280 per year. Residence fees were from $140 to $200 for a room and $360 for board per year.[6]

Betty Matula, one of eight lay faculty, Sister Mary Janet, and I made up the art department faculty. Betty became a supportive, trusted friend as we planned courses together and shared our delight and concern about our students. Our young artists were remarkably responsive, responsible, creative, and closer to me in age and interest than most of the faculty. I studied constantly to prepare experiences worthy of them.

Mundelein offered two art majors, a thirty-hour art major and a bachelor of fine arts degree that required sixty hours. The elementary schools were in such dire need of teachers that students with only two years of college were hired to teach; it was difficult to convince students to stay and finish their degrees. Almost half of our students were preparing to teach in the city's elementary and high schools, so they opted for the thirty-hour major.

Art faculty taught double periods, twice the number of clock hours in studio classes as in a lecture course, so we spent a great deal of time with the students. The B.F.A. degree required that half of one's college courses, sixty credit hours, be in the art department. And because studio courses met for double periods, faculty spent many hours in small classes with very creative students. Our friendships generated with some students have endured through many decades.

Jane Cordes Simanis, class of '58, who teaches watercolor classes in Washington, D.C., and exhibits widely in that area, recalls, "You expected much from us, and *we worked*. I remember especially one all-nighter, painting color charts." Alvena Schell, class of '58, remembers, "Everything seemed so well thought out and organized. I felt that I got a vision about how to make a living. Happily, that vision and direction stayed with me, and I am making a living with my paintings, both commissioned works and others that I sell out of my studio in the Torpedo Factory Art Center in Alexandria, Virginia."

Convent life was strictly observed in the college community. Sisters wore ankle-length habits of black serge with a very complex and time-consuming headdress consisting of a heavily starched "quilled border" (derived from a nineteenth-century dust cap) under a heavily starched "hood" (originally a sunbonnet). The hood folded into a box at the back. Over this, a hip-length black veil was pinned into the shape of an Irish coffin—a very heavy symbol! We wore our coffins all day, every day.

We lived in small cells in the convent, which were on the ninth through twelfth floors of the Skyscraper and marked *cloister* to assure privacy. Our daily schedule, or horarium, was patterned after life in rural Irish culture. We were awakened at 5:00 A.M. with a rising bell; we then dressed and appeared in the chapel by 5:30. We meditated for one half hour before Mass at 6:00. Breakfast followed, then preparation and classes. We gathered in the chapel at 5:00 P.M. for "Visits," assigned vocal prayers that include the rosary.

Prayers were followed by dinner. All our meals were taken in silence, with spiritual reading at dinner from some book chosen by the superior; conversation was allowed at dinner on Sunday noon, and also on Thursday nights because we made a holy hour after dinner and missed our recreation hour together. We ordinarily gathered for recreation (conversation as we mended our clothing) for an hour after dinner, then recited night prayers in the chapel. We retired at 9:30 P.M. That romantic Skyscraper building began to feel like a solemn limestone mausoleum.

We taught eight courses each year and were allotted college duties. The younger sister faculty were assigned turns cashiering in the tearoom. (I often slowed down the line by suggesting that milkshakes were the same price as the cottage cheese.) We were expected to take turns as receptionists operating the switchboard, which controlled the one phone on each floor of the building, and we operated the student elevators. For two years, I lived as a residence moderator, which included late nights and rising at 5:00 A.M. And all of this was spiced with college committee service. If all this sounds exhausting, it was!

We were allowed to walk down Sheridan Road with a companion, or to Granville Avenue two blocks away to shop. My favorite adventure was the hardware store on Granville, where I could buy stuff for classes and experiments. Because of my professional area I was allowed to take students and a sister companion to the Art Institute to see exhibits. When we received permission to go out, we were given a coin envelope with two bus tokens; we were never permitted to eat outside the convent.

We were granted a home visit of three days per year, with a companion. My mother and father came to visit in 1956 to tell me that they were selling our family home and moving to Boulder, Colorado, to be near my brother Bob and his family. My mother lived less than a year there. She died on the feast of the Sacred Heart in 1957; my father followed her three years later and was buried on the feast of the Sacred Heart. My two brothers were giving their energies to their jobs and families in Colorado and New York, so I seldom saw them. I put all my energy into Mundelein College: the art department, the students, my own painting, my colleagues on the faculty, and the B.V.M. congregation lifestyle.

We B.V.M.'s were a large group of religious. When I entered the congregation in 1944, we numbered 2,500 women.[7] Our members were highly educated as our only ministry was teaching. It was community policy to allow each woman to complete college after first vows as a religious or to pursue a graduate degree if she entered with a college diploma. I was allowed to begin a master of fine arts degree at the Catholic University of America in Washington, D.C., in 1949, attending the program part-time as my community duties allowed. I received a master of fine arts—or *Magisterius in Artibus in Elegantium* as it was printed on my diploma, which was all in Latin—in 1956, the year after I began teaching at Mundelein. The M.F.A. was a terminal degree for persons in the creative arts as no university offered a Ph.D. degree in this area.

Sister Mary Ann Ida Gannon was appointed president and superior of Mundelein College in August 1957, and we rejoiced. She was a young philosophy teacher with new ideas and new energy, who was challenging us to "take leaps." She enlarged the campus in the 1960s by building a new dormitory named Coffey Hall, for the original founder of the college, and by building the Learning Resource Center, which housed the library, audiovisual services, and faculty offices. Both buildings received large government grants. The college property expanded to include two apartment buildings, which were used as dormitories, and the Yellow House, a mansion south of the new library, which was used as a center for graduate religious studies. In 1957 Mundelein College had become the largest Catholic women's college in the United States.[8]

In the early 1960s Sister Mary Ann Ida selected bright young sisters during their first years of teaching at the college and sent them to prestigious universities for Ph.D. degrees. They returned with doctorates in philosophy, theology, Russian, English, history, administration, French, economics, music, and other areas. We became engrossed in conversations about change in the church, about education, and about the form that religious life would take in the future. Our students were part of these vigorous conversations, and Mundelein was an exceptionally stimulating environment.

The college began admitting older women into the continuing education program in 1965. These women brought much mature experience to our class discussions, which enriched the department immeasurably. Louva Calhoun, B.F.A., class of '70, writes, "My first class in the department was drawing with Gordon Goetemann. At that time he was very skeptical about the seriousness of these older housewives looking for an outlet, but later he defended us as being especially serious, dedicated, and creative students." Fern Samuels, B.F.A., class of '73, currently a professor at Columbia College in Chicago, writes, "Going back to school as an older student, I was very open to all that the art department had to offer, especially the classes in twentieth-century art history."

Lynn Botti, our first continuing-education art major, introduced me to Thomas Berry, a Passionist priest who was the president of the American Teilhard Association in New York. He would become an ally in my research and subsequent paintings influenced by Teilhard de Chardin, and he became an indefatigable supporter of the Institute of Creation-Centered Spirituality, which began at Mundelein in 1978.

The late 1960s and early 1970s were times of great upheaval on college campuses. The very unpopular Vietnam War caused much soul-searching among students, and some of this found voice in the teach-ins and sit-ins on campus. The most visible sign of unrest at Mundelein appeared in the red paint spilled over the heads of the two thirty-foot-tall angels named Uriel, "flame of God," and Jophiel, "beauty of God," who guarded the entrance to the college.

Part of the unrest on Mundelein's campus boiled over in concerns about the twenty-two courses required of all students for the liberal arts degree. In January 1970 the curriculum committee, with faculty, student, and administration representation, called for a three-day meeting to discuss changes. The process was called the Conference on Curriculum, or Con-Cur. Both white and black students convinced us that they should be responsible for choosing their own educational experiences. All required courses in liberal arts were deleted, but the required courses remained in the major sequences. Students were empowered to approve the syllabus for a class before a faculty member began teaching it, and students were elected to faculty committees.

Our faculty discussed our responsibility to the ever-growing black population in Chicago. We agreed to forgo salary raises in 1969 and fund scholarships for about fifty young black women. We also offered them tutorials as well as financial aid.

The black population in the city was becoming very active, and a Black Panther group from Northwestern University came to campus to organize black students, who then created the Mundelein College United Black Association (MUCUBA). They insisted on having a union of their own that no white person would be allowed to enter, and they were given space in the mansion on the lake, which had been the college library and is now Piper Hall. They asked for their own dining room, and were given room 100, which had been a faculty dining room. MUCUBA members were not allowed to speak to white people outside of the classrooms. Though many white students supported the black students in their practice of separatism, it was a painful experience for students and faculty.

After Vatican II, some B.V.M. sisters began to live in smaller groups, and in 1973 our living group moved to the top floor of the Northland apartments, which were used as a dormitory for residence students. The sixth floor was sparsely occupied because the students believed that it was haunted. Fourteen B.V.M.'s moved into the sixth floor to form a community. Some of us remained there until Loyola razed the building in 1991.

A storefront in the Spanish Manor, the apartment building west of the Skyscraper, became available, and I requested it as a studio space. It was the dry-cleaner's shop that had been our smoker when I was in college. This became my "Ming Tang Studio" (the *ming tang* is the top floor of a Chinese house accessible only by a retractable rope ladder). My studio space enabled me to paint and to prepare exhibits. It was a vital center for aesthetic discussions with students and artists about the relationships of art and life.

The writings of Pierre Teilhard de Chardin absorbed me when they were first published in English in 1959. Teilhard's vision of evolutionary history and its effect on theology intrigued me. I began reading his work because I was researching Hindu and Buddhist spiritualities. Teilhard didn't give me any insight into these spiritual traditions, but I became entranced with his cosmology, his perception of evolution, and his theology of creation.

The margins of my books filled with diagrams and drawings as I attempted to decipher Teilhard's language. I'm not sure that I would have persevered in this task, but the Jesuits at Loyola University Chicago were forbidden to read Teilhard (also a Jesuit), so this created an impetus for me. These marginal drawings became a series of paintings. I wanted the paintings to live, to breathe, and to glow with an inward light. The paintings grew into a body of work that I was asked to exhibit and talk about in 1968 as part of a regional Teilhard symposium at Seabury Theological Seminary, the Episcopalian seminary at Northwestern University.

In 1971 I received one of the first sabbaticals awarded to a member of the religious faculty at Mundelein. I planned to study the art and spirituality of East Asia: Japan, Korea, Thailand, Taiwan, and Hong Kong. (Mainland China was still closed to outside researchers.) The president told me that a sabbatical meant that I was given the time, but there was no money involved; I would need to find the money. The sisters of the Mundelein community arranged a fund, and I went to East Asia with a stipend of under $350 per month. (When I returned, we formed a committee to ensure that the sister faculty received the same sabbatical privileges as lay faculty.)

Blanche M. Gallagher, B.V.M., poses with *Homage to Teilhard: Planetization*, 1977. One of the paintings in her series Homage to Teilhard.

The School Sisters of Notre Dame offered me hospitality for seven months at their college in Kyoto, Japan. I studied in the monasteries and museums; learned about Noh drama, Kabuki theater, and the tea ceremony; and lived in a Tantric Tendai monastery on Mt. Hiei in order to incorporate the Shinto and Buddhist spirituality into my classes. Carmelle Zserdin, B.V.M., a potter at Clarke College, shared three months of this adventure with me. After seven months in Japan, I studied the spirituality and art of the Hindu and Buddhist traditions by traveling for three months in Taiwan, Hong Kong, Korea, and Thailand, living as a guest in convents with American sisters.

In 1975 Susan Rink, B.V.M., followed Ann Ida Gannon as president. Our enrollment had reached 1,427 and the college had tripled in size. Under Susan's presidency and with the great creativity of the faculty and of Mary I. Griffin, former academic dean, the very experimental Weekend College flourished on campus. We offered some art history courses, but were unable to propose many studio courses within the time format.

My research of the mandala as the basic ground plan of the Hindu temple made it possible for me to receive a Lilly Foundation grant in 1976–77 to do further research in India, Burma, Nepal, and Sri Lanka, where I crawled around, studied, and photographed fifty Hindu and Buddhist temples in these four countries. My itinerary packet held thirty-six plane tickets, for the government-owned planes flew from one city to another only once a day, and they carried a two-month waiting list. My Teilhard lectures were also well received in India and Nepal. Mary Donahey, B.V.M., professor of theology, spent the first six weeks in India with me.

When I returned from South Asia, Mary DeCock, B.V.M., acting chair of the graduate religious studies department that year, asked me to meet with Matthew Fox, O.P., who had submitted a proposal for a graduate degree that would ground theological education in aesthetics and creativity. He called it creation spirituality. Matt suggested a master of theology degree that embraced the arts of dance, painting, poetry, and music and that would discipline students to become mystics and prophets. We accepted his proposal and the Institute of Creation-Centered Spirituality (ICCS) was born on Mundelein's campus in the fall of 1978. Matt's vision changed my life, for it introduced me to the writings of Meister Eckhart, a fourteenth-century mystic. Matt gave me a copy of his fresh, new book, *Breakthrough: Meister Eckhart's Creation Spirituality in a New Translation*. It transformed my spiritual life, as well as my painting and teaching.

Frank Drew, M.A., class of '80, recalls: "The thing that stood out about Mundelein was the influence of the B.V.M. sisters and the faculty. They seemed to set a tone of open communication both in and out of the classroom. There was the sense that the faculty had a real interest in the well-being of each student and what each student could contribute through the open-minded exploration into many schools of thought, from many cultures and times."

As I realized the effect of Eckhart on my life and on the lives of our students, I wished that someone would package Teilhard in a similar way. I published *Meditations with Teilhard de Chardin* in 1988 through Bear and Company, the publishing company in Santa Fe, New Mexico, that Matt had founded. The book attempted to fit the writings of Teilhard into the four paths that Matt originated for Eckhart, and my book is in its fifth printing. I received a grant for a month at Ragdale, an artist's colony in Lake Forest, Illinois, where I completed the illustrations for *Meditations*.

I very much enjoyed working with students in our graduate program in religious studies, teaching the relationship between art and spirituality, but I realized my need for updated credentials in theology. So I applied for a sabbatical in 1980–81 and spent fourteen months at the Graduate Theological Union in Berkeley, California, to renew my studies in theology and to prepare myself to become a spiritual director (or mentor, as I prefer to call it).

Matt Fox left Mundelein in 1985 to establish the creation-spirituality program at Holy Names College in Oakland, California. I joined him in 1989 and taught in the program in Oakland while I was offering a semester course in Theology of Creativity at the Graduate Theological Union in Berkeley. Mundelein continued to offer courses in creation spirituality as an enrichment to their graduate degree.

By the 1980s, several senior faculty were troubled because almost half of Mundelein's students were business majors. We mourned the loss of the liberal arts basis for our college, though the arts at Mundelein had been eroding since 1970. We met to consider our options. We agreed that our students, many who were in the Weekend College, did need to have the assurance that they would be trained in business and would be able to make a living. So after five years of committee work, we developed a master of liberal studies degree, launched in 1983. We hoped that after our students became proficient in business they would become aware of their lack of integrated learning and would return. It worked. The M.L.S. degree grew and prospered with three required courses: Survival of the Planet, Survival of the Polity, and Survival of the Person. Michael Fortune, professor of English, and I taught the "Person" course together for five years; we had often team taught courses on the undergraduate level.

Miriam Ross, M.A., class of '91, a School Sister of Notre Dame, recalls: "Our course in creativity in song, writing, art, and ritual still lives in me. I've never learned so much. What I learned with and in my body I remember. I do not remember the words. These works opened me to basic truths that I hold today and use in my healing work as a spiritual director."

And Jennifer Kelly Connolly, M.A., class of '91, adds a story: "I remember how empowering my first class was for me. We stood with feet firmly on the ground and drew energy from the fireball at the center of the planet into our bodies. When I left to return to my car, a man tried to mug me. I opened my mouth and screamed; I was in awe of the energy coming from me. He ran away. This empowering essence summarizes my whole experience of Mundelein College."

After I celebrated my sixty-fifth birthday, I asked for a half-time contract to teach in the graduate programs. The art department had four tenured professors, and enrollment was too low to support that many faculty. This left me free for six months of the year to accept other invitations. I taught Painting as Meditation for Matt Fox in Oakland and Theology of Creativity at the Graduate Theological Union in Berkeley for one semester in 1988. The next

winter I returned to Berkeley and received an appointment as spiritual director at Grace Episcopal Cathedral in San Francisco from the Rev. Dr. Lauren
Artress, Canon Pastor, who was a friend from Mystery School.[9] Our students
over the years have moved all around the world and have been very generous
in inviting me to visit them.

The broad landscape of my life has spread over thirty-two countries in
Europe, East Asia, South Asia, the Americas, the Middle East, and Africa. And
through the depth level I have been nourished by the Christian and Hebrew
scriptures, the Catholic ritual and sacramental system, the Hindu and
Buddhist scriptures, and all the art, music, philosophy, theology, and literature flowing from them. My mother's adventurous Norwegian-Viking ancestry has challenged me to travel to explore the arts and spiritualities of this
planet, and my Irish father's gift of storytelling has enabled me to relate these
experiences to others.

When we view ourselves as more deep and mysterious than the galaxies,
we perceive how much we must expand our potentials as the dream flows
through us. My Mundelein colleagues, students, and friends constantly
stretched me toward that dream. What more can one ask of a college?[10]

Endnotes

1. Editorial, *The Skyscraper,* 22 January 1943, Mundelein College Archives (MCA),
   Gannon Center for Women and Leadership, Loyola University Chicago.

2. *The Skyscraper,* 20 November 1944, MCA.

3. *The Skyscraper,* 8 October 1943, MCA.

4. Doris Kearns Goodwin, *No Ordinary Time: Franklin and Eleanor Roosevelt: The Home
   Front in World War II.* (New York: Simon and Schuster, 1994). Goodwin gives a great
   deal of factual information about World War II.

5. *The Skyscraper,* 8 October 1943, MCA.

6. Mundelein College Catalog 1955–56, MCA.

7. As I write in 1999, we are less than nine hundred. We have buried or said goodbye to
   over sixteen hundred women during my time in the congregation. Thirty women
   have joined us in the past thirty years.

8. Sister Mary Cecilia Bodman, "Mundelein Then," pt. IV: 1957–69, MCA.

9. In 1985 Jean Houston, noted psychologist, established a Mystery School that integrated studies of new scientific mind-brain explorations with classical mythologies
   and ancient spiritual belief systems.

10. The full text of this memoir is available through the Gannon Center for Women and
    Leadership Archives at Loyola University Chicago or from the author.

A Tale of Two Mundeleins, 1947–1951

Mary Alma Sullivan, B.V.M.

It was the best of times; it was the best of times. Or so it seems from the perspective of nearly five decades. Families had settled back into the familiar practices of the prewar period, and many of them had discovered prosperity and the conveniences that came with better times. Young women, like me, coming of age in these families found opportunities for personal development and options in life choices beyond marriage. But the years 1947–51 in the United States were not without clouds for those in touch with events around the world.

This is where Mundelein College entered my picture, colored it, and shaped its dimensions. The college deepened my values and opened me to the wider world, though I could not discern that movement at the time. But I'm getting ahead of myself.

Finding My Niche

I really had no intention of attending Mundelein College. It had nothing to do with the reputation of the college, though I confess my information about Mundelein was limited to the fact that the same religious congregation—the Sisters of Charity of the Blessed Virgin Mary (B.V.M.'s)—that taught in my high school also taught there. And despite the fact that many of my high school classmates would go there, I thought that "going to college" meant going away to school.

Interestingly, Mundelein was not the choice of Margaret "Peggy" Egan Namovic, who would become a college friend. "In truth, I wanted to go to Marquette for two reasons: it was coed but equally important was that it was a Jesuit school." Though her father admired a Jesuit education, "my folks said, 'Mundelein is here in the city. The B.V.M.'s are here, and the B.V.M.'s are good.'" Peggy added, "They were not willing to send me out of town. But during my first year at Mundelein, I was so delighted to be there that I gave no further thought to Marquette."[1]

How I came to enter Mundelein in 1947, therefore, remains unclear. I suppose family finances were a factor. Perhaps it was partly the more conservative Irish-American family structure in place at the time, particularly as regards daughters: staying near home was safer. But the one factor I remember clearly is that my father was impressed with the intelligence, poise, and professional performance of B.V.M.-trained high school graduates employed in his law office.

We were a family of six. My father, an attorney associated with a large Chicago law firm, later served as an assistant attorney general for the State of Illinois. My mother had completed a year of training as a legal secretary at DePaul University in Chicago before their marriage. I was the eldest of four children and the only girl. By the time I entered Mundelein College, the family had been living on the North Side of Chicago in the community of Edgebrook for six years—and Mundelein was only a thirty- to forty-minute bus commute away.

Thus, I arrived with 307 other freshmen at the west door of the college in September 1947, with a schedule of my classes in hand. Classmates came from forty-seven different high schools, the majority coming from the city: St. Scholastica, St. Mary, Longwood, Visitation, Trinity, Marywood, Alvernia, Siena, Aquinas, Senn, and Immaculata, my own school. A few students came from other places: Indiana, Missouri, Ohio, New Jersey, Wisconsin, and Puerto Rico. I found out a month or two after we arrived that there were even four GIs in our class.[2]

Many faces were familiar. Close friends from high school were on hand to ease the tension of embarking on a new adventure and to increase the feeling of being at home: Jean Schaefer Wojiechowski, with whom I would travel to school daily until the demands of courses and cocurricular involvement intervened, Kathryn "Katie" Quinn Knowles, and Mary Ellen "Murnie" Ward Page, the latter two sharing with me a love of writing.

We had little control over which courses we took during freshman and sophomore years because the Mundelein College curriculum emphasized the core of humanities and science courses deemed requisite for any educated person as a prelude to specializing in a major field. For the most part, the biggest decisions entering freshmen made were not about the kinds of courses they would take, but about when to take the required courses.

I found the first years of pursuing a bachelor of arts degree challenging and exciting. As I look back on it now, there was an uncommon professionalism in the faculty I encountered. But at the time I imagine this impression expressed itself in eureka moments—"I didn't know that!" or "Wouldn't it be wonderful to know as much as she does about . . ."

Science and foreign language were especially challenging for me. Honestly, I would not have survived chemistry except for the patience and understanding of Professor Henry Budd, who commuted five days a week from the Milwaukee area and often appeared in class in mismatched trousers and suit coat because, as he explained to us, he dressed in the dark so as not to awaken his wife. Professor Budd was a prince of a man, who managed to coax me through smelly concoctions and opaque reading to an acceptable, though hardly impressive, grade.

Then there was the required language study. How I ever got assigned to a course in intermediate Spanish given the bumbling nature of my high school experience with the subject is beyond my comprehension. In addition to distressing tasks involving syntax and vocabulary, classroom conversation in Spanish about "the red cow at grandmother's door" didn't seem practical. Complicating my course performance was the fact that my instructor was also Mundelein's academic dean, Sister Mary Bernarda Welch. It never occurred to me to represent my cause or ask for a Spanish I course instead. Ironically, as a master's degree candidate in English at Loyola University Chicago years later, I chose Spanish to fulfill, successfully, the language requirement.

Sophomore year marked the real beginning of my college life and the beginning and end of elected public office. I found a focus for my studies when I took a newswriting course taught by Sister Mary Madelena Thornton, which brought me in touch with the staff of *The Skyscraper,* an eight-page tabloid published twelve times each academic year. My writing was also nurtured by the discovery of room 506, home to both *The Mundelein College Review,* a quarterly magazine, and *Quest,* the biannual poetry collection.

I was elected president of the sophomore homeroom in which about thirty of us had our religion class. The homeroom was also the place for students to hear all-college or class announcements, receive occasional reminders of decorum, and elect representatives to this or that committee. My election was a heady experience until I was instructed by Sister Mary Cecile Riordan, who presided over the group, that my specific tasks were generally to promote good order, start the homeroom activities should she be late arriving, and take attendance in homeroom and at assemblies. The last task meant I had to be present at every assembly, and they occurred sometimes twice a week.

There were about thirty-three assemblies in 1948–49—some required seniors to wear caps and gowns—with a staggering range of topics, including prayer, vocations, applied economics, ethical aspects of social security, and "the Palestine question." Some assemblies featured people in the news: novelist Bruce Marshall, scientist Glenn Seaborg, tenor Christopher Lynch, and Krishna Nehru, younger sister of the prime minister of India and a follower of

Ghandi. More appealing to me were the following: the presentation on Graham Greene's *The Heart of the Matter,* a lecture on Modern Art and the Old Masters, piano and lute concerts, and delightful performances by Cornelia Otis Skinner and the Catholic Youth Organization Theatre Workshop. Needless to say, it was a very long year at the end of which I determined to leave attendance and the promotion of good order to those whose political virtue was ironclad.

Meantime, literature and writing absorbed me. Though I made college friends among *Skyscraper* staff members and practiced a new format when I ventured briefly into newspaper writing, it soon became clear that the fascination with chasing news did not readily translate into an ability to meet *Skyscraper* deadlines. Reluctantly, I moved on.

The choice of my major entering junior year was never in doubt. It was English. While a few classmates labored over the decision—history or sociology? biology or chemistry?—and at least one person weighed faculty affability in her choice, mine seems, in retrospect, a seamless passage from the required courses of the first two years to a course of study that allowed me to study literature and learn more about writing.

Shakespeare. The English Romantic Movement. Contemporary Drama. World Literature. Dante. Courses that required writing essays, poetry, and short stories were taught by Sister Mary Irma Corcoran, my mentor on *The Mundelein Review* during college days and a source of encouragement and friendship throughout my life. Because it was a regular source of conversation in my family as I grew and because I took the words of Sister Mary Irma to heart ("Learning to write is one thing; having something about which to write is quite another"), I chose history as a minor field.

But my college life as a junior and senior was focused on room 506 and its activities. I remember it these many years later as a magical place where what we now call collegiality was present each day. Staff members, experienced and brand-new, sat around the table with Sister Mary Irma to plan the next issue of *The Review* or of *Quest* and to review material selected for an issue to determine a theme or placement of pieces. Editors and senior staffers— Katie Quinn, Virginia Volini Marciniak, Joan Holland, Marian Dwyer Gleason, Jeanne Pennie Goldstein—conferred over a piece one of them had completed and looked for ways to improve a poem or short story, or they labored over editorial suggestions on the work of some student who had submitted a book review or article for publication.

Mary Alma Sullivan (right) meets with staff writers about the publication of *Quest*, the biennial collection of student poetry.

The energy of room 506 was everywhere: in the damp recesses of the basement locker room first thing in the morning where, amid clattering locker doors, writing ideas for *The Review* were shared along with class notes and reserve books; on stairways between classes where manuscripts were exchanged or last-minute editing assignments made; even in the Mundelein tearoom or across the fence in the Loyola University student union where an editor could be summoned to room 506 to deal with a printing emergency.

Apart from the introduction to writing and editing, Sister Mary Irma challenged all the staffers and writers with subtle invitations to excellence. I recall one piece of advice that she gave after she had read the first draft of an essay I was writing on Sir John Tenniel, the illustrator known for his work in *Punch* and for illustrating the first edition of Lewis Carroll's *Alice in Wonderland*. She said, "I think that you would find a visit to the Newberry Library very helpful." The Newberry Library! I thought only scholars used its resources. But there I was—requesting a first edition of the book and related commentaries, occupying my own carrel, and returning to my own work the better for it.

Our 506 experience gave us the opportunity to glimpse that exciting, exacting world of publishing "out there." I discovered some of my own gifts and the gifts others provided that complemented my own, and I learned about the richness and satisfaction of working closely with others in a common endeavor and about responsibility to a project and to colleagues. Katie Quinn shared my enthusiasm for *The Review* experience: "Working on the magazine was the most satisfying activity in my college career. I loved to go to that office. I felt comfortable. Sister Mary Irma made it a welcoming place. She appreciated each of us and our tiny bit of talent. To think about *The Review,* to really do it, see it in print, and realize your thoughts have value."[3] Clearly, her challenge took root when Katie and I were recommended by the English department faculty for membership in Delta Gamma Sigma, Mundelein's honor society for writers.

It occurs to me now that even the preparation at the end of our senior year for the dreaded two days of final comprehensive examinations in English was eased by the fact that those of us who chose to study together transferred the collegial and organizational skills learned in room 506 to the new and crucial endeavor of pulling together all we had learned in our major field. For those of us connected with the literary publications, the final afternoon of the exam was the best part: to write an original poem, short essay, or story.

Sister Mary Irma Corcoran, B.V.M., pursues research in the National Library, Dublin, Ireland.

I would not want to leave the impression that Mundelein students were all about the rigors of the intellectual life and associated activities. For the most part, the college was commuter oriented, and even the few whose homes were not within the reach of Chicago buses and the El had to arrange for weekend lodging with a local relative or family friend. So we continued a social life in our local communities, but as each of our four years at Mundelein unrolled, the high school groups who had matriculated together at Mundelein embraced others and, more and more, socialized together. For some, finding a social niche was difficult in the face of so many who came with friends from their high schools. Again, Peggy Egan: "In high school I was not part of the mainstream—sororities and such. I felt alone. When I went to Mundelein, I resolved it would be with a new slate. I was going to be somebody. I knew I *was* somebody. . . . I found myself at Mundelein, and I found a lovely group of girls from Immaculata who included me. In fact, I had lots of little groups with whom I socialized."[4]

There were the college-sponsored events in which to participate: the Skyscraper Ball, candle-lighting ceremony, and postcandle-lighting class parties at Christmastime; the Sophomore Cotillion; first-night benefits, such as opening night at the Ballet Russe; teas to welcome new club members; myriad concerts; and intercollegiate basketball and volleyball games. Some students joined the stage crew for theater department productions, such as *Peter Pan* and *The Lute Song,* and were rewarded with an invitation to the cast party after "striking the set."

Informally, there was considerable interest in bridge games at the Loyola Union just across the fence; more than one bridge enthusiast passed up a class meeting of Philosophy 304 or English 410, reluctantly no doubt, when a fourth hand was needed. We linked with classmates for foreign movies—the new rage—at the old Cinema Theatre on Chicago Avenue or picked up a bite to eat at Hardings on Wabash before ushering for a performance of *The Lute Song* or *South Pacific* at a downtown theater. The old Edgewater Beach Hotel— only a mile or so from the campus—was not only the site for Mundelein class luncheons but a popular spot for strolling along the beach walk and cruising in the hotel lagoon with your date on a spring evening.

The Learning Environment

To anyone who did not attend Mundelein College, certainly in the 1947–51 period, it might appear that nothing else of influence was occurring on campus for me and my classmates other than the experiences of college publications work and academic courses. In retrospect, it seems that we were being informed and formed though our clubs, committee work, conversation with faculty, and activities to be women in and for the world.

Conversations with a few of my classmates from the class of 1951, as well as my meanderings through issues of *The Skyscraper* for 1947–51, prompt me to suggest that the educational environment—that is, the environment of Mundelein College beyond and around academic activities such as courses, majors, and minors—provided us with two parallel tracks which, though apparently contradictory, actually came together in the lives of graduates. To develop this idea, I focused research for this essay on the editorial pages of *The Skyscraper*, because what ultimately appeared in print in each issue reflected an important process: the faculty moderator and the staff discussed jointly what was newsworthy for the student body after which staff writers assumed the task of preparing editorials. As a result of this collaboration, editorial pages provided an integration of three perspectives: the interests of students, the attitudes, often unconscious, of the religious sisters who were their teachers, and the elements of institutional mission.

In examining these parallel tracks, perhaps the most obvious track was the traditional one, which reinforced the religious traditions of the Roman Catholic Church, including its social and political positions. In addition, this track followed a time-honored attitude toward woman's place in the world as wife and mother and homemaker. I do not doubt that my parents expected Mundelein to be a place where my formation in the Catholic faith would be deepened and strengthened and where, in addition, I would be trained intellectually to be an estimable companion to my future husband and a worthy educator for my children.

Also evident is the second track, which I perceived as I thumbed through the pages of *The Skyscraper* for those years. Despite the apparent peace and prosperity of the postwar era in the United States, ideas and movements were stirring about which students became aware even if they read only their campus newspaper. It appears that even as the image of the good Catholic woman and her place in society was frequently addressed in *The Skyscraper*, a parallel and less formal education assumed that Mundelein graduates would work in the world—in the public sector or in a business setting. At the very least, each of us would be citizens of the world with responsibilities for making it a better place than it was, for making it a place where justice and peace collaborated.

The classmates with whom I spoke agreed. "Mundelein gave me an excellent education. I learned to think. I learned compassion. I learned to take responsibility for my part of the world as well as for the people next door. Mundelein helped me to prepare very well for life's encounters."[5] Irene Meyer, who returned years later to Mundelein as a professor of psychology, viewed her experience in terms of her activism in later life. "A lot of what we were learning in class, such as being concerned about people who didn't have anything, led me to a concern later with civil rights, though it wasn't called that at the time, and to attempts to banish the death penalty."[6]

For Judith Terese McNulty, B.V.M., the friends she made at Mundelein developed the social outreach interests that accompanied their college years. "I have remained close to my Mundelein friends. They have not been static as far as their education about the world is concerned. When we get together, conversations center on issues in society, on the conditions in the world."[7] "Both my religious faith and my sense of social responsibility were encouraged at Mundelein," recalls Katie Quinn. "Of course, we actually had to take religion and philosophy courses. And so much of responsibility to others was inherent, just in the way that our teachers were and the way they treated us. I never thought about going out and doing good. It was just there. And I embraced teaching as part of that."[8]

Catholicism and Activism

An examination of the editorial pages of *The Skyscraper* over the 1947–51 period offers evidence of the reinforcement of traditional Roman Catholic social values espoused by the college and by parents alike. Under one guise or another, there were frequent reminders that beauty is in the soul, that Catholic college students aren't capitalizing on opportunities to promote their faith, that retreats are essential to prepare for meeting the world, and that making life choices requires strong faith. Understanding what a Catholic education is all about and how to create a Catholic atmosphere on campus and recognize the elements and significance of Catholic leadership were frequently addressed themes. In an editorial piece entitled "Letter to the Freshmen," students were reminded that "a spiritual life prevails in your school, a life that you must bring to others outside. A Catholic atmosphere strengthens and defends the kingdom of Christ in the lives of individuals, families, and all of society."[9] The following month a checklist was provided to assist each student in assessing her maturity as a Catholic who could explain church attitudes toward birth control, labor unions, divorce, papal infallibility, and confession to a priest.[10]

These observations in the student newspaper not only reflected why parents sent or encouraged their daughters to attend Mundelein College but also showed the strength of the religion program in the curriculum, which required that students enroll in religion courses throughout their four years. A marriage course was required of graduating seniors. An editorial declares that "we believe that 95 out of every 100 students here at Mundelein realize that the 'careers' they are planning for are really vocations, either to religious life or to marriage."[11] Yet most of my friends, if recollection serves me, were looking toward the world of work, not marriage.

A specific and persistent focus in the college newspaper from 1947–51 was devotion to Mary, the mother of God, as the model of purity, self-sacrifice, and devotion to Jesus for young Catholic women. Her feast days were celebrated variously in fact and regularly in the press. As the perception of the Communist threat grew, the regular recitation of the rosary was suggested to thwart the menace. "A chapel ringing with rosaries will be the best medicine in the world today."[12] Under the headline "Looking for a World-Wide Panacea? Our Lady Offers Rosary Cure-All," a reporter for *The Skyscraper* describes the plan being initiated by the Club Coordinating Committee for Mundelein's participation in the group rosary movement as "a deterrent to the extension of Communism and American materialism." As a convert to Catholicism, Irene Meyer had a special interest in learning all she could about church history and belief. She became a vital member of the Mundelein sodality as a way of enriching her faith, and this involvement "meant being in touch with people who . . . believed and weren't afraid to acknowledge, you know, publicly that they believed."[13]

Even the Pilgrims were fair game. "The Pilgrims had much to be grateful for . . . but we have something most—probably all—Pilgrims lacked. We have love for the mother of God, and trust in her love for us."[14] And perhaps the most imposing tribute to Mary from Mundelein College found expression in the annual Magnificat medal first presented in April 1948. Medalists were women who demonstrated humanitarian, aesthetic, social, scientific, philanthropic, or religious leadership. The medal was awarded annually through 1991.[15]

Lenten practices, as well as suggestions about how to celebrate Christmas or Easter in a religious spirit and how to model that spirit for others, were addressed as occasion demanded. And popular books, movies, and plays were examined in light of their congruence with Catholic values. An editorial in 1949 took on materialism, which it claimed underestimated the intangibles of our culture, such as service and simple living.[16]

As an expression of Catholic religious commitment, *The Skyscraper* editorials encouraged students to develop a spirit of service. Sometimes the focus was on internal service: serving on student government committees or as officers of classes or clubs, signing up for committees to plan an event, finding an outside speaker for a club meeting, or greeting new students and campus guests. More often than not, the focus was on external service: representing the college at conferences, symposiums, and tournaments; volunteering for parish activities; or tutoring in elementary schools. In the 1949–50 academic year, a service sorority whose members "welcomed all for all," was initiated.

Growing out of this emphasis, but framed by traditional Catholic values and practices, editorials decried the inertia of Catholic students in a needy world and extolled the importance of being persons of justice who would fight bigotry. As a practical demonstration of expressing justice for the needy, an editorial on February 19, 1951, urges students to contribute to a fund being established to support two women on campus who were displaced by the war in Europe.

Attitudes toward women and toward women in leadership roles are frequent topics in the editorials of *The Skyscraper,* and are, perhaps, the most compelling indicators of the two educational tracks I identified earlier in this piece: education for Catholic life and education for work in the world. As part of a Vital Speakers program, Mundelein collegians spoke on issues off-campus as a way of developing leadership in schools and parishes. While the women of Mundelein College were urged to emulate Mary, the mother of God, in their personal and family lives, they were also urged to be visible and vocal in the world.

A whole series of editorials announced college intiatives to promote student leadership, and to prepare for leadership in the local community and the world. For example, the May 10, 1948, issue features a reflection on the public-mission benefit of leadership-training sessions for everyone; two weeks later another editorial appeared entitled "Leaders Lead What?" The October 6, 1947, issue gives high praise for the introduction of group guidance to explore the leadership responsibilities of Catholic college students. Perhaps the most visible opportunity for practical leadership occurred when the student body approved a measure to affiliate with the newly established National Student Association (NSA). An October 6, 1947, editorial had urged students to attend informational assemblies about voting for this affiliation. Mundelein

College students went on to assume leadership in the NSA at both the national and regional levels, events reported on the news pages of *The Skyscraper.*

An extraordinary example of women's obligation to make a difference appeared in November 2, 1948, issue of *The Skyscraper:* "We're strongly feminist in most things, but we must admit that at meetings and in discussions girls are inclined to let the young men do the talking." The writer calls this "regrettable" and continues: "Not infrequently, the awed silence that accompanies [the resonant voices of young men] is not so much a tribute to their logic as it is an indictment of our timidity."

A similar theme is developed in the May 26, 1950, issue under the headline "The Case of the Vanishing Woman." The editorial reviewed an all-school assembly in which Walter P. Farrell, O.P., reminded students that women in our society are caused to disappear behind a psychological wall. Women are seen as merely decorative, as specimens of physical beauty or of intellect, or as appendages to their husbands. *The Skyscraper* piece urged students not to let this disappearance happen.

Reflecting on remarks by Cardinal Samuel Stritch on the occasion of presenting the Magnificat medal, an editorial rejects the "lazy thinker" among women, the one who will "relapse into the easy bromide of 'a woman's place is in the home'" and believe "woman has no place in activity outside her home." The writer continues that it is personally insulting to women and it is false thinking. "We are spending an important period of our lives being educated as women, we want to be able to apply our college training to community problems."[17]

It seems clear that there was the explicit expectation that we Mundelein graduates had a place in the world and that leadership and service in this arena were required, whether at the local or some other level. "Well-Tailored Leadership Discards Ready-Made Judgments" headlines a piece that uses the metaphor of ladies' fashion to deplore the fact that too many collegians make judgments without learning the facts or exploring the issues.[18] The "Credo of a College Student" begins with this paragraph: "We believe . . . that tomorrow will be better, . . . that beauty and truth and good can yet be found in the world, . . . that life is what we make it, . . . that life will somehow go on despite A-bombs and H-bombs and Red hordes and bungling politicians and indifferent electorates . . . not only that we can save the world, but that it is worth saving."[19] And our class was cautioned in an article titled "1951 World Is Chaotic" that "no flower-strewn path stretches before the 1951 graduate. There is much thinking, working, and praying to be done."[20]

Education for participation in life beyond college required editorials that addressed issues around the world. Through 1947–48 *The Skyscraper* commented on such items as the Marshall Plan and a Palestinian-Jewish conflict. In 1948–49 the newspaper discussed a meeting of the Conference of Pan-American States, the Italian elections and the Communist influence, and the primary elections in Chicago. Political comment through 1949–50 focused on the new West Germany, Red China, anti-Semitism, Poland's "martyrdom," peace and the opening of the jubilee year, continued support of the Red Cross wherever need occurs, the effect of television and advertising on children, and the meaning of bipartisan foreign policy. In our senior year at Mundelein, topics such as Tito versus Franco, the inconsistency of United States diplomacy, and India versus the United Nations were among those published. Not infrequently, editorials challenged pieces appearing in prestigious journals such as *The Nation* and *New Republic*. For example, a 1950 editorial reviewed an article on world Communism in the *New Republic* by historian A. J. P. Taylor. The student writer asserted that Taylor's approach to world Communism contains "factually correct but philosophically distorted reasoning" in believing "that there can be faith without a creed, hope without illusions, love without God."[21]

Living Our Stories

Long ago, Joan Holland and I penned an introduction to the volume of Mundelein College student poetry for which we served as editors. We began this way: "It may be said that some of our songs are off-key, that some of them are awkward and that they lack meatiness and strength. Still, because we believe in our songs, we will not apologize."[22] In the same spirit, and with gratitude to my professors and the 160 women with whom I graduated, these are some of my memories of the best of times.

Endnotes

1. Margaret Egan Namovic, interview by Mary Alma Sullivan, B.V.M., tape recording. 2 October 1998. Mundelein College Oral History Archives, Gannon Center for Women and Leadership, Loyola University Chicago. Taped interviews cited throughout this essay were done by the author and are located in the Mundelein College Oral History Archives of the Gannon Center for Women and Leadership, Loyola University Chicago.

2. *The Skyscraper,* 6 October 1947. Mundelein College Archives (MCA), Gannon Center for Women and Leadership, Loyola University Chicago. Hereafter, all citations, unless otherwise indicated, are from *The Skyscraper*.

3. Kathryn Quinn Knowles interview, tape recording, 15 December 1998.

4. Margaret Egan Namovic interview, tape recording, 2 October 1998.

5. Joan Holland interview, tape recording, 30 November 1998.

6. Irene Meyer interview, tape recording, 18 November 1998.

7. Judith Terese McNulty, B.V.M., interview, tape recording, 9 November 1998.

8. Knowles interview.

9. *The Skyscraper,* 2 October 1950.

10. 13 November 1950.

11. 8 May 1950.

12. 16 October 1950.

13. Meyer interview.

14. 13 November 1950.

15. Among the recipients have been the following: Patty Crowley (1963), cofounder with her husband of the Catholic Family Movement; Gertrude Ramsey Crain (1988) of Crain Communications, Chicago, in recognition of her civic and business leadership; Dolores (Mrs. Bob) Hope (1987) for humanitarian service; Mother Teresa of Calcutta (1981) for lifelong service to the poor, MCA.

16. 21 November 1949.

17. 23 April 1951.

18. 2 November 1948.

19. 22 January 1951.

20. 21 May 1951.

21. 13 November 1950.

22. Editors' Foreword, *Quest,* 14 (1950), MCA.

Working with the People: The Religious Studies Department, 1957–1991

Carol Frances Jegen, B.V.M.

Mundelein College has enjoyed a reputation for involvement with the community of Chicago and beyond. As a high school student I was aware of Mundelein's community influence, but only later as a Sister of Charity of the Blessed Virgin Mary did I realize why this community outreach was integral to Mundelein's mission. Mary Frances Clarke, foundress of the Sisters of Charity of the Blessed Virgin Mary, always wanted her sisters to be involved with the people.[1] It is not surprising that Mundelein's religious studies department has a history of involvement that is unique in the academic world.

Mundelein's religious studies department began in 1957 when Sister Mary Ann Ida Gannon, B.V.M., became president.[2] One of her major goals was the establishment of a theology department, directed by one of the B.V.M. sisters. Such an arrangement could not have taken place in Mundelein's earlier days because of the impossibility of women doing graduate work in theology.[3]

Preparation for the Second Vatican Council began toward the end of the 1950s. One of the ways to understand the community involvement of Mundelein's religious studies department is to relate its activities to the documents of Vatican II. Perhaps the key orientation would be expressed in the opening statements of *Gaudium et Spes,* often referred to as "The Pastoral Constitution on the Church in the Modern World": "The joys and the hopes, the griefs and the anxieties of the [people] of this age, especially those who are poor or in any way afflicted, these too are the joys and hopes, the griefs and anxieties of the followers of Christ. Indeed, nothing genuinely human fails to raise an echo in their hearts."[4]

This memoir, illustrating one major aspect of Mundelein's commitment to the "modern world," features five major sections: (1) department development, (2) the Mundelein Center for Religious Education, (3) Jewish-Christian relations, (4) the Hispanic Institute, and (5) peace studies. Corresponding references to the teachings of the Second Vatican Council will be included in each section. What cannot be included in this brief account are the complete records of the many dedicated persons whose involvements were necessary for these developments. Truly, this history was a work of the "people of God," to use a key designation of the Church as given in *Lumen Gentium,* "Light of the Nations," the Vatican II "Dogmatic Constitution on the Church." Perhaps, someday, a more complete history can be written.

Department Development

The year 1957 marked a major transition period in Mundelein College when Sister Ann Ida became president and the B.V.M. congregation inaugurated its scholasticate program on the Mundelein campus. Immediately after completing the novitiate, all sisters who had not completed a B.A. degree became scholastics with the opportunity for full-time study before being assigned to a teaching position.[5] Courses in philosophy and theology were given high priority.

At the time, I had completed the course work for an M.A. degree in theology at Marquette University's recently established summer program for laity.[6] Sister Ann Ida requested that the B.V.M. congregation send me to Mundelein to begin a theology department that would serve the whole college, including the scholasticate. Up to that time, the Mundelein B.V.M. sisters taught religion classes for juniors and seniors. A first major change occurred in the organization of a new course for freshman year in 1957. The entire freshman class gathered in the auditorium for my lecture, which was followed by discussion sessions with the other sisters in their respective advising groups. Gradually, this lecture/discussion format became a regular department pattern developed with the assistance of Sister Margaret Mary Whalen, B.V.M., and Sister Agnes Cunningham, S.S.C.M. Two diocesan priests, William Clark and Michael Dempsey (later to become bishop), continued to teach some upper-division courses.

Curriculum development could be a significant history on its own, especially because of the major breakthroughs in biblical and theological studies that were occurring at that time. In the summer of 1959 I was invited to a special meeting organized by then-Jesuit Bernard Cooke at Marquette University. Invited were eminent Scripture scholars, theologians, religious educators, and publishers. Some of the participants included Roderick MacKenzie, S.J., later to become director of the Pontifical Biblical Institute in Rome; Gerald Van Ackeren, S.J., founder and editor of *Theology Digest;* Gerard Sloyan of Catholic University; Maria de la Cruz Aymes, S.H., renowned catechist; and William Reedy of Sadlier Publishing Company.[7] All of the participants were concerned with the exciting new possibilities and challenges in catechesis at all stages of life.[8] This historic meeting influenced greatly the subsequent curriculum developments in the theology department of Mundelein College.

In 1960 the four B.V.M. provincials asked that a summer course be established for high school religion teachers. Sister Margaret Mary and I designed a program that was launched in the summer of 1961 in the new scholasticate building, now known as Wright Hall. The first seventy-five students included B.V.M. secondary and elementary religion teachers, along with fifteen diocesan priests sent to the program by Cardinal Albert Meyer.

This first religious-education summer session was a tremendous success. Students insisted that there be another session the following summer with two tracks: a beginner's course in Scripture, theology, and catechetics, and a second track for those who wanted to build on the first-year program. The ensuing summer offerings were opened to other religion teachers as well as to B.V.M. sisters. Several hundred students, mostly women religious, attended those courses during the following summers. A certificate in religious education was offered for the completion of three summers' courses. The request for graduate-level courses came from those students.

A major component of those summer sessions was a lecture series by eminent scholars who played a significant role relating to the Second Vatican Council. The Scripture scholar Barnabas Mary Ahern, C.P., and the moral theologian Bernard Haring, C.S.S.R., were two who graced Mundelein's campus more than once. Week after week, approximately five hundred or more persons came to the Skyscraper auditorium for those lectures. Each lecture was taped. Sister Margaret Mary organized a circulating system of those tapes for the entire B.V.M. congregation.[9] Eventually, Argus (now Tabor) Publishing Company continued this tape-recording circulation.[10]

The Mary Festival of 1983 could be considered the culmination of Mundelein's summer-lecture series. Designed as a celebration of the 150th anniversary of the Sisters of Charity of the Blessed Virgin Mary, the festival included seven major lectures by seven B.V.M.'s: Anne Carr, Margaret Irene Healy, Rose Marie Lorentzen, Mary Donahey, Mary Lauranne Lifka, Mary DeCock, and Carol Frances Jegen. Most lectures focused on a familiar Marian title from the Litany of Loretto. These lectures were published later by Sheed and Ward in *Mary According to Women*. In addition to the lectures, a music program was directed by Sister Frances Dolan, B.V.M., workshops and a candlelight procession were organized by Sister Maureen Cleary, B.V.M., and an entrance procession of 150 B.V.M.-elementary school students for a culminating Eucharist with Cardinal Joseph Bernardin was followed by a campus picnic. Truly, we experienced a festival in honor of Mary "in the Mystery of the Church."[11]

While these summer sessions were burgeoning, significant developments were also occurring during the regular academic year. In the 1960s two young B.V.M.'s were sent to Mundelein after completing their M.A. degrees at Marquette. Sister Anne Carr and Sister Mary Donahey made invaluable contributions before and after completing their doctorates. In that same decade Bill Hill and Nicholas Patricca joined the theology department faculty. Partly because of the growing need for interdisciplinary work, the theology department became a religious studies department, always with a strong theology core. A major was established in 1968.

The many requests for graduate study led to the formation of an interdisciplinary core graduate faculty that included Michael Fortune, English literature; Russell Barta, sociology; and Sister Eloise Thomas, B.V.M., economics. The graduate program in religious studies, Mundelein's first M.A. degree program, was launched in the summer of 1969 and continued throughout the regular academic year. After completing her doctoral course work at the University of Chicago, Sister Mary DeCock, B.V.M., joined the core faculty. A welcome fine-arts component was provided by Sister Blanche Marie Gallagher, B.V.M., of the art department. Dr. Stephen Schmidt, a Lutheran, brought an ecumenical dimension to the core faculty of the graduate program and to the entire department. Sister Mary Anne Hoope, B.V.M., served as a core graduate faculty member and as undergraduate chairperson before leaving for Ghana.

A final development occurred when then-Dominican Matthew Fox began the Institute of Creation-Centered Spirituality (ICCS) on Mundelein's campus in the late 1970s. After the institute was moved to Oakland, California, the Mundelein faculty developed a weekend program in spirituality. During three full weekends in each of Mundelein's three terms, a special theme was developed: creation, liberation, feminism.

During the 1980s, Mundelein's graduate program also served the Peoria Diocese. Faculty traveled to Peoria on weekends, thereby educating pastoral ministers for that entire diocese. For those students pursuing an M.A. degree, half of their course work was done in Peoria; the remaining courses were taken on the Mundelein campus.

More than seven hundred students received M.A. degrees in religious studies. Those students, along with undergraduate majors, have served throughout the United States, Canada, Latin America, India, Africa, the

Philippines, Korea, Taiwan, Australia, and New Zealand. May they continue to spread the Mundelein spirit!

The Mundelein Center for Religious Education

The Mundelein Center for Religious Education (MCRE) began in 1959, following a Marquette University meeting in June of that same year. Insights regarding curriculum development meant that throughout the meeting we focused on a need for audiovisual materials in schools. Mindful of our first scholastics' pending graduation in August, I wrote to our provincial, Sister Frances Shea, B.V.M., requesting that our young sisters have at least one week in catechetics before they were missioned to our elementary and secondary schools where they would be teaching religion. In that letter, I explained fully the issue of distorted (often Jansenistic) religious education that resulted in the anguish many adults suffered because of their childhood experiences. Referring to the recent tragic fire at Our Lady of Angels elementary school (December 1958) in which many children were seriously burned and ninety children and three sisters died, I pointed out that the entire world had expressed concern about the physical suffering of the victims of that fire. Even Pope John XXIII sent personal condolences. In that context, I raised the question as to when people would become at least equally concerned about the far greater psychological and spiritual suffering of children and adults whose basic relation to a loving God was being distorted by faulty religious education.

The request for the catechetics workshop was granted. In many ways, we were anticipating Vatican II's "Declaration on Christian Education" that stated: "In discharging her educative function, the Church is preoccupied with all the appropriate means to that end. But she is particularly concerned with the means that are proper to herself, of which catechetical training is foremost" (#4).[12]

Because such a workshop necessitated the use of some religious-education materials, sample textbooks and audiovisual materials were gathered from publishers, marking the beginning of what came to be known as Mundelein's Center for Religious Education. When I spoke with Sister Ann Ida, Mundelein's president, about developing a collection of materials, including newly marketed audiovisuals, she encouraged the venture, but added, "I have no money to give you." So along with Sister Margaret Mary and my relic of St. Francis of Assisi, we began to beg materials from publishers in Milwaukee, where we were studying at Marquette during the summers.

By 1961 when the first summer religious-education program had begun, the collection had grown considerably and included display materials on the walls of the scholasticate's second floor. Father Ted Stone brought German and Swedish posters from the historic international Eichstaat Conference on religious education. Fathers James J. Killgallon and Gerard P. Weber donated other materials as well as some financial assistance.

As the summer program and the collection developed, including some ecumenical and Jewish materials, the collection was moved temporarily to the Skyscraper. In 1966, with the strong support of Emily Flynn, B.V.M., the superior of the Mundelein sisters, the entire collection was moved to the newly purchased "Yellow House" that became the Mundelein Center for Religious Education, serving all Chicago-area religious educators. Member schools and parishes that paid a small yearly library fee could borrow the materials. For most of MCRE's history, the Jegen family funded the acquisition of materials.

From 1966 to 1973, the Yellow House could be described as a center for the implementation of many hopes and dreams of the Second Vatican Council. Numerous gatherings took place there, not only of Mundelein faculty and students, but also of parish groups, women religious, and ecumenical and interfaith gatherings.[13] With the help of Sister Marie Flynn, B.V.M., and Sister Maureen Patrice Fury, B.V.M., the MCRE became a hospitality center for pastoral ministers. In the summer of 1974, members of the United Farm Workers made the center their home.

Some of the most significant gatherings in those early years involved liturgical celebrations and developments. Many diocesan priests welcomed the opportunity to celebrate the Eucharist with small groups. Truly, in those exciting post–Vatican II days, Eucharists were the "summit and fount" of life in MCRE.[14] Largely because of my involvements in the Chicago Liturgical Commission and in the U.S. Bishops Subcommittee on Liturgical Adaptation, much of the initial planning for children's liturgy and for communal anointing took place in the MCRE. The struggles were many in bringing those liturgical plans to fulfillment for the whole church.[15]

In 1973 the Mundelein Center for Religious Education moved from the Yellow House to Piper Hall. There, under the leadership of Sister Jane Haslwanter, B.V.M., with the continued assistance of Sister Maureen Patrice and the added services of Sister Rose Phoenix, B.V.M., the MCRE thrived and developed. Sister Jane's numerous contributions included identifying materials according to age levels, developing an extensive catalog for participating members, and organizing a United Parcel Services delivery of materials to outlying areas. Sister Jane also conducted workshops on and off campus. Especially during this period, the MCRE continued to serve as a recruitment base for graduate students in religious studies. Piper Hall became home for the ICCS and for the weekend spirituality program. Saturday evening Eucharists were life-giving experiences for many Mundelein students and friends.

When Mundelein College became part of Loyola University Chicago in 1991, the MCRE's collection of religious-education materials became part of the Institute of Pastoral Studies (IPS). However, no budget was provided for a director. The materials were consolidated in one room on the second floor of Piper Hall. Sister Virginia Hughes, B.V.M., generously kept the circulation of materials in operation on a small scale until the decision was made to transfer the collection to the Archdiocesan Office for Religious Education (ORE).

At the Catechetical Awards Dinner in May 1996, in the presence of Cardinal Joseph Bernardin, Raymond Baumhart, S.J., made the formal announcement of the transfer. Under the leadership of Carole Eipers, ORE director, the decision was made to name the center after the Jegen family. Archbishop Francis George, O.M.I., dedicated the Jegen Center in September 1997.

Now, the Jegen Center for Catechetical Media and Research occupies the entire third floor of the Office for Religious Education. Its exciting new life is under the direction of Sister Judith Dieterle, S.L., and Sister Vivian Wilson, B.V.M., volunteers services on a regular basis.

In the open house following the dedication of the Jegen Center, I concluded my brief remarks in a way that also seems fitting for this brief history of the center.

> Our challenge as religious educators for the twenty-first century can be expressed quite simply and profoundly as continuing the dream of Jesus. He is the Way, the Truth, and the Life that can give meaning and hope to our world. We have ways and means to share this good news that have never been possible before in the history of the Church. In sincerest gratitude, joy, and trust, together let us make the dream go on.

Jewish-Catholic Dialogue

Mundelein College always welcomed Jewish students and faculty. But Vatican II's *Nostra Aetate,* "Declaration on the Relationship of the Church to Non-Christian Religions," opened the door for Jewish-Catholic relations in ways that never existed previously. One of Mundelein's first efforts was the formation of a Jewish-Catholic neighborhood dialogue group that met in the Mundelein Center for Religious Education. A Jewish woman participant remarked that for the first time in her fifteen years' experience in our neighborhood, she felt welcome on our campus.

As the dialogue continued, another Jewish woman suggested that in addition to our conversations for mutual understanding, she hoped we would find ways to pray together. This suggestion led to Seder celebrations, an event that continued for many years.

The first Seder celebration took place at our neighborhood synagogue, Temple Emanuel. Rabbi Herman Schaalman led us in that prayerful experience. Then, for several years, with the cooperation of B'nai B'rith women, Seder celebrations for Jews and Christians took place in McCormick Lounge on the Mundelein campus. Different Chicago rabbis presided. These gatherings influenced a Liturgy Training Publication booklet entitled *The Passover Celebration: A Haggadah for the Seder.*

Rabbi Schaalman was a precious gift to us. He lectured in classes and also in our summer lecture series. One memorable experience during those early summer sessions will never be forgotten. One day in the mid-1960s, more than one hundred sisters in traditional habits walked down Sheridan Road from Mundelein College and entered Temple Emanuel. During that synagogue visit, "our rabbi" explained many aspects of Jewish worship. We were privileged to see the Torah scrolls up close. Through the years, this synagogue experience with Rabbi Schaalman was repeated several times for Mundelein students.[16]

Another great Jewish rabbi friend was Dr. Byron Sherwin, renowned author and currently vice president and academic dean of Spertus Institute of Jewish Studies.[17] Before assuming his administrative responsibilities, Dr. Sherwin taught classes on Jewish mysticism and spirituality in Mundelein's graduate program in religious studies. His course on Rabbi Abraham Heschel was very popular and greatly appreciated. Rabbi Sherwin and I coauthored a book, *Thank God: Prayers of Jews and Christians Together,* published by Chicago's Liturgy Training Publications. In 1997 I was privileged to give the interfaith tribute to Dr. Sherwin at his twenty-fifth anniversary celebration at Spertus Institute.

Such experiences of Jewish-Catholic dialogue were background for the decision to host the archdiocesan celebration of *Nostra Aetate* at Mundelein College in 1985, the fortieth anniversary of that renowned document. In the early planning stages, representatives of the Jewish community requested that this special event be hosted at Mundelein because, they stated, "Mundelein is our college." That celebration was memorable in so many ways, including the presence of our brother Cardinal Joseph Bernardin on our campus again. The posters announcing the event featured pictures of John XXIII and Rabbi Heschel juxtaposed along with the date and place, Mundelein College. How proud and grateful we were to have Mundelein highlighted in this way.

Under Cardinal Bernardin's leadership, the Archdiocesan Catholic-Jewish Scholars Dialogue was established. Approximately fifteen scholars from both communities were invited to participate, I being one of them. The experience has been extraordinary in developing mutual understanding and genuine friendship.[18] Usually, we meet at the Jewish Federation Building. As a result of this involvement, I was one of the Christian Leaders Group invited by the Jewish Community Relations Council and the American Jewish Committee to participate in the first week-long visit to Israel in August 1991. As the leader of prayer on the Mount of the Beatitudes, I incorporated some prayers, including the Magnificat, from our recently published book, *Thank God*. Our Jewish friends joined us and commented that this experience witnessed to the prayerful spirit we needed to bring back home to Chicago.[19]

Perhaps the most fitting way to conclude this brief history is to thank God for the ways Mundelein College responded to *Nostra Aetate*. A brief section from that document can remind us how we endeavored to respond to its call. "Since the spirituality patrimony common to Christians and Jews is thus so great, this sacred Synod wishes to foster and recommend that mutual understanding and respect which is the fruit above all of biblical and theological studies, and of brotherly [and sisterly] dialogues."[20]

The Hispanic Institute

Mundelein's Hispanic Institute began in the early 1970s with a noncredit evening course taught in Spanish by Sister Dominga Zapata, S.H.[21] Within a decade, the Hispanic Institute was flourishing with its own year-round schedule of courses, a summer lecture series, and an annual fiesta. Almost all courses were taught in Spanish by prominent faculty, including pastoral theologian, Casiano Floristan, director of the Instituto Superior de Pastoral at the Pontifical University of Salamanca, Spain; Maria de los Angeles Garcia, associate director of catechesis for Hispanics in the Archdiocese of Newark, New Jersey; and Virgilio Elizondo, director of the Mexican American Cultural Center in San Antonio, Texas.

One of the institute's unique features was its four-level participation. In the same classroom were noncredit, certificate, undergraduate, and graduate students, both Hispanic and Anglo. Students participated according to their background preparation. Credit students enjoyed extra sessions with the instructors and wrote papers after an extended period of time. This pattern was a unique one, designed to accommodate the Hispanic population, especially the women who often did not have the equivalence of secondary or even elementary education in this country. A special committee of the institute's students and faculty designed the certificate program, Capacitación Pastoral. A series of six courses, including the writing of brief papers, acted as a bridge from noncredit to undergraduate participation.

Some of the Anglo graduate students preparing for Hispanic ministry appreciated this pattern for another reason. As one of them remarked, we had brought the field-education component into the classroom. Those students valued their contacts and discussions with Hispanics from various parishes, neighborhoods, and countries of origin. All participants treasured the sharing of experiences, insights, and concerns.

The Eucharistic celebrations that Sister Dominga included in the first summer program soon developed into a glorious annual fiesta. Usually, Father Casiano assisted the people in preparing the liturgy, which featured a unique dramatization of the gospel. The participation of Hispanic people originally from Mexico and from many Caribbean and Central and South American countries was an extraordinary celebration of Christian unity, attuned to some of the hopes of Vatican II's *Liturgy Constitution*.[22] The generosity of these people in providing food and entertainment to complete the fiesta was amazing year after year. The Hispanic Institute fiestas provided the basic pattern for the several Archdiocesan Festivals Cátolicos celebrated with Cardinal Joseph Bernardin. One such memorable event was held on the Mundelein campus at the request of the Hispanic Catholics in Chicago.

A very significant feature of the Hispanic Institute was the formation of the Comité del Pueblo. Members of this committee helped organize the institute's entire program. In its own way the Comité del Pueblo was a school of leadership, providing experience for several who were later appointed archdiocesan Hispanic leaders, including Enrique Alonso, director of the Hispanic Diaconate Program; Angelina Marquez and Araminta Martinez of the Hispanic Ministry Office; Virgilio Bonifazi of the Office of Religious Education's Hispanic Program; and Alicia Rivera of the Hispanic Family Ministry Office.

Three of today's women leaders who received M.A. degrees through the Hispanic Institute deserve special mention. At the urgent request of Cardinal Bernardin, Sister Dominga Zapata accepted the position of director of Hispanic Ministry for the Archdiocese of Chicago. Sister Dominga had served previously as the founder of the ORE Office for Hispanic Ministry and as the director of the Midwest Hispanic Office of the National Conference of Catholic Bishops (NCCB). She had also served on the board of directors of the Catholic Theological Union and on the advisory council of the Catholic Bishops of the United States. Her influence continues to be widespread throughout the United States and beyond. Largely through her leadership, the National Catholic Commission for Hispanic Ministry was born at Piper Hall on the Mundelein campus.[23]

Olga Villa Parra has been another outstanding Hispanic woman leader known in many Hispanic circles. Olga directed the NCCB Midwest Hispanic Office before she joined the Lilly Foundation as the key Hispanic adviser.

Sonya Rendon returned to her native country, Ecuador, to found Nuevo Mundo, a unique education endeavor that she developed as her final M.A. degree project. Some students who attend this elementary school are able to pay tuition and help support other students who are quite poor and unable to meet tuition costs. This school has functioned through the generosity of many benefactors, including some B.V.M. assistance as teachers and supporters.

This brief history of Mundelein's Hispanic Institute would not be complete without including Mundelein's support of Cesar Chavez and the United Farm Workers (UFW). Then-B.V.M. Prudence Moylan marched with Cesar on the historic Sacramento march in California and continued her support in Chicago. Mundelein students and faculty helped make known the farmworker cause through many marches, picket lines, and frequent billboard messages on Sheridan Road. After committing civil disobedience, I spent two weeks with the farmworkers in the Fresno Prison farm. I helped in the day-care center at LaPaz, the UFW headquarters in California dedicated to Our Lady, Queen of Peace. I assisted in the legal department in Delano. During the summer of 1974, farmworker families lived in the Yellow House and helped welcome Mother Teresa of Calcutta to the Mundelein campus. The climax of our involvements took place on November 1, 1979, the fiftieth anniversary of the ground breaking of Mundelein College. Cesar Chavez joined us for a most memorable Eucharist in McCormick Lounge and gave the homily.[24] Sister Dorothy Dwight, B.V.M., planned the beautiful bilingual liturgy with special music. After Communion, Cesar turned to me and said, "Sister, this is so beautiful. Now, I have the strength to go on."

Throughout all of the efforts of the Hispanic Institute, the strength to go on has come from prayer. The challenges of poverty continue. Without some small grant assistance, including some financial help from the B.V.M. community, the institute's work could not have continued. Now, as this ministry continues as the Instituto Hispano of Loyola University Chicago's Institute of Pastoral Studies, under the direction of William Spine, S.J., our prayerful support continues as well.[25]

Peace Studies

Peace studies is a new discipline in higher education. In 1970 there were three such programs in the United States. By 1990 there were two hundred fifty. Mundelein College was one of the forty-four colleges and universities to inaugurate the national Peace Studies Association.

Mundelein's involvement in the peace movement can be traced to participation in the Catholic Association for International Peace. As early as 1934, Emilie Barron, a Mundelein representative, attended a national meeting of this association at Catholic University.[26] How significant that one of the committees was peace education.

Another significant moment in Mundelein's history of nonviolent action was the Selma march with Martin Luther King Jr. Several Mundelein faculty and students traveled to Selma, Alabama, by bus and joined Dr. King in that historic event in the civil rights movement.[27] This nonviolent precedent of the 1960s influenced greatly our nonviolent involvement with the United Farm Workers in the 1970s. Then, as Pax Christi began to be organized in the United States, the call for peace education became stronger.[28] In 1983 the United States Catholic Bishops' pastoral letter, "The Challenge of Peace," gave strong encouragement to peace education. Our bishops wrote: "We are confident that all the models of Catholic education which have served the Church and our country so well in so many ways will creatively rise to the challenge of peace" (#305).[29]

During the 1980s, under the leadership of the religious studies department and with full support of Mundelein's administration, an interdisciplinary committee was formed to plan a minor in peace studies. The departments of biology, English, history, philosophy, psychology, and sociology were represented.[30] The decision to plan a minor, rather than a major, in peace studies was prompted by the desire to have students in various departments become knowledgeable about ways of peacemaking and become aware of the urgency to find paths to peace in a world of increasing violence and of threats of unimaginable nuclear devastation.

When the faculty approved the minor, eighteen students joined the program immediately. A generous grant of $100,000 from the John D. and Catherine T. MacArthur Foundation enabled us to expand our peacemaking efforts. Two of the first graduates completed internships in Europe: Karen Veverka studied in Sweden's Life and Peace Institute and Joyce Platfoot became involved in the Pax Christi International office in Belgium. Two peace scholars resided on the Mundelein campus, Margreta Inglestom from Sweden and Petra Heldt from Israel.

The MacArthur grant also assisted in the program of the recently established Mundelein Center for Women and Peace. Sister Mary Evelyn Jegen, S.N.D., became part-time director, having served as Pax Christi USA's national coordinator and Pax Christi International's vice president. In its brief history, the Center for Women and Peace established many contacts with peacemakers throughout the Chicago area and beyond. The center sponsored a supper-lecture series that brought to campus many women who shared concerns, hopes, and plans for peace. The book *A Dwelling Place* was published and included photographs and stories of women from varied ethnic backgrounds who were involved in Mundelein and were committed to peacemaking efforts.[31] In the months preceding the Persian Gulf War, the center organized a weekly prayer service for the prevention of that conflict. More than once, Dr. Haider-Ghulam Aasi of the Islamic College joined us in prayer.[32]

When Mundelein's affiliation with Loyola University Chicago occurred in 1991, the Center for Women and Peace was unfortunately discontinued. However, the peace-studies minor was brought into Loyola through the strong support of Dr. Kathleen McCourt, dean of the College of Arts and Sciences. Soon after the public announcement of the pending affiliation, Dr. McCourt arranged a meeting of the Mundelein peace-studies faculty committee with Loyola faculty from comparable departments. A new joint committee was formed. After three years of meetings, the peace-studies minor was approved by the necessary Loyola faculty committees and administrators. Dr. William French of the theology department became the new director of peace studies.

In concluding this brief sketch of Mundelein College's religious studies department, it is important to mention once again that without the prayerful support of every person involved in the department, none of this history would have taken place. The many challenges and struggles demanded "staying power" from everyone involved. Let me conclude on a note of sincerest gratitude to each person who made this history a reality, particularly those who shared administrative responsibilities.[33] Together, all of us nurtured the spirit of Mundelein as we reached out to the people in the spirit of B.V.M. foundress, Mother Mary Frances Clarke.

Endnotes

1. *My Dear Sister,* is a collection of letters of Mary Frances Clarke, edited by Laura Smith-Noggle and published in 1987 by Mount Carmel Press, Dubuque, Iowa. These letters bear witness to Mary Frances Clarke's unrelenting concern for the people to whom her sisters were ministering in their schools.

2. The lead article in the 1996 Anniversary Edition of *PACE (Professional Approaches for Christian Educators)* is entitled "Ann Ida Gannon, B.V.M.: A Legacy of Leadership." In this article I highlighted her support for the developments in Mundelein's religious studies department. In writing the article, I learned that Sister Ann Ida had requested that I come to Mundelein to start a theology department.

3. See my article, "Women in Theology" in *Listening* 13:2 (spring 1978) for a brief history of the pioneering efforts of Sister Madaleva, C.S.C., at Saint Mary's College, Notre Dame, as well as the efforts of Saint Xavier College and Mundelein College to educate women in theology.

4. *The Documents of Vatican II,* ed. Walter M. Abbott, S.J., (New York: The America Press, 1966), 199.

5. Because the B.V.M. congregation wanted some Scripture courses to be incorporated into the new sister-formation program, a special curriculum design was established at Mundelein College. In the early days of the scholasticate program, the Chicago Benedictines and Felician Sisters joined the young B.V.M. sisters at Mundelein.

6. After the doctoral degree program was established at Marquette and our theology department was launched, I began doctoral studies in 1964.

7. Sister Maria de la Cruz Aymes, S.H., William Reedy, and I were three of the thirteen delegates sent by the United States Catholic Conference of Bishops to the First International Catechetical Congress in Rome in 1971.

8. It is important to distinguish the word *catechesis* from the word *catechetics,* which refers to the more basic catechetical aspects of religious education. *Catechesis* is a much broader term, referring to all the experiences involved in developing a mature faith life, such as theology, liturgy, social action, and prayer. In 1996 when Cardinal Bernardin presented me with the Chicago Medallion for Excellence in Catechesis, all those factors were considered. I was the first woman to receive this award.

9. When Marie Augusta Neal, S.N.D. de Namur, surveyed women's religious congregations in the late 1960s, she discovered that the Sisters of Charity of the Blessed Virgin Mary possessed the highest level of theological competency. This circulation of tapes along with the summer courses at Mundelein were largely responsible.

10. The original tape recordings are now in the archives of the Jegen Center in the Chicago Archdiocesan Office for Religious Education.

11. The final chapter of Vatican II's "Dogmatic Constitution on the Church," *Lumen Gentium* is entitled, "The Role of the Blessed Virgin Mary, Mother of God, *in the* Mystery of Christ and the Church" [emphasis mine].

12. Abbott, 642–3.

13. One example of women religious' gatherings would be the planning sessions led by Sister Ethne Kennedy, S.H., for inaugurating NAWR, the National Assembly of Women Religious.

14. Perhaps the climactic, often-quoted statement of Vatican II's *Constitution on the Sacred Liturgy* is section 10: "Nevertheless the liturgy is the summit toward which the activity of the Church is directed; at the same time it is the fountain from which all her power flows" (Abbott, 142).

15. With the invaluable assistance of Godfrey Diekmann, O.S.B., one of the key authors of Vatican II's *Constitution on the Sacred Liturgy* and member of the U.S. Bishops Subcommittee on Liturgical Adaptation, our plans for Children's Liturgy were finally accepted and promulgated by the Vatican. However, we were not as successful in changing the age for the first reception of the sacrament of reconciliation, even though our U.S. bishops had already set in motion the plan for a later age than that for first Communion.

16. Several times Rabbi Schaalman and I presented a "dialogue-lecture"for audiences of Jews and Christians. He was chairman of the Chicago Board of Rabbis and our rabbi on the 1991 Israel trip. Often, he and I sat together in the front seat of the tour bus. I will never forget the experience of the Jewish Farewell Prayer Service for Cardinal Bernardin, organized at Holy Name Cathedral under his leadership. Jewish and Catholic leaders sat together in the sanctuary. When Rabbi Schaalman stood to begin his beautiful tribute, along with other Jewish leaders, he reminded everyone that we were witnessing an historic event—the Jewish community paying heartfelt tribute to a dearly loved Roman Catholic Cardinal, Brother Joseph, in the cathedral of a Catholic archdiocese.

17. Earlier relations with Spertus included the teaching of some of their courses on the Mundelein campus.

18. When the Auschwitz convent controversy erupted in Europe, we received word that all Catholic-Jewish dialogue there would cease. On hearing of this decision, Rabbi Hayim Perlmuter of Catholic Theological Union, one of our most distinguished scholars, remarked, "Even if we receive such a directive in the United States, we could never stop our dialogue, because we are friends."

19. In addition to Rabbi Schaalman, Michael Kotzin, director of the Jewish Community Relations Council, and Jonathan Levine, Chicago Chapter of the American Jewish Committee, accompanied us.

20. *Nostra Aetate,* #4 (Abbott, 665).

21. At the time that I invited Sister Dominga to teach a course for Chicago's Hispanic people, I also invited Sister Teresita Weind, S.N.D. de Namur, to teach an evening course for Chicago's African Americans. Although we continued African American course offerings for some time, we did not develop a program comparable to the Hispanic Institute.

22. "Even in the liturgy, the Church has no wish to impose a rigid uniformity in matters which do not involve the faith or the good of the whole community. Rather, she respects and fosters the spiritual adornments and gifts of the various races and peoples" (#37) (Abbott, 151).

23. Sister Dominga first came to Mundelein's religious education courses as a young sister from Puerto Rico. With the help of Sister Josetta Phoenix, B.V.M., who taught her English, Sister Dominga completed both her B.A. and M.A. degrees at Mundelein College. She was largely responsible for the research component of the Hispanic Alliance with Mundelein, DePaul, and Loyola that was funded by the Ford Foundation. At the time Ford investigated the Chicago area for a possible grant, Mundelein's Hispanic Institute was the only existing program in the three institutions. Our brochure was instrumental in securing the Ford Foundation grant.

24. A tape recording of Chavez's homily is in the Gannon Center archives.

25. Small grants enabled the Hispanic Institute to employ the services of the following directors: Sister Rosalinda Ramirez, M.S.C.; Tomas Bissonnette; and Kenneth Ortega.

26. See archival letter dated 29 March 1934. Another Mundelein representative was Miriam T. Rooney who was a member of the Ethics Committee. Loyola University representatives included Frederic Siedenburg, S.J., on the Economic Relations Committee.

27. Selma marchers included twenty-eight Mundelein students, eight faculty members, and two guests (a priest and a doctor) as reported in *The Skyscraper,* 7 April 1965. Although I requested to go from Marquette, where I was in doctoral studies, Sister Ann Ida thought it wise for me to stay in Milwaukee.

28. Sister Mary Evelyn Jegen, S.N.D. de Namur, played a significant role in influencing Mundelein's peace-education efforts. As her sister, I learned much from her organizational efforts for Pax Christi, the international Catholic peace movement.

29. "The Challenge of Peace: God's Promise and Our Response" (Washington, D.C.: United States Catholic Conference, 1983), 93. On the evening this historic document was passed by an overwhelming majority of our bishops, several Mundelein representatives were present in the hotel's "upper room," where a prayer vigil was organized
by campus ministers of the Chicago Catholic colleges and universities. After the vote, Bishop Raymond Lucker of New Ulm, Minnesota, joined us in a special prayer of thanksgiving.

30. Faculty members included Anthony Gramza, Peter Brogno, Prudence Moylan, Thomas O'Brochta, Lois Leidahl-Marsh, Mary Sparks, and Carol Frances Jegen, B.V.M. Patricia Bombard, B.V.M., assisted us as a most efficient secretary and grant

writer. Prudence, Mary, and Carol Frances continued on the Loyola committee until the minor arrangements were complete.

31. *A Dwelling Place,* edited by Patricia Bombard, B.V.M., and Mary Evelyn Jegen, S.N.D.; photographs by Christian Molidor, R.S.M. (Mundelein College, Loyola University Chicago, 1992).

32. Dr. Aasi is a part-time member of Loyola's theology department and continues to be a faithful friend.

33. Undergraduate chairpersons: Carol Frances Jegen, B.V.M.; Mary Donahey, B.V.M.; Mary Anne Hoope, B.V.M. Graduate program directors: Carol Frances Jegen, B.V.M.; Mary DeCock, B.V.M.; Stephen Schmidt; Clarisse Croteau-Chonka; Avis Clendenen. In addition to Ann Ida Gannon, B.V.M., we could rely always on the wholehearted support of Presidents Susan Rink, B.V.M., and Mary Breslin, B.V.M., along with academic deans: Mary Griffin, Mary Pat Haley, B.V.M., Jean Sweat, and Mary Murphy, B.V.M. And in countless ways, especially for the Mary Festival and graduate religious studies graduations, we enjoyed the faithful, generous assistance of Jean Dolores Schmidt, B.V.M.

A Class Apart: B.V.M. Sister Students at Mundelein College, 1957–1971

Ann M. Harrington, B.V.M.

My life as a student at Mundelein College hardly fits the typical coed story, or for that matter, the typical Mundelein story. A transfer student, I arrived at the college in 1960 from Dubuque, Iowa, having just finished three years of training as a Sister of Charity of the Blessed Virgin Mary (commonly known as B.V.M.'s), including two years of study at Clarke College, our B.V.M. women's college in Dubuque. With me were fifty-three classmates, all of us in Chicago to complete the last two years of college. My classmates and I all dressed alike: a full-length black serge habit, a black veil held to our head by a white coif to cover our hair, and a long rosary affixed to a black belt and hanging from our left side. We lived together across Sheridan Road from the Mundelein Skyscraper in the ten-story scholasticate (today Wright Hall). We took our meals together there, prayed together, played together. Our rising and retiring were on a common schedule. A B.V.M. companion had to accompany us when we left the grounds. While there were a few native Illinoisans in our group, most originated elsewhere—Wisconsin (my home state), Iowa, New York, California, Minnesota, Florida, Missouri, Kansas, Nevada, Hawaii, and elsewhere. We were B.V.M. *scholastics,* the term used for B.V.M. sister students, about to begin our junior year in college. We were joining forty-one other scholastics already at the scholasticate who were about to begin their senior year. They too dressed like us and like the B.V.M. sisters who taught at Mundelein College.

How did it come to be that so many B.V.M. sisters were studying at Mundelein College? What did it mean and what was it like to be a class apart? How did the life of a scholastic change over time? How do we, today, assess our educational experience at Mundelein? What difference did it make that Mundelein was a women's college? This essay explores these questions and, at the same time, highlights faculty and administrators who emerge as role models. My own experiences at Mundelein College are fleshed out in what follows through a nonscientific sample of B.V.M.'s who earned their degrees over the fourteen years of the scholasticate program. I surveyed persons from each class, I tried to sample a variety of major fields, and finally, I identified respondents who are still members of the Sisters of Charity of the Blessed Virgin Mary and respondents who have left the congregation.[1]

These scholasticate years from 1957 to 1971 encompassed massive changes in the United States, the Roman Catholic Church, the B.V.M. congregation, and Mundelein College. Understanding the origins of these changes can help one to sort out why so many B.V.M.'s happened to be studying at Mundelein College. The story starts with a bit of history. Into the 1940s, many teachers in the public- and private-school systems began their grade school and high school teaching before they had earned the professional training we take for granted today. While certification demands were growing, they varied by state. Sisters who had completed their college education were first to begin agitating for all sisters to earn their college degrees before entering the classroom. The issue gained some notice in 1948 through the college and university department of the National Catholic Education Association (NCEA) under whose auspices the Teacher Education Section was established.

Sister Madeleva Wolff, C.S.C., president of St. Mary's College in South Bend, Indiana, was one of the most vocal proponents of sister education. At the 1949 NCEA convention, she gave a paper entitled "The Education of Sister Lucy" in which she challenged religious congregations of women to look toward the future. She said, "If all our religious communities begin this year to complete the education of our young sisters before sending them out to teach, practically all of our immediate generation will have their degrees and licenses in two or three years."[2]

The idea had its critics. Some believed that sisters should have some teaching experience before earning a bachelor's degree. Others saw no need to earn their undergraduate degrees when 45 percent of the public-school teachers were without degrees. Still others felt religious communities needed more time to ensure that sisters, once educated, would remain in the congregation. One of the most difficult issues was the two- to three-year time span when no young sisters would be going out to teach if this plan went into effect. How would pastors, who had to secure staff for the schools, respond to this? The question takes on added significance when one considers these March 19, 1957 statistics: 1,282 B.V.M.'s taught 66,766 children in 146 elementary schools; 478 B.V.M. high school teachers staffed 46 community, parochial, and diocesan secondary schools, teaching 14,691 high school students; and 88 B.V.M. sisters taught a total of 1,499 students in the two B.V.M. colleges.[3] Finally, how would college life be integrated with the demands of religious life?[4] Being a sister at this time in the life of the church was the same for most religious congregations. Obviously, integration of college life and religious life would need extensive discussion.

The impetus for the education of sisters received a boost from an address given by Pope Pius XII on September 15, 1951, to the first International Congress of Teaching Sisters in Rome, sponsored by the Sacred Congregation for Religious (SCRIS). At one point he said,

> Many of your schools are being described and praised to Us [sic] as being very good. But not all. It is our fervent wish that all endeavor to become excellent.
>
> This presupposes that your teaching sisters are masters of the subjects they expound. See to it, therefore, that they are well trained and that their education corresponds in quality and academic degrees to that demanded by the state. Be generous in giving them all they need, especially where books are concerned.[5]

The mother general of the B.V.M.'s, Mother Mary Josita Baschnagle, learned of this meeting through a letter dated August 17, 1951, from Amleto G. Cicognani, archbishop of Laodicea and apostolic delegate. His letter requested "any materials, suggestions, ideas, methods, experiences, etc., which may contribute to the work and success of the meeting."[6] Given that the International Congress was "concerned with questions connected with the formation of young sisters in religious communities dedicated to education,"[7] Mother Mary Josita's reply dated September 12, 1951, gave evidence of some irritation. She said, "Your letter . . . was our first notice of this meeting, and gave us little time to prepare any points for it." She mentioned one point that relates to this essay, namely "provision for a juniorate [a course of study for the sisters under temporary vows] after first profession, as soon as we can see our way clear to such a program financially."[8] It should be noted that the pope's directive carried no financial support.

Mother Mary Josita's letter to the apostolic delegate marks the first indication of the B.V.M. congregation's attention to a full college education for sisters before assigning them to classrooms. On May 10, 1952, Mother Josita moved on the idea in a letter addressed to provincial superiors, the novice mistress, presidents of the two B.V.M. colleges (Clarke and Mundelein), registrars of the colleges, and those who were directing the student-teaching program of young B.V.M. sisters. "I am asking you to please come to Mount Carmel [the B.V.M. motherhouse in Dubuque, Iowa] to deliberate with me and the councilors on the question of the study program of our young religious."

The intention was to discuss "our weaknesses and our strengths and ways in which we might improve our present program and lengthen the period of religious formation and intellectual development before assigning our young sisters to the demands of the classroom."[9]

The development of the Sister Formation Movement at the Teacher Education Sectional Meeting of the NCEA college and university department in April 1952 marked the next significant step nationwide. By 1953 there was a Sister Formation Committee; at the NCEA meeting in 1954 in Chicago, this committee was made official as the Sister Formation Conference. The committee took as its task to sponsor regional conferences on sister formation. Sister Mary Richardine Quirk, B.V.M., served on the first national committee (1954–62), chaired by Sister Mary Emil Penet, I.H.M.[10]

The 1955 Eighth General Chapter of the B.V.M.'s in enactment 30 directed that "present plans for extending and enriching the spiritual and intellectual formation of our junior professed sisters are to be further developed and completed by March 1957."[11] To activate this directive, an education committee was formed comprised of the following B.V.M.'s: Sister Mary Frances Patricia Shea, member of the general council; Sister Mary Teresa Francis McDade, council member and directress of education for the congregation; Sister Mary Ann Ida Gannon, representative of Mundelein College; Sister Mary Adorita Hart, representative of Clarke College; and Sister Mary Leo Hogan, mistress of novices. The committee first met in the summer of 1956, then later at Thanksgiving time that same year, and again during the summer of 1957.[12]

By the end of the summer of 1956 Mother Mary Consolatrice (Helen) Wright was able to announce to the B.V.M. congregation that "the total period of formation of our young sisters will be five years in duration. The two and one-half years of novitiate will be followed by the scholasticate, two and one-half years of postprofession study. This program will be put into effect in March 1957."[13] By March 1957 the committee had decided that Clarke College would cover any courses over the first two and one-half years, most of these offered at the motherhouse. The group chose Mundelein College for the last two and one-half years for two reasons: first, sisters would meld more easily into the larger student body; second, the Chicago area offered advantages both for student teaching and culture. Projections for a building to house scholastics in Chicago were revealed in a March 9, 1957, letter from Mother Consolatrice.[14] Finally, the entire scholasticate study plan was circulated more widely through a new publication of the congregation called *Vista*, which charted the life of a fictional B.V.M. from her entrance into the B.V.M.'s on August 2, 1957, to the completion of her undergraduate degree at Mundelein College.[15] Those of us who entered the B.V.M.'s in 1957 were the first set (name used for all who entered in a given year) who would live out the entire plan. However, those who entered in 1954, 1955, and 1956 were melded into the plan midstream.

So it was that in August 1957, the first group of forty-eight scholastics arrived at Mundelein College. Because the projected residence would not be completed until 1959, scholastics lived initially in the Skyscraper building on the ninth and tenth floors. Sister Margaret Zonsius (Sister Mary Frederick Cecile) recalls that "if there was a good-sized single bedroom, TWO beds were put in it; if there was a double room with space, THREE beds were put into it."[16] When the second group of scholastics arrived, they lived in Aquinas Hall on the east side of Kenmore (now part of the Loyola University Chicago parking lot) and they lived in Philomena Hall (now the Coffey Hall parking lot). By the time my set arrived, the scholasticate was completed, and we moved into our first private rooms in the congregation; for some of us, they were the first private rooms in our young lives.

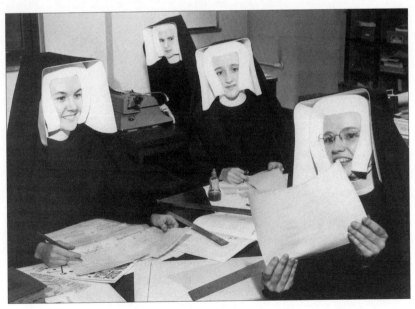

Serving on *The Review* staff are (left to right) Sisters Frederick Mary (Patricia) Nolan, Mary Theodora Stanton, Mary Georgianne (Marilyn) Quinlan, and Mary John Bosco (Sheila) Houle.

Having settled into our new home, what were our experiences as a "class apart"? We were allowed very little interaction outside class with the B.V.M. sisters who taught us—for that matter, with any of the faculty at the college. Nor could we socialize with other students, and for the most part, we were not allowed to join departmental or extracurricular clubs or to participate in extracurricular activities. In the eyes of many in the congregation, we were being given incredible privileges. Most sisters prior to 1957 were on the eighteen-to-twenty-year plan in terms of earning a bachelor's degree—summer school every year, and/or Saturday or after-school classes until the requisite number of credit hours had been earned. Speaking for myself, I took my education, that is a bachelor's degree in five years, for granted. Many of my respondents did the same. B.V.M.'s for the most part were teachers, so to become a B.V.M. meant further education. For others, the only thought was to enter the B.V.M.'s, and they were open to whatever work came with that choice. Several realized that, had they not entered the B.V.M.'s, college would probably have been financially impossible for them. Few of us, it appears, realized what a dramatic departure the scholasticate program was for the congregation, and at what cost to the sisters teaching in the schools, to say nothing of the financial costs to the congregation.

A letter from Mother Mary Consolatrice to the sisters at Mundelein College responded to concerns voiced to her. "Several have stated fears that the influx of sisters will make Mundelein into a 'sisters' college and that the word will 'spread like wildfire' that only sisters attend it." She allays these fears with the following summary statement:

> Of the present enrollment at Mundelein, the 68 percent in the lower division will not be in classes with sisters. The 32 percent in the upper division will not have sisters in two-thirds of their classes. The sister students in 1957 will form less than 14 percent of the number of upper division students (45 of 327) and less than 5 percent of upper division class enrollment. Two-thirds of their classes will be for sisters only.[17]

She also mentioned that it was a department decision whether or not scholastics join the department club and added that several departments had already voiced the desire to have the sisters as part of cocurricular activities. It appears that this integration never came to be, as not one of the persons I consulted on their experiences as a scholastic alluded to belonging to a department club. There were areas, however, where there was significant interaction with other students because of the nature of the study, such as those scholastics on the college-newspaper staff, *The Skyscraper,* and those in music, art, and science.

The message to scholastics was conveyed clearly—maintain a low profile. Dressed as we were, this task was not easy. Some directives, never written that I can find, assisted us: we were to enter and leave the college through a side door not often used by other students, we were not to move in big groups, we were to avoid using the elevator for floors one through five (we got a lot of exercise), we were to go the library or back to the scholasticate immediately after class. Classes that constituted core courses or courses that all of us had yet to take, such as metaphysics and educational psychology, were offered at the scholasticate or at off times at the college so that we would not overwhelm any class. Our physical-education requirements were completed apart so that no one would see us out of our religious habit. Members of the first group of scholastics remarked on how stressful their lives were; there was a feeling of living in a glass house with the entire congregation observing.

With this less than full immersion into the life of the college, what of our education at Mundelein? My own experiences as a French major were enhanced greatly because of the 1957 launch of the unmanned Soviet space-craft *Sputnik.* Quickly, the United States responded with federal monies for the study of math, science, and languages. When our group arrived in August 1960, the language division was chaired by Sister Mary St. Irene Branchaud (1904–68). She was a dynamic individual whose passion for the French language and literature is legendary. Of French-Canadian descent, Sister Mary St. Irene was bilingual from the age of three. She earned her M.A. degree in French at McGill University in Montreal and her Ph.D. degree in Old French from Fordham University. Shortly before our arrival at the college, the French Ministry of Education recognized Sister Mary St. Irene's contribution to French culture and letters by awarding her Les Palmes Académiques in February 1960. She had already received the Chevalier d'Académiques (Knight of the Academy) award in 1954, making her an *officier de l'instruction publique,* or an officer of public education.

One of Sister Mary St. Irene's pioneer projects in Chicago was language education through the use of foreign film. Early on, Mundelein students had access to first-rate films from France, Spain, Italy, Germany, Austria, Japan, Mexico, Canada, Argentina, and Sweden. A number of my interviewees mentioned attendance at these films as memorable. (Yes, this was an activity that we were allowed to attend.) One of the films I remember best is *Ikiru (To Live),*

Jean Beliard, French consul general to Chicago, presents Sister Mary St. Irene Branchaud, B.V.M., with a medal, designating her an *officier de l'instruction publique.*

a Japanese film directed by Akira Kurosawa. Along with each film came a discussion sheet and spirited exchanges after the viewing. I recall being fascinated by the symbolism that came to light for me as we talked; this kind of film analysis was new to me. Kathleen Antol, B.V.M., class of '68, a biology major, talks of the "arty, foreign films of some import and a discussion after. This truly provided me with a new way of viewing film and with a desire to see creative, artistic films and read good literature. Until then, I had not thought of film as art at all."

Sister Mary Elsa Copeland, B.V.M. (1922–93), another of our French professors, had just returned from a Fulbright summer seminar at the Sorbonne for teachers of French. Possessing endless energy and enthusiasm for French language and literature, she followed Sister Mary St. Irene as a recipient of the treasured Palmes Académiques in 1978. Having spent her early years teaching in elementary schools, she had a veritable treasure trove of methods to make classes interesting and lively. She introduced us to much of French culture through music, poetry, and story. We also learned how to do *explication de texte* (textual analysis the French way) using books designed for students in French schools. Sheila O'Brien, B.V.M., class of '62, says, "Sister Mary Elsa really taught me how to teach." At the end of our first year at the college, however, Sister Mary Elsa went off to Paris with another Fulbright to finish her Ph.D. degree at the Sorbonne. We felt we were being put to the ultimate test when she was replaced by Madame Lilian and Monsieur Gerard De Joubécourt, who were, as you might suspect, native French speakers. This was one of Sister Mary St. Irene's plots to improve our pronunciation.

And she had other plots up her sleeve. The Théatre du Vieux visited from Paris and presented Molière's *L'Ecole des Femmes* on the Mundelein stage. While outings from the scholasticate were few and far between in those days, she managed on occasion to get us "liberated" for French theatrical productions in the city. We joined Sister Mary Elsa, at least a few times, on Belmont Avenue in helping out at the newly opened (1959) Chicago office of Little Brothers of the Poor, an organization to serve the elderly, founded in 1946 and headquartered in Paris. The personnel at the time were all French speaking, so this outreach had double motivation. Sister Mary St. Irene had in fact met the founder, Armand Marquiset, in France and invited him to speak of his work at Mundelein. Cosponsored with Loyola University Chicago, the first talk was in May 1958, and the second in May 1959.[18]

The Alliance Française in Chicago used Mundelein's Social Room, 206, for Sunday afternoon get-togethers. Of course, Sister Mary St. Irene arranged for French majors to visit with them. At the time we viewed it as torture, but once in our own classrooms—better yet, in France—we appreciated the experience. One final remembrance of Sister Mary St. Irene's efforts on our behalf, or perhaps more on behalf of the preservation of the French language, was her insistence that when teaching in our high school French classes we use *Voix et Images*, the St. Cloud method of tape, filmstrip, and text published by Chilton, which centered on the life of the imaginary Thibaut Family. The French that students (and teachers) heard over and over was, yes, native French. She never stopped. What anyone who majored in French in those days will attest to is that we were challenged from the beginning to the end of our studies, capped with a massive comprehensive exam. To this day, I do not know if it was meant as humorous that the exam ended by challenging us to do an analysis and a translation of excerpts from Victor Hugo's poem "Waterloo."

Mundelein's reputation for excellence in languages can be seen in the Spanish department as well. Spanish majors praise the work of Nina Sokaloff and Beatriz Medrano, but Sister Mary Terese Avila Duffy, B.V.M. (1917–70), seemed to have had the most impact. Kateri O'Shea, class of '59, in the first group of scholastics, says of her that she "helped me learn to think critically, awakened in me my social consciousness, and taught me to love literature. She was also a superb model for me as a Spanish speaker and Spanish teacher." Theresa Gleeson, B.V.M., class of '61, credits Sister Mary Terese Avila as the one "who truly inspired me to want to teach or at least pursue Spanish later on." Sister Mary Terese Avila benefited from NDEA monies for work on her Ph.D. degree at the University of Wisconsin, Madison. Additional NDEA monies allowed her summer study of Portuguese in Brazil.

Sister Mary Terese Avila's own social consciousness emerged most tangibly in her work in the mid-1960s with the United Farm Workers and their boycott in 1966 against the California grape growers, her work with migrant workers during the summers of 1968 and 1969, and her founding of the Hispanic Institute at Mundelein for teachers of the Spanish speaking.[19] Unfortunately, cancer took her in 1970 at the young age of fifty-two, but her spirit lives on in her students.

Scholastics who were English majors consistently mention Sister Mary Philippa Coogan, B.V.M. (1908–84). She was noted for her courses on Beowulf, Dante, Chaucer, and Shakespeare. Anita Montavon, B.V.M., class of '61, referred to her as "the wonder of wonders." Mary Nolan, B.V.M., class of '63, says her "final integration course was cosmic and difficult—only 'thinkers' survived. Her vast knowledge and dry wit made it bearable."

An English minor, I somehow missed the opportunity to take a course from Sister Mary Philippa, but I, like others, remember vividly my courses from Sister Mary Anne Leone Graham, B.V.M., and Patricia O'Donnell Ewers. Sister Mary Anne Leone gave me a love of Shakespeare that I have to this day. Mary Nolan, B.V.M., refers to her as "a walking Shakespeare." I remember writing a paper in which I compared themes from Jean Racine, the seventeenth-century French playwright, with themes from Shakespeare. Feeling quite smug and knowledgeable, I quoted extensively in French only to get the paper back with each missing accent filled in neatly in red ink! She did, however, like the paper. And Marilyn Wilson, B.V.M., class of '65, credits Sister Mary Anne Leone with finally teaching her how to write.

American literature to this day evokes for me the name Patricia O'Donnell Ewers. She was a young mother working on her Ph.D. degree. Again, a humbling memory drifts back. Our assignment was to write an essay on one of the authors we had studied, based on a book we had not read in class. Patricia Ewers warned us that if we did not understand symbolism, we should steer clear of Melville. That was all I needed to choose Melville's *White-Jacket*.

Three-fourths of the way through the work, I'd had it and said so in my paper, which included the arrogant statement that it was not even necessary to finish the novel. Needless to say, I learned my lesson and a lot more about symbolism! Jacqueline Powers Doud, class of '62, remembers Ewers as always enthusiastic and knowledgeable, and Janet Desmond, B.V.M., class of '63, says that she adapted her notes from Ewers' class in her high school teaching.

Sister Mary Crescentia (Margaret) Thornton, B.V.M. (1910–89), merits the most mention among history majors during the early years of the scholasticate. Mary Ann Kehl McGinley, class of '62, writes that "taking classes from Sister Mary Crescentia Thornton was the most challenging part of my studies at Mundelein. . . . Of all the teachers that I have ever had in my life, none has ever surpassed S. M. Crescentia." Another says that she "was one of those 'gently demanding' teachers that got more out of you than you thought possible" (Mary Cleary Krauss, class of '62). Finally, Kathleen Conway, B.V.M., class of '65, says that she "loved writing papers for S. M. Crescentia. She made learning fun and creative. She taught us the discipline we needed to learn and to continue learning after graduation. . . . She was by far the best teacher I ever had and one who continues to influence me to this day."

What of the sciences, a field that benefited from *Sputnik* as much, if not more, than the languages? Biology majors single out Sister Mary Cecelia Bodman, B.V.M. (1905–82), Patricia Cullen, and Claudia Carr. Sister Mary Cecelia was head of the department in the early years of the scholasticate program. As one person said, "I could not have been placed with a better woman, teacher, and religious. From day one, she did her best to fill in the discrepancies in our backgrounds." She goes on to describe a wise and humane woman: "She insisted that during vacations we needed to relax and do other kinds of reading. I still remember the first book she gave me was Dorothy Sayers' *Gaudy Night*" (Alice Kerker, B.V.M., class of '59). Studying general biology with Sister Mary Cecelia made Monica Seelman, B.V.M., class of '63, "aware of ecodiversity, the relationship between form and function in the living world and in architecture." Kathleen Antol, B.V.M., remembers Patricia Cullen and Claudia Carr as providing information that is still remembered. The latter Antol extols because of the types of exams she gave, which enabled Antol "to realize that I could actually use my mind to think out, create, DO science myself." Chemistry major, Joellen McCarthy, B.V.M., class of '65, remembers that Sister Marina Kennelly, B.V.M., "presented chemistry in a beautifully integrated and logical fashion."

Two persons stand out in mathematics during these years, Sister Mary St. Ida (Katharine) Forsyth, B.V.M., and Sister Mary Neal Moran, B.V.M. (Cecilia Moran Cooper). Sister Katharine is remembered as someone who put students first. Maureen Sheehan, B.V.M., class of '61, remarks that "her intensity was over-powering but she was truly interested in us as students and persons." Her math knowledge and the lengths to which Katharine would go to see that students really learned impressed Barbara Tadin, class of '61. Sister Mary Neal's teaching style is described as outstanding and creative by one scholastic graduate of 1965. And Joellen McCarthy, B.V.M., says that she "made me want to learn all the calculus I could absorb."

In the fine arts, music majors recall the teaching of Sister Mary Josette Kelly and Sister Eliza Kenney, both B.V.M.'s. They "were marvelous and so patiently empowering,"commented Roberta Ellis Flaherty, class of '65. Another scholastic of that same class mentions that she took lessons downtown at the American Conservatory during her senior year, and she also had the opportunity to go to Ravinia with a group of music majors. Dorothy Dwight, B.V.M., class of '65, remembers that these were afternoon trips, where they listened to Igor Stravinsky and Aaron Copeland warm up with the Chicago Symphony Orchestra. The only night concert allowed them during those two years was at Symphony Hall where they attended a performance of the *Messiah*. Also mentioned by several music majors were B.V.M.'s Sister Mary Louise Szkodzinski and Sister Julie Tracey. Diane Forster, B.V.M., class of '69, praises them along with Sister Josette and Sister Eliza. "These were outstanding teachers who continued their own practice, learning and reading constantly, and who respected students and expected a lot." Bette Gambonini, B.V.M., class of '65, felt encouraged. "They pushed me to go beyond where I was and affirmed me in my studies."

Art major Marilyn Feller Wasmundt, class of '62, found her education "more than an academic experience; it was a life-awareness experience. As I gained more information, the total picture began to take shape. I learned history through art, and social studies and religion through art. Even the math was easier to understand as everything fell into place. There was unity."

There were, of course, certain courses that we all had to take, as teaching, for most of us, was our mission. Education courses varied, obviously, depending on whether we were preparing to teach in the elementary or secondary schools. Whichever it was, those of us who arrived at Mundelein in 1960 were enlisted to help the education department chair, Sister Margaret Irene Healy, B.V.M., prepare for an extensive self-study in preparation for a proposal to seek accreditation from the National Commission for Accreditation of Teacher Education (NCATE). In 1962 Mundelein became the first Catholic college in Illinois to receive accreditation. This meant that any state that accepted NCATE accepted us as teachers with no further education needed (by 1964, twenty-eight states did). For scholastics being assigned across the United States, it made our Mundelein degree very mobile indeed.[20]

For many, education courses and student teaching were memorable. Mary Ann Kehl McGinley mentions Sister Mary Joan Therese Scanlan, B.V.M., as "dynamic, interesting, and incredibly practical." Her five-hour primary-education class, she says, was the most interesting education course she ever took. "She did not tell us what to do, she made us do it. We had to tell stories to the class, write experience charts, write on the board, and explain work-sheets to our peers. Sister used the textbook as a jumping-off point, but she used her experience in the classroom as our real text." Mary Nolan, B.V.M., says of Sister Mary Joan Therese that her "enthusiasm, energy, and expertise were contagious." Anne Kendall, B.V.M., class of '64, writes that "I came into my own as a person, thanks to Joan Therese Scanlan, B.V.M." Judy Callahan, B.V.M., class of '63, credits Sister Joan Therese and Sister Jean Dolores Schmidt, B.V.M., with her love of teaching. And Sister Jean Dolores and Sister Mary Sharon Rose, B.V.M., get kudos from Kathleen Antol, B.V.M., for their team-taught courses Teaching of Reading and Children's Literature. Also in the education department, Sister Mary St. George (Helen) Thompson, B.V.M., was seen by Marilyn Wilson, B.V.M., as "visionary and really gave me a philosophy of learning."

Our theology classes served a double need for us scholastics: continuation of our religious training and continuation of our teacher training, as many of us would be teaching religion in either elementary or secondary school. Across the broad range of respondents, this aspect of our education gets rave reviews. Most credit is given to Sister Mary Carol Frances Jegen, B.V.M., who arrived at Mundelein in 1957. Only in retrospect did many realize that we were exposed to the most up-to-date theology of the time, which prepared us for the changes brought about by Vatican II. Roberta Ellis Flaherty, class of '65 says the following about her training in theology:

> What I savor more than anything at this point in my life is the fact that
> the B.V.M.'s who responded to Pope John XXIII's call to aggiornamento
> provided scholastics (and perhaps the regular student body, as well)
> with a wealth of experts in the field of Scripture study and in the nature

of the church . . . , who gave us insights into the books of Amos and Hosea, the Exodus experience, the Gospel writers, the letters of Paul . . . , and they walked us through the changes in the liturgy. We were introduced to people who passionately loved the Scriptures, who knew and understood the liturgy. . . . We grew up in the United States during Vatican II (and the great social revolution of the 1960s); we became knowledgeable and, therefore, were not afraid of the changes asked by the church.

I remember a paper I wrote for a class taught by Sister Mary Carol Frances in which I traced the image of Mary in Islamic religion. This was my first acquaintance with the Qur'an. Sister Mary Carol Frances's own essay in this volume demonstrates what so many respondents speak to. What the essay does not show the reader is that almost all respondents refer to Sister Mary Carol Frances as an inspirational and dynamic teacher whose work has left an indelible impression on them to this day. Respondents who graduated in the later 1960s also mention Anne Carr, B.V.M., Mary Donahey, B.V.M., and William Hill. Phoebe Van Hecke Segal, class of '70, a religious studies major, says "it was a very avant-garde department at the time—rebellious and fun."

Perhaps one of the biggest changes over the years in training scholastics began around the end of the Second Vatican Council in the 1964–65 academic year. Outreach service was encouraged, which resulted in scholastics teaching religion and other subjects at Cabrini Green and at St. Dominic School in the Cabrini Green area and helping out at the Kiwanis Boys Club on Diversey. Elizabeth Avalos, B.V.M., class of '67, recalls involvement with the Upward Bound program, which took her to various sites in the Chicago area.

Glimpses of events that rocked the nation during the 1960s were certainly very much part of the academic discussion in classes during these years, but for the most part, the scholastics viewed the action from windows across the street from the college. Peggy Nolan, B.V.M., says, "I saw the buses from Mundelein take off for Selma in 1964, and I yearned to go. I was glad S. M. Ignatia [Mary Griffin] went if I couldn't!" And from Phoebe Van Hecke Segal: "One totally memorable experience was looking out my eighth-floor window at the scholasticate to see a huge 'Free Kent State' sign and red paint on the two angels at Mundelein's front doors." She remarks that even though convent life was in great transition at the time and her access to the city of Chicago was an important part of her education, she still felt that the new freedoms were scorned by some and thus she felt "pulled in many directions." Peggy Nolan, B.V.M., says that "Harvey Cox's 'secular city' was at my fingertips, almost like a laboratory. I couldn't get enough of it." During her time at Mundelein, the self-study directed by Vice President Norbert Hruby called for a curriculum change from semesters to trimesters, and she says, "At this time, the cutting edge was calling for concentrated study, in-depth exploration. I bought it all!" Jean O'Keefe, class of '69, actually went to the University of Chicago with a professor from the English department to protest the police violence at the 1968 Democratic National Convention in Chicago. By this time, however, some scholastics were living at other B.V.M. houses in the city, so there was more freedom of movement (Jean lived at St. Mary High School her senior year and had a part-time job at the Veteran Administration Hospital). As society and the nation changed, so did Mundelein College and the B.V.M. congregation.

Anita Montavon, B.V.M., voicing our situation in the parlance of the late 1950s and early 1960s, says that we were "in the world but not of it," as we were reminded in our religious-life training. The same was true for us scholastics at the college—in the college but not of it. Our single focus at Mundelein was the intellectual life, but that always had to be second to our life across the street—the continuation of our training to be B.V.M. sisters. Thus, our intellectual life was not celebrated in the early years of the scholasticate program. Within the first year of the program, those scholastics who earned a place on the dean's list ceased being recognized in *The Skyscaper.* Was it because the students referred to us as the D.A.R.'s (the darned/damned average raisers)? Was it to prevent intellectual pride? Or were there perhaps some other reasons known only to the times? When our grade cards arrived, we were to look at them and then drop them in the mail slot next to our mailboxes on the tenth floor of the scholasticate, where only our religious superior had access. The grade cards were never to be looked at again or spoken about with others.

Did the fact that Mundelein was a women's college make a difference to us? In the first years of the scholasticate program, it was somewhat taken for granted by scholastics, I suspect. In the days before Betty Friedan's *Feminine Mystique* (1963), few of us would have been thinking of the discrimination against women in our society. Views changed somewhat into the mid- and late 1960s, but the civil rights movement and the Vietnam War were much more center stage during these days. What does become clear in hindsight is the impression left by excellent, qualified women faculty and administration. The name of Sister Mary Ann Ida Gannon, B.V.M., who was president of the college during the entire scholasticate years, comes up again and again. Many found her interest in the scholastics both heartwarming and refreshing. Her extemporaneous talks, her compassion and kindness, her warmth, her charisma and wisdom, her brilliance and vision, and her ability to run the college are some of the ways she is remembered. She was named a member of the planning committee for the program by the B.V.M. congregation in 1955, and she became president of the college at the same time the first scholastics arrived in 1957.

Sister Mary Assisium (Mary) Cramer, B.V.M., dean of women and professor of history, had less contact with scholastics, but several speak of her. She is remembered for the cultural events sponsored by the college, such as the concert and lecture series. Featured in the series while I was a scholastic were the following: folksingers Joe and Penny Aronson, Philip Scharper on "Love in the Intellectual Life," the Gold Curtain Festival Singers, poet John Fredrick Nims, Irish baritone Michael O'Higgins, and last in the series that year, *Karla, Woman of India* performed on the Mundelein College stage. The name of Sister Mary Ignatia, B.V.M. (Mary Griffin, 1916–98), academic dean, is mentioned often as a person who was articulate and spoke of interesting world issues. On September 19, 1961, Sister Mary Ignatia and Sister Mary Assisium addressed the Mundelein student body on "The Role of Women in the World Today." There does not appear to be an extant copy of that talk. Kathleen Antol, B.V.M., however, remembers Mary Griffin saying, "An educated woman reads avidly. She listens to the news. She knows what is going on in the world and is able to articulate many different kinds of ideas. An educated woman reads a book a day."

To round out the activities beyond the concert and lecture series and the foreign film series mentioned earlier, we avidly took advantage of performances staged by Mundelein students. In December of 1961 music students presented *Amahl and the Night Visitors* as the annual Christmas cantata; in February, students brought James Thurber's play *Many Moons* to the Mundelein stage; finally, the glee clubs of Mundelein College and John Carroll University presented a joint concert at Mundelein in April. A final expansion of our education revolved around guest speakers brought into the scholasticate to address us on various issues. Related to our future life as teachers was the presentation by Ruth Kittle, author of *Kittle's Penmanship* (1961). Our religious life was enhanced by John L. MacKenzie, S.J., who spoke on "Theology and Education." Finally, our intellectual life got a boost from George Klubertanz, S.J., the author of the text we were using for our Philosophy of Man [sic] course.[21] In the years that followed, many famous and influential speakers and performers found their way to Mundelein College.

The fact that it was women who planned the rich extracurricular activities at the college, women who held all the major offices in the college, and mostly women who were our teachers, instilled in us an unconscious and, perhaps only later, clear recognition that our horizons as women were limitless. Women could do anything they set out to do: be president or dean of a college; earn a Ph.D. in the sciences, social sciences, or humanities; publish newspapers and creative-writing magazines; become lawyers or medical doctors.[22] For Letitia Close, B.V.M., class of '63, Mundelein was a launching place for women, who were provided with a quality education, breadth, and depth. She says, "I would have recommended the college to anyone." For Dorothy Jean Donahue, class of '61, "[My] life has been profoundly influenced by . . . Mundelein College. . . . My liberal-arts education gave me vision of life and for life, not just training for employment." Kateri O'Shea sums it up well: "My life has been irrevocably, deeply, significantly influenced by my Mundelein experience. It made me a strong, well-educated woman, aware of the world and how I could serve it. The strong women models from that experience have been a source of inspiration for me throughout my life."

One question keeps returning to me as I reflect on the scholastics' presence at the college. What if we had not been in the habit? Would it have made any difference? It was not until the last year or so of the scholasticate program that B.V.M.'s were given the choice to change to a modified habit which, quickly for most, turned to wearing secular dress. Certainly, our presence in classes and in the halls of Mundelein would not have stood out as it did. Mundelein would not have had the worry of being viewed as a "nuns'" college. But the change did represent a visible movement within the congregation in line with the suggestions coming out of Vatican II. I believe it also freed us as women to recognize our own individuality, and perhaps as we experienced the lifting of the stereotype that accompanied the habit, we also became more conscious of the stereotypes of women of the day.

In retrospect, our existence was a strange one indeed—a part of such exciting times, and yet a "class apart." Very few of us questioned the strict rules and regulations, but rather saw our lifestyle and the confining setup of the times as part of the demands of religious life. Looking back, most respondents expressed some regret that we were not afforded more opportunities to socialize with other Mundelein students, more access to the city of Chicago, and more outreach to the surrounding community. Even as I write these words, I think of the parents of college-age students who would probably love to have their children semicloistered until they earn the diploma that comes at such an exorbitant cost today.

Despite the restrictions on our outside activities and the relative "hothouse" existence most of us led, almost all respondents place great value on their Mundelein education. In fact, a couple of respondents now see the restrictions as having helped focus them on the education they were receiving (Margaret Geraghty, B.V.M., class of '65, and Jerry Snider Delaney, class of '66). Certainly, there were classes that some among us found boring or useless, but in evaluating the overall education, the words *excellent, superb,* and *challenging* appear over and over again. "Mundelein was a great formative influence on me. It gave me knowledge of and respect for my field of study, and it gave me self-confidence and the ability to work with others; in short, the foundations upon which I have built a career in education" (Mary Martens, B.V.M., class of '59). Kateri O'Shea says, "Excellent education. I was extremely well prepared in my field because of the strong academic program and superb teachers. That enabled me to be a good teacher . . . the broad liberal-arts background provided a basis for lifelong learning that continues to this day." Judy A. Mayotte, class of '62, writes that "the fine education we received allowed me to open other doors in my life and gave me the courage to do things I probably would not have otherwise done."[23]

Among those respondents who went on to further education, which includes almost all, several remarked that their graduate classes were easier than their undergraduate classes. An example is the following from Rita Basta, B.V.M., class of '65, who writes, "My math education was excellent—so much so that my study at Notre Dame for my master's degree was very easy." Graduates of the mid- to late 1960s emphasize other elements of the experience, again reflecting the changing times. Peggy Nolan, B.V.M., says, "Mundelein helped me to take learning out of an ivory tower and put it to work at street level. To this day, I consider myself a learner." And Kathleen Antol, B.V.M., saw Mundelein as "a hotbed of change of all kinds. It made me a thinker, a considerer, a weigher of situations. It brought me out of myself. It really had great influence on the rest of my life and how I would live it." I could supply many more statements from respondents. I will add my own, which is echoed by many as well. When I went into my own classroom to teach at Mount Carmel Academy in Wichita, Kansas, I felt confident and well prepared for the challenge. The quality of my Mundelein education has never been a question for me; it has served me well in my graduate studies and in my life in general.

After graduation from Mundelein in 1962, I taught in high school for the next seven years, one year at Mount Carmel Academy and six years at Xavier High School in St. Louis, during which time I became deeply involved in Japanese studies. In 1969 I returned as a faculty member to a very different Mundelein College, a Mundelein in the throes of civil rights struggles and deeply involved in the Vietnam War protests. I remained on the faculty through our affiliation with Loyola University Chicago in 1991. But that is another story for the next book.[24]

Endnotes

1. Where given permission by the respondent, the completed questionnaires are available in the Mundelein College Archives. Approximately sixty-five questionnaires were sent out and forty-eight returned. It should be noted that twelve other congregations of women religious sent sister students to Mundelein during these years. For reasons of space, their experiences are not included here. Also not included is any comment on the excellent education provided by Clarke College during our first two years of college. I have used the full title for sisters, as we did in those days. Among ourselves, we often referred to each other and our B.V.M. teachers by religious name alone, without the "sister."

   As scholastics, most of us were given the freedom to choose our major. Initially, a theater major was allowed, but because scholastics were not allowed to perform on stage, eventually those interested in theater were told to choose a different major. English seemed to be the alternative most chose.

2. Marjorie Noterman Beane, *From Framework to Freedom: A History of the Sister Formation Conference* (Lanham, Maryland: University Press of America, 1993), 7. See also, Mary L. Schneider, O.S.F., "American Sisters and the Roots of Change: 1950s," *U.S. Catholic Historian* 7 (winter, 1988), 55–72.

3. *The Education News,* April 1957, 5. Mundelein College Archives (MCA), Gannon Center for Women and Leadership, Loyola University Chicago. The total number of B.V.M.'s at the time was 2,194. That means that 1,848 B.V.M.'s would have to wait a year, and more likely two, to get replacements for sisters who might need to retire from the classroom. In July 1956, Mother Mary Consolatrice sent a letter to the pastors in parishes where B.V.M.'s taught, explaining the enriched educational experiences planned for the sisters and asking that in the first year of the program "will you consider the release of one Sister by securing an additional secular teacher? The following year, a Sister will be returned to your school if you cannot continue to make the sacrifice" (Mother Mary Consolatrice, Correspondence, Sisters of Charity of the Blessed Virgin Mary [B.V.M.] Archives, Mount Carmel, Dubuque, Iowa [B.V.M. Archives]).

4. Ibid, 10.

5. "Counsel to Teaching Sisters," trans. N.C.W.C. News Bureau in Rome (Washington, D.C.: National Catholic Welfare Conference Publications Office, n.d.), Sister Formation, Box 2.7, B.V.M. Archives.

6. Sister Formation, Box 2, B.V.M. Archives.

7. Ibid

8. Ibid. In the B.V.M. congregation of that time, sisters pronounced their vows of poverty, chastity, and obedience, renewed them annually for five years, and then took perpetual vows. After that point, they were no longer "junior" sisters. According to Ann Ida Gannon, B.V.M., archivist for the Mundelein College archives, B.V.M.'s chose the term "scholastics" for the sisters in study to stress the role involved, not the status or age in the congregation. The word was also used by the Jesuits.

9. Ibid.

10. Beane, 138.

11. Scholasticate Box, B.V.M. Archives.

12. From a taped interview with Frances Shea, B.V.M., conducted by Rita Benz, 1989.

13. Letter, 18 August 1956, Scholasticate Box, B.V.M. Archives.

14. Scholasticate Box, B.V.M. Archives.

15. *Vista,* 1:1 (December 1957): 2 ff.

16. Mary Therese Rink, "The Scholasticate Years," a paper presented as part of a "Report on the History of Wright Hall," to the B.V.M. Heritage Society, 20 June 1998, Wright Hall: 1. The buildings that were Aquinas Hall and Philomena Hall no longer exist.

17. 29 January 1957, Scholasticate Box, B.V.M. Archives.

18. Sister Mary St. Irene and Sister Mary Elsa continued to befriend and support Little Brothers as they began their work in the city. Today, they are known as Little Brothers—Friends of the Elderly and the executive director of the Chicago office is a Mundelein graduate, Mary Christina (Tina) Stretch, class of '67.

19. This was a program held the summers of 1968 and 1969 at Mundelein College and was the first of its kind in the city of Chicago to use leaders of the Spanish-speaking community as resource persons.

20. I arrived in Wichita, Kansas, in 1962 to teach high school and was told I needed to take a statistics course to be certified in Kansas. When I questioned this and my NCATE certified teacher training was verified, I was immediately certified. It is interesting to note that Loyola University received NCATE approval in 1963 and DePaul in 1964.

21. This list of speakers was taken from Annals of the Scholasticate, August 11, 1961, to August 3, 1962. Scholasticate Box, B.V.M. Archives. There are annals for the years 1961 to 1971.

22. Five Mundelein graduates have become college or university presidents: Patricia O'Donnell Ewers, class of '57, Pace University, New York; Mary B. Breslin, B.V.M., class of '58, Mundelein College; Alice Bourke Hayes, class of '59, University of San Diego; Jacqueline Powers Doud, class of '62, Mount Saint Mary's College, Los Angeles; and Marilou Denbo Eldred, class of '63, St. Mary's of Notre Dame.

23. Judy Mayotte's colorful life to date is summarized in the *Chicago Tribune,* 5 April 1998, and in an article by Helen Gourlay, B.V.M., in the B.V.M. publication, *Salt* (spring 1995), 16–17. As a teaser, I'll tell you that she was a recipient of a MacArthur Foundation "genius" grant.

24. Unfortunately, I could not use all the material I received. For example, both Sally Holland Griffith and Frances Connolly Leen majored in speech correction. Since I had comments from only two graduates of the program, I decided to leave it out of my discussion of majors.

A New Dean Sweeps Clean, or Adventures with the Academic Dean

Gloria Callaci

In July 1961 the already beloved Pope John XXIII was in the Vatican, the recently elected President Kennedy was in the White House, and the newly graduated me was looking for a place to work. When Peggy Roach, a friend and fellow alumna who knew both Mundelein and me well, phoned to ask if I would consider working for Mundelein's academic dean, I was surprised by her question. The dean under whom I had just spent four years at Mundelein was a staid, elderly B.V.M. professor of Latin and Greek, in whose office I could not imagine being closeted as I began my career climb in the world. "Oh, no," Peggy laughed, "there's going to be a *new* dean, Sister Mary Ignatia Griffin. She's brilliant, dynamic, and everybody loves her! She just finished her Ph.D. degree in English literature at Fordham, and she'll be here in August."

Peggy was right on all counts and I took the job. It was a difficult time for me because, after a long struggle with cancer, my mother had died in May just three weeks before my graduation. My brother had just graduated from high school, my sister was only twelve, and my father was overwhelmed. I postponed "going out on my own" plans in order to help take care of my family and our household. In return, I granted myself a lifelong dream—planning a trip around Europe the following summer with a group of friends. This would require a two-month leave of absence from my job, which was readily agreed to by my new boss, the academic dean.

Even though Sister Mary Ignatia had graduated from Mundelein the year I was born, she quickly became the big sister I never had and certainly needed at that trying time. And I became her "court jester," a title she soon bestowed and I readily accepted because Sir Thomas More, a favorite saint of both of ours, had highly valued his jester's ability to provide comic relief at difficult times. We also had very compatible senses of humor, and we both loved to tease. Besides, she explained to me, I couldn't possibly be her secretary because I didn't type well enough.

My official title was assistant to the academic dean. When asked exactly what I did in this capacity, my standard reply was, "Everything the dean does, only less of it and for less money." Everyone knew the latter part of that statement couldn't possibly be true, modest though my salary was. Actually, I did have some specific assignments, including the supervision and administration of all standardized tests given at the college, primarily the Scholastic Aptitude Test (SAT) and the American College Testing Assessment (ACT), which was a fitting task for a psychology major. In one of the briefing sessions I held for members of the faculty, my former philosophy teacher in whose after-lunch seminar I had often unavoidably dozed did me the same "honor." I also became the source for all information on foreign-study programs and a major cheerleader for students who considered applying for graduate grants and fellowships.

Sister Mary Ignatia would ensconce her tall and graceful black-robed figure in a newly acquired orange upholstered chair behind her formidable desk. Initially, that inspired Mary Ann Annetti, a member of the economics faculty who worked part-time in the dean's office, and I to refer to her among ourselves as "the Great Pumpkin." But after receiving dozens of memos signed "S.M.I.," I began calling her "Smi."

I soon learned that changing things at the largest Catholic women's college in the nation was one of Smi's major missions. My "But it's never been done like that before!" in reference to academic procedures or ceremonies, would elicit her "All the more reason to do it differently!" One of her first changes was to give more students the opportunity of a college education by no longer granting scholarships to Mundelein at a uniform amount, but adjusting the amount to each student's individual financial need. To further her goal of academic excellence, Smi proposed several curriculum changes.

Incoming 1962 freshmen with exceptional intellectual promise would be invited into the Mundelein Honors Program. They would work in the humanities their first year and the exact sciences, the history of ideas and contemporary philosophy, and theology in succeeding years. Intended to resonate throughout the college community, these creative and more challenging courses would offer participants honors grades and lead to an honors degree. Qualified students at all levels would be eligible for a new interdepartmental symposium where they might study one of the Great Books or select a fundamental idea and trace its influence in the history and literature of the past. Incoming freshmen with exceptional experience or knowledge of a particular area of study would be tested in that subject and could be awarded college credit, advanced placement, or both.

Upper-class students of high scholastic standing would be encouraged to pursue independent study or research in their major fields, and arrangements would be made with Loyola University for qualified Mundelein seniors in their final semester to begin graduate work while still completing their undergraduate degrees. New interdepartmental courses for all students would be built around a core of required courses, all to begin with the 1962–63 school year.

Smi was particularly excited about the "Early Bird" summer-school program she created for June high school graduates who wanted to complete college in three to three and one-half years, as well as for incoming high school seniors with high recommendations from their school. The seven courses offered to Early Birds included Russian and Greek, United States history, European history, art, and physics. And if these bright summer Birds decided to nest long-term at Mundelein, so much the better.

All these changes were bound to ruffle some feathers, and the newly minted Fordham Ph.D., who still got homesick for New York at the sound of a Manhattan street name and who could flawlessly imitate a Bronx boy calling out to his buddies, was reminded that in her native Chicago it's clout that makes things happen. We learned that department chairs under siege have powerful survival instincts and that the academic adage "Changing a curriculum is like moving a cemetery" is bitterly true. Adding to the pressure of intramural jousting with faculty members whom she also lived with night and day were the extramural demands of what I came to call "deaning."

Deaning meant time, travel, and intellectual and physical energy devoted to local, national, and sometimes international meetings, conferences, seminars, and symposia, as well as to academic and Catholic committees, commissions, boards, and associations. We decided that, like the prime minister and queen of England, there should be a working dean and a ceremonial dean. But as there was only one, and she could become very frazzled by all the conflicting demands, she would find some comfort in my reminding her, "After all, what you're doing is not brain surgery. No one's going to *die* because of you!" As the daughter of a physician, Smi appreciated the distinction. We both learned a lot about perspective that first year.

In June we carefully proofread, checked, rechecked, stacked, and finally gave 177 Mundelein diplomas to Cardinal Meyer to bestow into the graduates' eager hands. And I left for fifty-one magical days of touring eleven European countries with thirteen friends.

"Sit down for five minutes and tell me *all* about your trip!" was Smi's way of welcoming me back on August 1 and alerting me that there was much work to do to prepare for the 1962–63 school year. There were twenty-one new faculty members: five sisters and sixteen lay teachers. The new honors program had attracted thirty-two gifted and eager freshmen. And while I was in Europe, a radical change had taken place in the college administration.

I was introduced to Dr. Norbert Hruby, former director of the adult-education branch of the University of Chicago and now Mundelein's vice president, a post created to meet the increasing needs and challenges of the college. Dr. Hruby's position and gender were unique to a Catholic women's college at that time. When someone would come rushing up to him and Smi at an academic meeting and gush, "So, this is your new *male* vice president!" Smi would deadpan, "No, we just dress her that way." Dr. Hruby's official title was vice president of development, a position traditionally associated with fund-raising. But Smi, Dr. Hruby, and Mundelein's president, Sister Mary Ann Ida Gannon, had a radical concept of development—the total restructuring of the college!

This monumental three-year project was designated the Institutional Analysis. Its key components were lengthy, detailed, anonymous question-naires regarding the college's past, present, and future to be answered by faculty, administrators, students, alumnae, and even the husbands of alumnae. The hundreds of probing questions ranged from the purpose and goals of a college education, to the effect of an alumna's college major on her later life, to how great an impact a husband felt Mundelein had made on his wife. When the questionnaires were completed, several study groups—each composed of faculty, administrators, and students—were to inquire in depth into every aspect of the college and then apply the questionnaire responses to the area under review. A high-powered advisory committee was formed, consisting of Dr. Bernice Brown Cronkhite, vice president, Radcliffe College; Fr. Will Dunne, executive secretary of the National Catholic Educational Association; H. Marston Morse of Princeton's Institute of Advanced Study; Dr. George Schuster, United States representative to UNESCO and former president of Hunter College; and Dr. Joseph Sittler, University of Chicago Divinity School professor and a leader in the Protestant ecumenical movement. These distin-guished educators and scholars would oversee the entire process and react to the reports of the study groups, adding their impartial expertise to the think-ing and experience of the college community.

In the midst of launching and overseeing this tremendous project, Smi was very touched by the kind gesture of a young history teacher who headed one of the faculty/administrator teams. The seven team leaders were to take turns choosing faculty members and administrative staff to join them, a com-petitive system which could mean some of the oldest sisters might be hurt by being among the last chosen. However, this man used a precious early choice to draft a very elderly nun who worked in the registrar's office saying, "I certainly want her on my team because I know she'll work harder than anybody else!"

Between her academic duties, Smi began stealing out of the office for an hour or so to take some lessons of her own. Because she had to be mobile for meetings and, at that time, few members of the order drove, her good friend Sister Mary Donatus was teaching her how to drive a car. When Smi had difficulty mastering the art of precision gear shifting, she and Donatus suffered the indignity of a car full of young men yelling at them, "Get a horse!" Donatus appealed to Smi's artistic nature by reminding the former music major—who was famed for writing the official college song—that, just as she used both feet while playing the organ, she needed to use both feet in a smooth rhythm to harmonize the brake, gas pedal, and clutch. Smi was soon licensed.

In those ancient days before computers, the preregistration system for correlating students' desired courses with the realities of teachers' schedules, with class numbers and times, and with the assignment of classrooms depended on the tedious processing of hundreds of punch cards. First, Mary Ann Annetti and I would take each student's card in hand and punch out the requested course numbers and sections printed along the edges of the card. How many incoming sophomores wanted to take Survey of English Literature on Monday, Wednesday, and Friday at 2:00? Align all the sophomore cards, stick a long needle through the appropriate hole for that class and lift. All the cards punched for that class would fall to the desk, and you would have the number and names of students for the potential class. Besides being primitive and time consuming, this system was very messy—all those hole punches and falling cards. Once, when Smi remarked that my outer office desk might be kept a little tidier, I couldn't resist protesting that that was like expecting a coal miner to keep a clean mine. She didn't argue.

Although my duties rarely involved overtime work, Smi and I spent several evenings in the spring of 1963 plotting summer-school course schedules for older teaching nuns who were still some credits short of a college degree. Having enjoyed the advantage of more progressive planning by the order in her educational formation, which had culminated in her doctorate, Smi sympathized with these sisters from a previous era. Many of them had decades of teaching experience but had to return to college for basic courses. A few years later, she would initiate the Degree Completion Program for older women returning to college that gave college credit for life experience.

At the end of her second year as dean, Smi announced another policy change to benefit students. By basing the amount of scholarship grants on demonstrated need the previous year, she had enabled the college to support twice as many scholarship students as in the past. Now, in order to encourage talented students to choose more challenging courses and to participate more actively in student affairs to the benefit of the entire college, she reduced from 2.5 to 2.0 the grade point average needed for scholarship renewal. She said she wanted to enable students "to benefit from their education by studying for the sake of learning rather than for the sake of grades." She was always radical.

Our second academic year ended with a laugh. Mundelein's distinguished commencement speaker, Dr. Glenn T. Seaborg, chairman of the Atomic Energy Commission and the Nobel prize–winning codiscoverer of plutonium, was chased away by a maintenance man when he tried to park his car near the east door. Somehow, he made it to the graduation ceremony anyway.

In June of 1963 I just missed a place in history. A young member of Mundelein's psychology department had recruited me, with Smi's eager endorsement, to join a picket line in front of the Illinois Club for Catholic Women, housed at Loyola University's Lewis Towers. Although the club allowed Loyola students to use its swimming pool, a black student had been refused admission to the pool. The civil rights movement of the 1960s was in its earliest stages, and when a handful of Franciscan nuns joined our picket line—the first nuns ever to do so—photographers, reporters, and television-news crews rushed to the scene. The scandalous photo that appeared the next day on the front page of the *New York Times,* the Chicago papers, other major newspapers around the country, and later in weekly newsmagazines, featured the nuns among the picketers but excluded me by inches.

When I called Smi from a nearby phone booth after our protest ended, I decided to tell her I'd been arrested and was in jail, since we had debated the pros and cons of this radical act. "I don't even know who you are," she replied. "I thought so!" I retorted. "You encourage me to do something dangerous and then desert me when I'm in trouble!" I think we were both teasing. Less than two years later Smi would lead a group of Mundelein students and faculty members to Selma, Alabama. They joined Martin Luther King Jr. and many others from across the nation in their historic march to protest the outrageous treatment of southern blacks. I did it first, but she did it bigger and better.

Even though she said she would be glad to keep her court jester on the job, Smi felt it was time for me to consider a change of role. She began encouraging me to look ahead to a job that would take me away from Mundelein, where I had studied or worked all my adult life. She told me she envisioned me in a creative and challenging job that would put me in touch with bright young people not wearing habits.

For my second summer off I spent six weeks at Georgetown University's Institute of Languages and Linguistics taking an intensive Russian course. Russian had been one of my minors in college, and I had decided to participate in an exchange program to the Soviet Union the following summer. My third year in the dean's office would be my final one.

In keeping with Smi's continuing pursuit of academic excellence, the 1963–64 school year began with 28 new faculty members, bringing the total number of instructors to 105, and eight new courses "to expand and enrich the present curriculum." These new courses included such innovations as a Chicago alderman teaching a course in municipal government and a professor from the American University in Cairo providing a survey of the Islamic Near East.

I, too, had become a student of sorts, improving my Russian skills with early morning study in Mundelein's language laboratory. I also had the opportunity to sit in on a class session on F. Scott Fitzgerald taught by Smi. She had arranged her schedule to allow for a long-desired return to the classroom to teach one course. An hour of listening to her lively, engaging presentation made it clear to me why so many students past and now present flocked to her literature courses. I had to remind myself that she benefited the education of more students by being an innovative dean than she possibly could by being a star member of the English department. I knew she had to remind herself, too.

In spite of the many demands on her, Smi certainly knew how to enjoy herself, even within the confines of the dean's office. A popular comic record had recently come out featuring a parody of John F. Kennedy's administration and family with dead-on imitations of the voices of JFK, Jackie, and other pioneers of the New Frontier. One afternoon in the fall of 1963, Smi and some of the other sisters who shared her love of devilish humor were listening to the record in her inner office. It was my duty to fend off intruders. How persuasive was it to tell students, "I'm sorry, but the dean is in a meeting now," as uproarious laughter escaped over the partition between our offices? Sadly, a few weeks later, the Mundelein community and the world were mourning the loss of that dynamic young president.

By the start of the second semester in January 1964, Smi lost no time in implementing the results of some of the students' responses to the Institutional

Analysis questionnaire. With the faculty, she had devised four new courses designed to cross departmental lines. She saw these seminar courses as one of the distinct advantages of a small college, a new way to bring faculty and students more closely together for the exchange of ideas. She was also proud to announce that, for the first time in Mundelein's history, the college would offer summer-school study and travel abroad—a university program in Spain undertaken in partnership with Loyola. Later that year Smi was elected to the executive committee of the American Conference of Academic Deans at their annual meeting in Washington. She had the honor of representing Mundelein as the only Catholic women's college on that committee.

But that very same month demonstrated not only how far she had come as a modern nun, but also how far there still was to go. The college newspaper had carried an enthusiastic student review of the film *Tom Jones,* an adaptation of Henry Fielding's rollicking, picaresque eighteenth-century novel. I had seen the film and thought it a brilliant, fast-paced, and visually stunning version of the literary classic; I desperately wanted to share the experience with Smi. However, in those days, nuns were not allowed to attend movie theaters, certainly unthinkable for a famously ribald film. Smi could read the novel, teach it, but not see the film version. Mary Ann and I devised a clever plan that would avoid all scandal. We would go to an outdoor theater with Smi swathed in blankets in the back seat, thereby concealing but not removing her habit. To our disappointment, she declined. How ironic that a few years later, as the cataclysmic changes of the 1960s accelerated, *Tom Jones* was chosen to be featured at Mundelein's film series for the entire college community.

In keeping with change as one of the major themes of the decade, before the academic year ended, Smi introduced more innovations. As a result of further evaluation of the Institutional Analysis questionnaires, now recognized as "a gold mine of information," experimental major changes in the curriculum were to begin immediately. These ranged from breaking centuries of tradition by introducing non-Thomistic philosophy courses to offering a forward-thinking new educational elective, "Living and Learning in the Inner City." Overall, the students now had a much wider choice of courses and more flexibility in meeting degree requirements.

Among the major changes in my life at that time was the end of seven years of study and work at Mundelein. In late June I would leave for a two-month stay in the Soviet Union, the first time the Experiment in International Living was being allowed to send a group to that enigmatic country. It might have been an occasion for dramatic good-byes, but I preferred a low-key departure. I knew I would see Smi and my other friends at Mundelein in the future, and I did.

I went on to a career as a television writer and producer, the "creative and challenging job" Smi had wished for me, although it took me a few years to find it. I lived in Paris for a year, traveled personally and professionally to my heart's content, and finally married at the age of thirty-seven, in time to raise many eyebrows and a son and daughter.

In 1968 Smi left the deanship after seven years of service, did postdoctoral work as a research fellow in English at Yale and was then a visiting professor of English at a small historically black college in Mississippi for three years. She returned to Mundelein in 1973, where she developed a coeducational Weekend College in Residence for adults with full-time work and family responsibilities, the first such institution in American higher education and one that became widely imitated. Smi left the B.V.M. order in 1974, but remained a member of the Mundelein faculty. Now known as Mary Griffin, she wrote *The Courage to Choose,* an acclaimed autobiographical memoir offering her perspective on changes in religious life and the church. She continued to attract numerous academic awards and honors until her retirement. These included being named in 1986 as one of the top twenty educational leaders among college and university faculty by the American Association for Higher Education and the Carnegie Society for the Advancement of Teaching.

Through all those years we kept in contact and got together as our divergent lives permitted, often at Mundelein events. My husband and I had the honor of participating in the wonderful eightieth birthday celebration given to Smi in December of 1997 by her great friend and fellow alumna Jane Trahey. In the spring of 1998 Mary and I spoke and joked by phone, and we agreed to get together soon for one of our infrequent lunches. Three days later, I learned that she had died of a brain aneurysm. What a sudden and unexpected loss to so many people! And I mourned the first and best boss I ever had, my beloved Smi.

Remembering 1962–1969

Joan Frances Crowley, B.V.M.

When it was suggested that my contribution to the Mundelein College History Project should take the form of a memoir on my eight-year tenure as director (later, dean) of the college's resident program, the idea seemed reasonable enough. I envisioned an introduction by way of a brief overview of the history of the program from its inception in 1934, with just thirty-five students housed in a mansion directly adjacent to the main building, to its evolution into a full-fledged program in 1962 when we welcomed students from throughout the United States. This would preface what was to be the focus of my presentation, an introduction to my lived experience with these students as they reacted to the explosive events of the 1960s. Again, the assignment did not appear to be formidable. Eight years of living among and interacting with over one thousand Mundelein women had provided me with a wealth of experiences on which to draw.

Sorted and categorized, the experiences would furnish the examples validating my interpretations of the days of the assassinations, of racial unrest turned violent, of changing sexual mores, and of the horrors of the Vietnam War. Permeating this era as well was the work of Vatican Council II. Its ongoing study and resultant implementation of changes in doctrines and practices that had been part of Catholic life for centuries caused a profound upheaval as American Catholics reacted to a modernized church. Moreover, Mundelein students were not living in a bucolic setting removed from immediate contact with the realities of this decade. Instead, they were situated in a major city, a city long noted for its racism. They dated friends from universities throughout the city and its environs, schools where the Vietnam War was raising the specter of a draft that would send young men into a war many believed unjust. I felt I could tell this story.

My work did not go smoothly, however. Memories that were very personal to me and, at times, painful, began to intrude. Vatican II, the horrors of the Vietnam War, increasing racism, and the assassinations had deeply affected my life as well. These memories were insinuating themselves into what was to have been a reflection on student reactions to these historic events. However, in a discussion with a group of our writers, Mary Griffin, distinguished and beloved professor of English at Mundelein, described for us what constitutes a memoir. She termed it "a piece of historical writing that is deeply personal as well as historical." She cited several outstanding memoirs, including Frank McCourt's *Angela's Ashes* and Jill Ker Conway's *The Road to Coorain* and *True North,* as exemplars of this approach. Unfortunately, she is no longer here to judge whether I have properly interpreted her definition, as my personal reactions become, at times, a part of the students' story.

Neither the Sisters of Charity of the Blessed Virgin Mary nor Cardinal George Mundelein, archbishop of Chicago, collaborators in the establishment of Mundelein College, had in mind a resident college when they settled on a North Side location with Loyola University Chicago as a next-door neighbor. In 1930, just a year after ground breaking, the doors of a fifteen-story building, the Skyscraper, opened to 378 students, all of them commuters. But within another four years, in 1934, thirty-five resident students moved into Philomena Hall, a newly purchased twelve-room mansion located east of the main building next to the library (what is now Piper Hall). The demands of Chicago and suburban commuters for whom the long daily ride to the far North Side was too time consuming necessitated that students live on campus Sunday afternoon to the close of classes on Friday. During the following decades, in addition to Philomena, residents would be housed in various floors in the Skyscraper and in Lourdes Hall at the corner of Sheridan and Winthrop. When the B.V.M. congregation built a ten-story building directly across the street from the Skyscraper, it was to serve as a house of studies for the young religious who were completing their degrees. For a time, however, three floors of this scholasticate also became home to Mundelein residents. Despite the limitations of the early residency plan—which, among other disadvantages, limited the attendance of residents at many weekend Loyola social and athletic events—the fond remembrances of alumnae attest to the success of this somewhat makeshift arrangement.

During the next several decades as the college population increased, President and Superior Sister Mary John Michael Dee, B.V.M., as well as her successor, President Sister Mary Ann Ida Gannon, B.V.M., recognized the growing need for a full-scale residence program. By the 1950s Mundelein College had become the largest Catholic women's college in the United States, although in the early 1950s, 85 percent of the student body was still drawn from within the city limits. During this decade of its existence and under the forward-looking leadership of the B.V.M. congregation, the college's reputation for academic excellence had spread well beyond the city of Chicago. It was graduating well-educated women who had, in many instances, exhibited their talents during their collegiate years. In this same decade, Mundelein gained worldwide notice when the scientific community chose Mundelein to house the Foucault Pendulum, at that time the largest instrument in the world for measuring the rotation of the earth. The pendulum was named for Jean-Bernard-Léon Foucault, a nineteenth-century French physicist, who was the first to use a pendulum to demonstrate the earth's rotation. The placement of this nine-story high instrument was under the direction of Sister Mary Therese Langerbeck, B.V.M., an astrophysicist and chair of the physics department. In 1953, Mercedes McCambridge, drama major, class of 1937, added luster to the Mundelein name and to that of her mentor, Sister Mary Leola Oliver, B.V.M., when she won the Oscar for the best female supporting role in *All the King's Men.*

The appointment to the presidency of Sister Mary Ann Ida in 1957 is a significant moment in the history of the college. After a summer session at Harvard, offered as an orientation program for new college presidents, she returned to Mundelein with a heightened awareness of the role women's colleges must assume in educating students to a realization of their potential as women. Thanks to a number of faculty, female and male, lay and religious, the "women theme" found a prominent place in course curricula. Even more important, faculty, especially in liberal arts courses, were teaching their students to develop a more critical attitude in their study of the role of women in societies, past and present. Given the promising record of the young college, it was deemed the right moment to take action on a long-recognized need to expand the resident program. The first step was taken in 1961 with the ground breaking for a residence, Coffey Hall.

I was appointed to the history department of the college in January 1962. Although the midyear assignment came as a surprise, my classes in European history had gone well and at the close of the academic year in June, I felt a sense of satisfaction; in fact, I was secretly smug. The teaching had gone well. Mundelein and I were a good fit.

My sense of satisfaction was short lived. After chapel one evening, Sister Mary Ann Ida invited me to join her in the east parlor. Still wallowing in feelings of a job well done, I had the temerity to assume that she might be going to express her satisfaction with my academic performance. That did not prove to be the case. Instead, she informed me in a most gracious manner that I was to become dean of residence and that I should be ready to move into Coffey Hall as soon as the last brick was in place. In equally gracious language I tried to explain that directing a residence program was not one of my competencies.

I don't recall her response. I do recall her kind words of confidence in my ability as she stood and brought the meeting to a close. On the following morning my new position became a reality when I received a phone call from the manager of our student laundry service. What were to be the days for the weekly pickup and delivery of the girls' sheet/towel packages? And could he see the room in the new building where the laundry lockers were located? Such procedures were a mystery to me. Furthermore, I had not even ventured into the building that was to be my home and my responsibility. I informed him that such serious decisions had yet to be made and urged him to call me later in the month.

I have little recollection of the rest of the summer. I do recall attending a history seminar at Northwestern University because I was to continue my teaching schedule. I also contacted several of the incoming senior resident students and invited them to join me in a discussion of the rules and regulations that were currently in use. This action was a canny move on my part. The invitation was a cry for help rather than a social gesture. I also visited a doctor who assured me that my sudden attack of peculiar physical symptoms was not a sign of serious illness but rather of a severe anxiety attack.

The meeting with the students was successful and greatly eased my apprehensions. They were a charming group, excited about the move to the new building. They were also full of funny stories about resident life under the leadership of my predecessor, their much-loved Sister Mary Agnesita Whelan, B.V.M. Especially amusing were their descriptions of the bare and ugly smoking room on the fifteenth-floor attic of the Skyscraper. Their youthful wisdom and my trust in their efforts to guide me away from excessively strict regulations resulted in a new handbook of rules that received an enthusiastic reception when presented to the Coffey Hall household. To my surprise, the announcement that 10:00 P.M. lights out had been abolished, received an ovation. Only on one other occasion was I the recipient of such applause. On March 23, 1963, the Loyola University Chicago basketball team won the NCAA basketball championship with an unbelievable last-second shot. Jubilant Loyola students took to the streets that night, and I had the good sense to "order" our entire and equally jubilant resident body to join the snake dance down Sheridan Road. A moment of glory for both Loyola and me. Sometime later, my former student advisers paid me a visit, unable to resist the temptation to describe our first meeting and their realization that in me not only did they have a new director but that a novice had come to preside over their resident world.

The doors of Coffey Hall, named to honor the institution's first president, Sister Mary Justitia Coffey, B.V.M., opened to 208 resident students in September 1962. The new building was situated directly on the lakefront, separated from the water by a small stretch of grass and a walkway along the seawall. To those of us who were its first inhabitants, it was a magic space. The elegantly furnished lounges, located on the east end of each of the four floors, offered stunning views of Lake Michigan, from Evanston on the north to Chicago's magnificent skyline to the south. On clear days the east view provided glimpses of the Indiana shoreline. Of equal importance, especially to those whose rooms faced north, Loyola University's leafy campus afforded an attractive vista and was a source of encouragement to those whose ideas of higher education included interaction with the male segment of society.

When graduates recall Coffey Hall, it becomes evident that close proximity to the lake had played a somewhat intangible but important role in their student years. A walk along the seawall at the end of a hard day—a day when one knew for certain that faculty, all of them, lacked even a semblance of the milk of human kindness, or a roommate's increasingly poor attempts at housekeeping had gone far beyond the dictates of civilized society—at such times a stroll along the waterfront might prove a soothing palliative. And on those gray, cold, and windy Chicago days when it was more prudent to view the awesome violence of raging waves from the safety of lounge windows, perhaps a sense of the mystery of God or the meaning of human existence itself might serve to shrink the size of one's problems to a more manageable state.

The pressure of finding my way in a new position meant long days and longer nights. Gradually, perceived student needs began to take precedence over what should be the heart of B.V.M. community life, the coming together in common prayer and the company of other B.V.M.'s. My prayer life was not neglected but was fitted into a busy schedule. At times, praying alone and missing the companionship of my B.V.M. sisters, I felt the isolation keenly. Equally troubling was the realization that at a time of important changes in the life of the church as well as within many American religious congregations, I was not a part of the dialogue. Through some of the leading journals and campus lectures I kept abreast of Catholic thought but found little time to join in the exchange of ideas with my colleagues. Had I asked for some assistance, it would have been quickly forthcoming. Instead, I saw myself as just one of sixty-four B.V.M.'s, all with heavy teaching or administrative schedules. Moreover, I liked what I was doing. In the novitiate I had read a book by Monsignor Ronald Knox, title long forgotten. One sentence, however, had touched me deeply and had become a motivating force in my approach to teaching. "Every human relationship involves an eternal responsibility." This perspective had carried me through many happy classroom years, and I was finding the same approach was easing my entrance into resident life.

As anyone who has experienced resident life knows, students live in a time warp uniquely their own. It has nothing in common with life as lived by the great majority on the planet. God has provided us a perfectly rational setting to ease our way through life. The morning sun is symbolic of our rising to a new day so that, fortified with breakfast we are ready and able to give our best to the tasks of our working day. Throughout at least five days of the week we carry out our duties fortified by a lunch break and, at day's close, enjoy an evening meal and some relaxation. Then, in the words of Samuel Pepys, "and so to bed," at a reasonable hour.

Not so for collegians. Freshmen soon become children of the night, the very late night, infected by the insidious examples of their elders in the dorm. Mornings are a mystery to all but one's roommate. Perhaps she is drafting a term paper, a book critique, or preparing for a quiz. Or perhaps she is still abed after a long night in the lounge. Like the Agora of the Greek city-states, the lounges on each floor were the social centers, places of learning for first-year students and, at times, for me. Here advice was given to the uninitiated on a number of important matters. Things to be avoided could include invitations to certain fraternity houses, single dating with older students, and professors whose seemingly inhuman reading lists could destroy one's GPA. Conversely, ringing endorsements were given to faculty amenable to accepting a late paper or who were readily available for some needed tutoring. (I strongly suspect that, in my absence, the characteristics and seeming idiosyncrasies of the dean of residence were also noted and suggestions made as to how one might best remain in her good graces.) Years later, when many seniors opted for off-campus housing, the disappearance of this offhand but often valuable free counseling service made the work of resident assistants much more difficult.

For many years predating Coffey Hall, residents had gathered for a 10:00 P.M. night prayer. Thanks to the influence of those who had experienced this custom, the practiced continued for some years. A floor officer rang a bell at 10:00 P.M. Most students responded by appearing at their doors in various stages of dress and undress, hair in big curlers, a la the style of the 1960s, and usually clutching a coffee mug in one hand and perhaps a pack of cigarettes in the other. Prayers were brief and often included the needs of a sick relative or friend. A good number of the students then made their way to the lounge and I to my rooms where, if no one had need of me, I corrected papers, prepared a morning lecture, or just luxuriated in my first private hour of the day. When those on my floor and I began to know each other, I was often urged to join them in the lounge. Thus, I gradually became a fairly frequent member of the lounge crowd. Here, I learned to eat pizza at midnight, developed an ear for the music of the Beatles, and learned the real meaning of the words to "Lucy in the Sky with Diamonds." I think these nights were well spent. My neighbors were young adults coming of age amidst the challenges of the 1960s. Some were struggling with the meaning of sexual freedom. Others were already engaged in a sexual relationship, were troubled, and wanted to talk about it. A myriad of other problems became a part of late-night discussions in my rooms, sometimes with just one student, sometimes with a group.

When parents deposited their daughters and mounds of luggage at Coffey Hall for the first time, I was always a bit uncomfortable at their utter confidence that all would be well with their offspring in a college managed by "the sisters." These first-year students, still adolescents and away from home for the first time, were very vulnerable. Sometimes, their roommates' values were a far cry from their own. In high school, for the most part, their boyfriends were classmates or members of parish groups. Coffey Hall on weekends drew fellows from St. Joseph, Rensselaer, Notre Dame, IIT, and, of course, Loyola. Years of reading *Seventeen* magazine had taught American girls to equate college life with an endless series of phone calls leading to library dates leading to frat parties leading to proms and on to the perfect romance.

The most sobering realization that came with the position of developing and directing a resident program was the phrase *in loco parentis*. With this Latin phrase, the college assumes the responsibility of a parent for those living in their resident halls. It follows that the rules and regulations governing their daughters' lives must be compatible with those in any well-ordered home. My initial solution was to check in all residents after dinner, lock the doors, and pull up the drawbridge! Wiser heads, in the persons of my resident advisers, prevailed. We worked out a reasonable, in fact, quite liberal, "hours" policy, and I was spared early retirement from my new position. Crucial to the life of most students was the question of "hours." How late on weeknights? What time on weekends? It was a matter of steering between Scylla and Charybdis to give them the freedom they felt they deserved as responsible young women and to judge the limits of that freedom in terms of in loco parentis. All of us who served in the resident program shared the anxieties that came when students violated this policy. We learned what it meant to experience the anxious parents' role when a student was several hours late in returning to her residence hall. Such incidents were handled by a student committee, the sanctions board, in conjunction with the resident assistant on whose floor the culprit lived. In serious incidents involving the possibility of dismissal from residence, my voice was included in the final decision.

So that I would experience what I would be asking of our resident assistants, I took weekend night duty for six months. The essence of this job was to be an unobtrusive but prevailing presence until the last student signed in at 1:00 A.M. The final task of a long, long evening was to close the house for the night. As the students signed in, it was my duty to ease their dates out. At first there was no problem. Polite good-nights to me and they exited. As I got to know them, however, this routine changed and I became the subject of a "persecution" I thoroughly enjoyed. Instead of leaving promptly they began pleading for extended time with their dates. I remained adamant and was accused of destroying young love, coming between two people whom God had ordained for eternal union, or some other marvelously inventive accusation concerning my cold heart. One fellow established a regular Friday night act, threatening to throw himself across the threshold of Coffey Hall until I relented. I became very proficient at answering all such pleas and threats with a single word, politely uttered: "Out." I was feeling rather proud of my mastery of late-night duty until I discovered that good-night kisses were being exchanged in the lobby, a brightly lit area that could not be seen from the sign-in desk but was clearly visible from the Skyscraper windows. Morning phone calls from a few B.V.M.'s, some indignant in tone, made me aware that I had much to learn. I had no objection to the good-night kisses, but did not like the impression that a very naive director was running a rather risqué residence hall.

Mundelein had an excellent counseling staff, but perhaps because those of us who lived in residence were more easily available, we were occasionally the ones to whom students turned for advice or, more often, just to serve as good listeners. Problems with roommates, boyfriends, professors, and even with parents came our way. I do not demean what sometimes troubled them. I learned that young people can fall in love and suffer deeply when things don't work out. I learned that some students frequently went home on weekends because their parents had little to do with each other unless their daughter was home to make it a family at least for a few days. Sometimes, however, being a good listener went far beyond the call of duty. One cold winter night during Christmas break when I was enjoying the peace of an empty dorm and in the midst of a great read, my phone rang. The caller was an Annapolis midshipman currently dating a Coffey Hall resident. He said he knew she was home in Arizona, but he wondered if he could stop by to talk with me. I agreed, thinking it must be a serious problem while secretly groaning, Why me, Lord. As we settled down in a freezing McCormick Lounge, heat turned off as a gesture toward economy, I learned that he just wanted to talk about her with someone like me who knew how wonderful she was and would understand his feelings for her. Needless to say, I have never let her forget what I suffered in her name, and no, they did not marry and live happily ever after.

Several years ago I received a note from a Mundelein graduate who had lived in Coffey Hall during my first years as resident dean. To make sure I remembered her, she reminded me of our common bond through Hugh Hefner of *Playboy* fame. I surely did remember this charming and attractive senior and remembered my decision regarding the invitation she had received to spend a few hours at the Playboy mansion on Chicago's Gold Coast. The invitation came through her boyfriend whose former high school teacher, a priest, was writing his master's thesis on "The Effect of Reading *Playboy* Magazine on Teenage Boys." Apparently he had had several interviews with Hefner, and as a result of their conversations, the latter expressed a desire to meet a Catholic collegian whose standards were so different from many of the women who worked for him. Of course, my first response to Kay's request was, "What do your parents say?" Her very Irish father had his own question: "What does 'the sister' say?" I recall that she was not overwhelmed by the invitation and was quite willing to accept my decision. I saw no problem. It was to be a weeknight meeting, and we agreed that she would hold to the regular weeknight curfew. During the meeting she phoned to ask to extend her visit by another hour. She told me later that Mr. Hefner seemed utterly amazed at such a phone call, and to a Catholic nun, no less. Because my quarters were on the lake side of Coffey, I did not see her arrival home in a Playboy limousine. Neither do I recall her description of the evening other than her report that Hefner and I shared an addiction to colas. Months later, as we chatted at the Mundelein graduation reception, she claimed that after her famous night on the Gold Coast, she made a point of attending Sunday Mass in the sisters' chapel, always taking a pew within my sight, to reassure me that her virtue was unscathed. She was joking, of course, but it made for a wonderful end to the story.

The Northland, a six-story apartment building just a few steps west of the Skyscraper, opened as a residence hall in 1963. The college was unable to take possession of the building until perilously close to the opening of the fall semester, so only with the full-time help of the young sisters in the scholasticate were we able to get the building into somewhat presentable shape for the arrival of the students. Some of them were obviously disappointed as they and their parents rode up in a sturdy but rather eccentric elevator, traveling ever so slowly to their appointed floors. Residents and our maintenance staff soon discovered that there were problems other than a reluctant elevator. Some windows didn't close completely; others didn't open. A leaky roof was quickly repaired, but not before sixth-floor residents suffered damage from the rain.

Within a short time, nevertheless, Northland took on a unique personality. Coffey Hall with its beautiful lounges and dorm rooms resplendent with matching drapes and bedspreads and lovely vanity sinks was not envied but scorned by Northlanders. Coffey's dormitory walls, splendidly pristine, were clear of posters, pictures, signs, all that usually typifies student quarters. Instead, a nicely framed, moderately sized bulletin board provided space for whatever its inhabitants could fit within its borders. In stark contrast, Northland's apartment units reflected the variety of personalities and interests of their inhabitants. The college supplied only beds and desks, leaving the students free to express themselves in any way they wished. Some created rooms worthy of *House Beautiful*. Others produced a glorious melange of nonmatching everything, a wondrous sight to behold. I never refused an invitation to a Northland apartment. There was a warmth and a delightful ambiance in their rooms that made one feel very welcome and very special. During the basketball season I attended several Northland parties. Each year Coffey Hall would be challenged, beaten, and forced to attend the winners' victory party on the sixth floor, where most of the athletes resided. At these events, I had to pin a big "N" on my habit as a sign of our defeat.

Technically, Northland came under my jurisdiction, and in serious matters, it did. A few years after Northland's opening, Mundelein and I, however, were fortunate enough to gain the services of Betty Prevender, a Mundelein graduate completing an advanced degree at the University of Chicago. Working with an outstanding staff, Betty directed the Northland operation skillfully. She understood and worked well with students and was relentless in pursuing the business office with demands for attention to problems of cracked walls, leaky radiators, and all that made life uncomfortable for her household. She was determined to make the building a home for them. For me she was an invaluable listener and friend. She was also quite at ease in calling my attention to instances when I overstepped the chain of command I myself had established. She once denied a freshman the right to have a private phone in her apartment unit, wisely seeing that it would be unfair to her roommates. I knew nothing of this exchange so that when the student's mother phoned and made the same request I very graciously agreed. Some time later, I received a very short phone call from Betty. She asked me who was in charge of Northland. She also informed me that the telephone installer had been sent on his way. I am sure that she and her staff handled many problems about which they told me nothing and for which I am eternally grateful.

One of the most potentially tragic but amusing incidents occurred early in the history of Northland in pre-Betty times. One early October evening a Northland freshman literally ran through the glass door leading to Coffey Hall's Lewis Center. At the time I was attending Holy Hour in the college chapel when my guardian angel nudged me into noticing that all the sister resident assistants were also in chapel. This meant there was no adult presence in Coffey Hall. I left chapel and arrived in time to see an ambulance pull up. Fortunately, the students who were on the scene had acted quickly, calling an ambulance, trying to locate me, and, most fortunately, stanching the flow of blood from the girl's arm using a handkerchief borrowed from a Loyola boy standing nearby. The paramedic replaced the handkerchief with a proper tourniquet and handed the bloody cloth to a student. As they eased the stretcher into the ambulance, the patient spoke softly but clearly to the girl with the handkerchief. "Wash it and save it until I get back. We can return it and maybe meet some guys." I climbed in with the driver and directed him to St. Francis Hospital in Evanston. As we sped down Ridge Avenue with siren howling, the driver informed me we were breaking the law by not going to the nearest hospital. Horrified, I asked why he was defying the law. He answered with a simple, "Because you're a sister." So much for the fruits of a Catholic education!

In Northland's early days, another less than amusing incident occurred. I received a phone call from a resident assistant reporting that a freshman had not signed in and was now two hours late. After a few hours of anxiety, she was discovered tossing pebbles at her apartment window, hoping to get in without being seen. When I talked with her, she seemed frightened but insistent that she had been held against her will in a nearby fraternity house. I phoned the house and talked with the fraternity president, a young man I knew. He and the boy she accused came over immediately. The latter firmly denied the charge. Our student held fast to her story, even identifying a first-floor room in which she said she had been held. To my undying shame, I accepted his story. The fraternity president thanked me profusely and two very relieved young men departed. They had reason to be thankful. The fraternity was on probation and this incident could have had serious repercussions. After they left, I urged our student to admit the truth, go before the sanctions board, and accept her punishment. She refused to alter her story. Within a few days, I received another call and another visit from the two boys, this time to tell me that the girl's story was true. Needless to say, I apologized profusely to the young woman, utterly ashamed of my role in her ordeal.

It is always a mistake to become confident that the situation is in hand when one is dealing with youth. At the end of the academic year, it had become a custom for graduating seniors on my floor to have a final lounge session. My presence was mandatory, not to receive paeans of praise for what a blessing I had been to the house, but to reveal what they had been able to get away with. One such group took enormous delight in their ability to have nurtured for nearly seven weeks a group of wild, newborn rabbits found on campus. Housed in a big bath towel under the beds of roommates who lived directly across from me, the rabbits were carefully checked on by a bevy of student caretakers on a twenty-four-hour schedule. The latter were advised by a staff member of the Lincoln Park Zoo. The girls had discussed their clandestine adventure with members of the college biology department who had advised them to call the zoo for directions. Zoo administrators became quite interested in the project because wild animals rarely survive in such an alien environment. Had they lived another week, some sort of record would have been broken. The babies went off to bunny heaven, however, when their caretakers, no longer able to bear the odor emanating from under the bed, removed the towel that had been a surrogate mother for the little brood, and its removal led to their deaths. What seemed to delight the seniors was the fact that the comings and goings of the caretakers, as well as of student visitors who were in on the secret, went on in such close proximity to me.

The students on that same floor gained national publicity when they saved a lovely little dog from sure death as he floated on a large chunk of ice just below our seawall. A student having early morning coffee in the lounge spotted the animal and rushed to the hall phone to call the Humane Society. When she received a rather lackadaisical response from them, she phoned the "Dick Biondi Show," a popular radio talk show and related her tale to millions of Chicago listeners. The response was immediate. A Northwestern student driving north on Sheridan Road to class sped into the Mundelein parking lot and ran toward the seawall where a crowd had gathered. One courageous girl, clutching a long window pole, was preparing to be held by the ankles and let down over the wall. The young man held her by the ankles while she snared the ice cake with the hook end of the pole and pulled the little animal to safety amid the delighted shouts of the bystanders. Newspaper photographers were busily snapping pictures of dog on ice, girl hanging from seawall, dog saved and frantically wagging his tail. These pictures were given full coverage not only in *Chicago's American* but also in newspapers throughout the nation. It made a wonderful human-interest story in the aftermath of Chicago's terrible winter of 1967.

When I returned from class, knowing nothing of the dramatic rescue, I noted some commotion in the lounge and walked in on a scene of doggy bliss. Wrapped in a towel and sporting a big red bow, he was cozily sandwiched between two enthralled girls who were feeding him sandwich cold cuts. A born diplomat, he immediately jumped from the couch and rushed to give me a joyous welcome, wisely recognizing that I was the lady of the house and must be won over. Though I was completely charmed, I had to take on the role of the wicked witch. "No, there is no way we can keep him." And "No, his owner must be found." I left the room feeling cloaked in an icy silence. Late that evening the dog left us, happily trotting at the side of his grateful owner.

Some memories are sad ones. One afternoon I was called to a nearby hospital emergency room. A transfer student, only in residence for a semester, had made a pathetic suicide attempt. When we talked, I asked her why she had not sought my help. Her reply, that I always seemed too busy, troubled me and made me question our staff policy on entering students' rooms without being invited. I had been aware of the young woman for some time because her room was just a few doors from mine. She had seemed rather withdrawn and in my judgment not eager to have her privacy invaded. Her father added to my sense of failure by expressing his disappointment that I had not been sensitive to his daughter's needs. She did not return to finish the semester nor did she return the following year.

Living for nearly a decade with members of the infamous 1960s generation, I have vivid memories of their generous and compassionate response to the needs of others. At times, when I expressed this to them as a living out of Gospel values, they looked a bit bemused at my interpretation of what they saw as merely doing the right thing. Certainly, they could be insensitive to each other in petty matters. Resident assistants had to deal with complaints about loud stereos, noisy room parties at inappropriate hours, and bitter denunciations of those who monopolized the hall phones. But when one of the group received bad news, she was likely to be comforted by the very resident whose stereo had been on maximal decibels. There was only a single exception to this that I can recall. A student whose academic duties were never allowed to interfere with her social life was in frequent emotional turmoil made public to all and sundry on her floor. She was either in the throes of despair over a broken romance or in the process of dismissing a former flame whose successor she was in process of snaring. Her neighbors, reduced to cynicism, responded merely with offers of Kleenex or with mere groans as she announced a new romantic crisis.

One of the most memorable examples of these young people's sense of spontaneity toward their neighbors occurred when a fire broke out in the Beach View Convalescent Home on Sheridan Road, almost directly across from Coffey Hall. The fire was quickly extinguished but not before Coffey Hall residents had carried some patients to safety. As I emerged from our building, they were helping frightened patients across the street, heading toward Coffey Hall. One of them shouted to me that they were bringing all patients who weren't being hospitalized to McCormick Lounge. They continued to take control of what proved to be a most bewildering but highly successful afternoon for some forty Beach View residents. With a student or two at their sides, they became a delighted audience as a group of guitarists and singers swung into action. Another student group raided the floors' refrigerators and their own store of snacks and cold drinks. These patients were in varying stages of mental and physical condition. I wondered what their nurses would say if they could see the weird melange of foods they were happily devouring. One student, a German major, took over the care of a patient who spoke only that language and was in desperate need of a bathroom. I was deeply moved by the scene and what it revealed about these young women. Euphoric about the events of the afternoon, I barely alluded to the fact that I would somehow have to cajole the maintenance staff to take over the restoration of the lounge before they left for the day. The next day an irate group of students burst in on me with the news that the nursing-home supervisor was refusing to let them visit their new friends. Apparently, the firemen had reported the slovenly condition of the home and city inspectors had been notified. Beach View closed shortly after.

Throughout the history of the residence program, the college was blessed with an outstanding group of resident assistants, first, of B.V.M. sisters and, later, with senior resident students who served for that purpose. Certainly, in my years in residence, they were highly respected and well-loved members of the floors on which they lived. Without them I would not have survived. In the spring of our first year in Coffey Hall, an unusually vicious storm hit the Chicago area. For us on the lakefront, it meant waves reaching nearly to the second-floor windows and winds of frightening velocity. In the middle of the night, I received a call from the night watchman. The roof of McCormick Lounge was leaking. When I arrived on the scene, he also called my attention to the magnificent, nearly two-story high windows, which, he pointed out, were bending inward from the force of the winds. He thought to calm my fears by assuring me that the glass was specially treated to withstand winds of seventy-five miles an hour but, he cautioned, if the winds continued to rise, we were in trouble. Not wanting to suffer alone, I phoned Sister Eloise Thomas, B.V.M., in charge of the third floor. She had served in residence for several years with Sister Mary Agnesita and, in her quiet way, was a pillar of strength to me in my first year. She appeared within a few minutes, called maintenance to set up pails, phoned the weather bureau, which allayed our fears of shattered windows, and then she suggested we both return to our beds. This was only one of the many times that her quiet wisdom reduced my problems to a manageable size.

Other sisters who served in the resident program included one who her students claimed played the best saxophone in the city. High compliment in a city noted nationwide for its jazz. Whenever she played, the lounge quickly filled with an enthralled audience. She was keenly missed when she left for Georgetown University to complete a doctorate in linguistics. Her successor on that floor was another talented B.V.M., this time a high-stepping Irish dancer. Thanks to her impromptu performances both in Coffey Hall and in the tearoom, many a Mundelein student became a devotee of Irish dancing long before the advent of Michael Flatley's *Riverdance* show. Regrettably, she, too, was lost to the program when she went on to complete her studies in the field of Spanish language and literature.

Mundelein College was the first Catholic college in the area to make use of resident seniors as resident assistants. Although at first, some members of the administration expressed concerns, I was convinced that mature young women, who had lived in residence for several years, could handle the duties the position entailed. The experiment worked well. Their authority was respected, their advice sought, especially by younger students, and in every way they were an asset to our program.

Like credit must be given to the officers elected to resident-student government positions. Their job often required the skills of a diplomat. They had to keep both the students and the resident dean happy. On campuses throughout the country, complaints about food were a constant. Mundelein was no different. Irate students complained to their officers, and they in turn complained to me. The menu was boring and lacked variety. There wasn't enough of it, or there was an unjust relationship between the cost and the quality of what the dining-room staff called "food." The officers and I cleverly relieved ourselves of this burden by creating a menu committee. Their duties included scheduling regular meetings with the dining-room director, discussing complaints and possible solutions, polling the students for menu suggestions, and, in general, freeing us from what had been an onerous task.

A memoirist, however, must not flinch at the truth. Officers were not always pillars of strength to their dean. One such incident remains in my memory, and I never fail to remind certain former officers of an instance of their perfidy whenever we meet at alumnae reunions. A small group of first-year Loyola students carried out a very weak and short-lived panty raid on the second floor of Coffey Hall. The boys entered the building by climbing to the roof of the entryway linking the dormitory to Gannons, now Piper Hall, then entering through an open window. They were able to take just a small haul of lingerie before being spotted and forced to flee. My instinct was to play down the entire incident, thus depriving the miscreants of any publicity. Both my officers were in hearty agreement. Unfortunately, two victims of the raid expressed outrage at the incident and demanded retribution. Reluctantly, I phoned my counterpart at Loyola. He responded the following day. The guilty had been identified, the stolen items had been recovered, and the young men had been ordered to appear in my office, loot in hand, and apologize.

I had no intention of facing alone what I correctly imagined would be a rather ludicrous situation. The two victims who had called for justice had legitimate excuses to absent themselves from the meeting. My officers, however, were prepared to let me face the situation alone. Their cowardly argument was based on the fact that they would be unable to control their laughter and would destroy the solemnity of the scene. I indignantly refused to accept their excuse. Both of them were dating Loyola men, and I accused them of not wanting to have their names connected with a situation that might become a source of amusement on our neighboring campus. They groaned and surrendered. The three of us faced a truly frightened group of young men on the following day. After offering fervent apologies, the boy with the laundry bag of lingerie tried to hand it to me. Coldly, silently, I pointed to a nearby chair where he then hastily deposited it. I then dismissed them, closed the office door and the room exploded with our laughter. Nevertheless, years later when I was a guest at their weddings, I was unforgiving enough to remind them of their callous attempt to abandon me.

The decade of the 1960s had a profound significance for Catholic students. They were members of a church in revolution. Its leader, seventy-six-year-old Cardinal Roncalli, was elected pope in 1958. Within six months, on July 25, 1959, this gentle, charismatic man startled the Western world with the announcement of his plan to call the church's twenty-first ecumenical council; its goal, aggiornamento, a renewed Catholic Church brought into harmony with modern society, yet faithful to the essence of Catholic belief. This Second Vatican Council, sitting from 1962–65, produced the sixteen decrees embodying most of the goals envisioned by Pope John XXIII and the council fathers.

Catholic collegians were, for the most part, a confident lot. In their understanding of themselves as Catholics, they were not their parents' nor their grandparents' heirs. Unlike their forebears, they suffered little anti-Catholicism. Theirs was the church of the Kennedys, Senator Eugene McCarthy, and the Golden Dome of Notre Dame.

But discussion of church affairs immediately preceding, during, and after Vatican II was not high on the agenda of Coffey Hall residents, at least in terms of conversation in the lounge. One heard negative reactions from a few to such practices as receiving the host in the hand and the proposal to remove altar rails and reposition the altar itself. A few, including myself, groaned over the guitar-accompanied music at the 4:30 student Mass at Loyola. Forever in painful memory is the hymn with the jazzy refrain "eat my body and drink my blood" that accompanied us to the communion rail.

What did elicit student response were the theses of some of the speakers who graced the Mundelein podium during these years. Among them was Harvey Cox, author of the nationally acclaimed *Secular City*. Several departments had placed the book on their required reading lists, so a good number of their students were prepared for him. To Cox's obvious delight, they offered insightful questions to his thesis concerning the effects of a growing American secularism on society and on Christianity itself.

Another speaker who captured his audience's attention was Michael Novak, then a young lay intellectual and professor of philosophy and theology at Stanford. At the time a fiery Catholic liberal, he was impatient with what he saw as a matriarchal church. (Today, he ranks as one of the church's most noted neoconservatives.) I had problems with his forceful attack on papal maternalism and his insistence that Catholics must cut the umbilical cord that bound us to Rome and hindered our development as mature Christians. The documents of Vatican II had just been published. I groused to myself, "Why not focus on some facets of the Vatican II resolutions that were being lauded throughout the Christian world?" However, in the discussion period that followed each of his lectures, it was obvious that his student audience took his critique in stride. They dialogued with him, peppered him with questions, and demonstrated a good grasp of some of the problems facing the modern church. Like all Catholic colleges, the Mundelein curriculum included a number of required courses in theology. Novak's student audience reflected the excellent quality of teaching provided by our B.V.M. theologians, most of whom had studied at Marquette University, at the time a leading center for theological studies in the United States. In the following decades, a number of these women would rank among the country's most noted theologians and philosophers.

I did not join the numerous faculty and student groups who lingered to talk with Professor Novak at the close of his final lecture. I returned to my quarters, somewhat abashed by the students' easy reception of his challenging analyses and annoyed at finding myself almost a loner among a very receptive audience. And yet, as I reviewed what had been an uncomfortable experience for me, I realized that many in the audience had been or were students in my classes. Their assigned readings had included Catholic scholar Desiderius Erasmus's *The Praise of Folly,* a work replete with a witty but devastating attack on the clergy, the hierarchy, and the papacy of the time. They had listened to lectures on the papacy during the reigns of Popes Leo X and Alexander VI, and they had heard a very sympathetic treatment of Martin Luther and his struggle against a scandalous sixteenth-century church. It was some time before my resentment of theologian Novak cooled and I could admit to myself that both of us spoke out of a common love of the church.

One aspect of Vatican II the students did identify with was the sexual revolution. Although it would be an act of temerity on my part to offer any judgments, I learned a great deal from listening and dialoguing with some of them. Certainly, they were affected by the overwhelming change in sexual mores that were in progress throughout the Western world. I do not know whether the problems I dealt with were typical of difficulties some young people in late adolescence and young adulthood have always faced. What was new, I believe, was the openness with which many of them discussed such intimate issues. I think this openness was best exemplified for me in an editorial that appeared in *The Skyscraper.* The writer was responding to Pope Paul VI's announcement that he found it necessary to delay his decision on contraceptives as a means of birth control and that until a decision was reached, Catholics were bound by the church's traditional teaching. In the editorial, the writer is respectful of the need for further study on a matter that will affect issues such as marriage, the family, the Church's influence in these areas, and the matter of individual conscience. But she cites and then questions Paul's much-quoted statement to a society of Italian gynecologists in which he declares that the magisterium was in no doubt about the question of contraceptives as a means of birth control. Why the need for further study if there is no doubt, she questions. She concludes with a warning that "unless a positive statement on birth control is forthcoming, this one point of contraception is volatile enough to call church allegiance into grave question for a large number of Catholics."[1]

The problem of racism has been a tragic feature of American life since the days of the young republic. On the eve of the millennium, the United States, now the most powerful nation in the world, has yet to achieve for its citizens the equality promised by our constitution. The Kerner Report[2] of 1968 stated what many Americans already knew: "America is moving toward two societies, one black, one white, separate and unequal." But despite nearly a decade of growing racial turmoil, I was slow to link Kerner's dire observation with life in the residence halls of Mundelein College. In 1964, at a meeting of deans of residence from the Chicago area, I was asked how many blacks lived in our dormitories and was a bit disconcerted that I had to answer that we kept no such count. One dean came to my rescue, turning my ignorance into a compliment by praising Mundelein for not compartmentalizing its students by race. By design, the Mundelein resident application form made no reference to race. In assigning roommates to freshman and transfer students, I used the brief essay each of them was asked to write, matching students by their stated interests. It seemed to work well. Many kept their same roommates throughout their resident years.

A consideration of racism as it might exist in the Mundelein resident halls divides quite naturally into two periods separated by the assassination of Martin Luther King Jr. on April 4, 1968. The first period I thought could be easily summarized. I could remember no instances of racial clashes during these years and was confident there were none. On one floor where I lived for several years, the most popular girl was black. She often double-dated with white friends and was a frequent guest in their homes. I remembered an evening in the lounge when the discussion centered on what was the best popular music of the 1960s. When I announced that songs by Simon and Garfunkel could not be surpassed, a black student reacted in mock horror and insisted I come to her room to hear what real American music was all about. That night I learned to appreciate her favorite recording, Isaac Hayes' *Presenting Isaac Hayes,* though I stubbornly clung to *Where Have All the Flowers Gone* as music par excellence.

Yet, as I recall those days in terms of race, I became painfully aware of what, in retrospect, was my failure to see what was there. I could remember no lack of courtesy or friendliness on the part of black students, but neither could I remember incidents where any one of them, except those who were my students, had felt free to flop into a chair in my office just to chat. Given the times, I should have been alert to any sense of alienation these students might be experiencing in our white world. I should have been but I wasn't. Blacks were just part of the Coffey Hall community and all was well with us.

But I was mistaken. I should have noted that black freshmen did not join their classmates to attend mixers at Notre Dame, St. Joseph's, and Loyola. And when Mundelein played hostess, few black students took to the dance floor. In a *Skyscraper* interview in 1968, after the death of King, junior sociology major Diane Allen, a black student, described what she termed a "subtle kind of discrimination when you have mixers, or going to Notre Dame or St. Joe's when there are few blacks. The mixers are white, middle class, exclusively."[3] She characterized Mundelein students as prejudiced because they don't know any better and indicted the Rogers Park community as unfriendly toward and fearful of blacks. In commenting on the black community's conduct after the assassination of King, Allen paid great tribute to President Ann Ida Gannon's understanding and support as she and her black sisters throughout the country began to find their voices in protest against a racist American society.

Yet on March 23, 1965, twenty-eight Mundelein students and eight faculty boarded a bus for a twenty-hour ride to Selma, Alabama. They were en route to join King and his contingent who were marching from Selma to the state capital at Montgomery. The thirty-five thousand who joined in this massive march for social justice included students and their professors from universities and colleges throughout the country. At Mundelein, those of us unable to join this historic march took turns keeping vigil in the college chapel, our prayer a plea for social justice as well as for the safety of the travelers. We learned later that prayers for the latter were needed as the marchers

Mundelein students and other collegians rally on behalf of interracial justice.

experienced the hostility of Montgomery citizens. Forced off the sidewalks and given false directions when they lost their way, the marchers felt the depth of southern resentment at their presence and bitter contempt for their cause. A painful prelude to the trip occurred in the form of a student protest against the student council's decision to allot $218.39 to each student traveler, the funds to be drawn from student-activity fees. Some based their protest on their opinion that the march was a useless gesture. Others resented the use of student funds for a cause that did not have the support of the entire college community. In a final and obviously symbolic protest, a small group of these dissenters lay down in front of the bus before letting it get underway.

Two of the protesters were upperclassmen, prominent members of Coffey Hall, and my good neighbors and friends for several years. It seemed important for them to justify their actions to me. Their conduct, they explained, was not a racial gesture but rather a protest against what they felt was the council's violation of the powers of their office. Aware of current college politics, I understood their position, but we clashed over my interpretation of their conduct as at least an apparent racial gesture that had no place on our campus. The subject was never broached again, and with the return of our exhausted but exhilarated travelers, the entire incident became a matter of college history.

Mundelein College students and faculty members in Selma, Alabama.

The night before the death of King, a gala birthday party was given for a popular black Northland resident by her white roommate. It was a big, noisy affair because she had many friends. Twenty-four hours later, after the horrifying news of King's death, all black resident students gathered in Northland apartments and remained there, incommunicado, well into the following day. When they did emerge, Mundelein College residents were of two constituencies, and one, black, no longer acknowledged its white sisters. It was painful to have a black student refuse to return a greeting in the dining room or have her pass by silently on campus. When my Isaac Hayes friend cut me cold, I realized the depth of black anger at white America. This young woman's snub was meant to hurt and it did.

Within a short time, the black students demanded a meeting with Mundelein faculty and students. Galvin Hall was filled to capacity by a puzzled and somewhat anxious crowd. I was more than puzzled and anxious; I was frightened. The previous evening I had had to confront a black student about her language when speaking on the hall phone on her floor. The student was a refined young southerner with a background of private education. The sudden shift in her conduct became apparent after the assassination. She was now spending long periods on the phone, speaking about racial problems and using loud and ugly language. The matter became my responsibility when white students' resentment reached fever pitch. To my relief, we had an amicable meeting and I felt a crisis had been averted. But as a group of black students gathered at the dais in the hall, I was shocked to see that this student was to speak for her black sisters. I awaited her attack. Instead, the young woman presented the list of demands of what she termed "the black community." I and many others were struck by her use of this new designation. I wish I could report that I shouted out my rejection of a separate Mundelein community. Instead, I was a relieved listener as they stated their perceived needs for special quarters where they could celebrate black culture and announced their decision to schedule and run their own dances. The meeting ended quietly. I longed to join the faculty at lunch where they would be digesting the significance of the meeting along with their lunches. Instead, I was scheduled to lunch with a group of visiting high school seniors, potential members of next year's freshman class. One of these young women had managed to sit in on our historic meeting. It was some time before I was able to appreciate the humor of her innocent remark that the meeting was fascinating and that she was anxious to see how things would work out when she returned to begin her freshman year at Mundelein.

Shortly after this painful meeting, the administration received a bomb threat. The president acted wisely, correctly suspecting that it was a hoax. Government authorities were immediately contacted and, at her request, arrived without siren accompaniment. The bomb squad quietly evacuated the Learning Resource Center (LRC), where the bomb supposedly had been placed. This building housed the library, audiovisual center, faculty offices, and a few classrooms. Rabbi Milton Kantor, a member of the religious studies department, left his black attaché case and its contents behind as he and his students departed the building. When the squad saw it, they slowly, carefully, skillfully lassoed the suspicious object and rendered it harmless. Opened, the rabbi's running shoes and shorts proved to be the sole contents of the case. His children were so delighted with their father's adventure that they pleaded to keep the case and its contents on permanent display in the family's living room. The administration tried to minimize the importance of the incident, but several Coffey Hall residents from Chicago and suburbia decided to move home early and commute for their last days of class.

With the opening of the fall semester, relations within the dorms seemed to have returned to normal. The college provided the second floor of Gannons as a cultural home base for black students. Black dances were introduced and a black student organization, MUCUBA (Mundelein College United Black Association) was organized. When I left residence, it was with a bittersweet memory of those years before and after the death of King. Twenty years later, long after my Coffey Hall days, MUCUBA invited me to speak at their annual celebration of his birthday. Until the evening of the program, I was not aware that there was to be a cospeaker, a minister from one of Chicago's black churches. I had no problem with sharing the podium. Several of the black students in the audience were in my classes, and I felt well prepared and looked forward to an inspirational evening. I spoke first. My thesis was simple, based on the message of the New Testament, that we love one another as Christ loved us. I opined that if we in the Mundelein community lived this law of love, future Mundelein students would one day ask why there had ever been a need for such an organization as MUCUBA. I returned to my seat quite satisfied with my performance. Then the minister took the "pulpit." His was an eloquent, rip-roaring sermon in what I imagined was the style of the Old Testament prophets. I had remained demurely behind the podium as I spoke. He, on the other hand, strode from one end of McCormick Lounge to the other, sweeping us along in the spirit of his impassioned words concerning the goodness of God. Both of us were roundly applauded, and over coffee, we lavishly praised each other's message to the students.

The other problem of the 1960s that challenged the whole Mundelein tradition was the Vietnam War. During World War II, Mundelein students gave wholehearted support to the United States and the Allies. Their war effort began with a student vote to begin each class with a prayer for victory and peace. For the next four years, student life included taking short courses in such government-requested subjects as first aid, air-raid precautions, flight observation and principles, and groundwork aeronautics, to name but a few. Some faculty and students accepted appointments to the Chicago division of the Office of Civil Defense. Even before the government had asked, student leaders launched a campus defense drive. Profits from the junior prom were contributed to the defense stamp drive, and President Roosevelt was sent a recorded message of support from the Mundelein student body. Such an outpouring of support continued until the Allied victory in 1945.

Nearly a quarter of a century later, numbers of Mundelein students became active opponents of a war that pitted the most powerful nation in the world against a national peasant revolutionary force in Vietnam. Unlike their predecessors' behavior in World War II, the response to war of this group of students included antiwar assemblies and marches, sit-ins and teach-ins, and in union with schools throughout the nation, an attempt to boycott college classes.

These were painful years whether one supported or opposed the war. Feelings ran high within the college community. Some faculty avoided any mention of the terrible conflict, while, for others, it was the first topic of conversation broached at table. In November of 1966 some Mundelein faculty joined with colleagues from Loyola University and the University of Chicago for a teach-in on the war. Situating themselves in front of the federal building in downtown Chicago, these academics attracted an appreciative audience as they presented their arguments for an immediate withdrawal from a patently immoral war.

For most Americans, 1968 was an especially appalling year in the history of the war. In March the slaughter by American soldiers of many helpless Vietnamese in the village of My Lai shocked a nation already troubled by the war's violence. It was the year of the Vietnamese National Liberation Front's Tet Offensive, a powerful though unsuccessful attempt to seize Saigon. It sent a strong message to the American government that it was far from victory in its war against a peasant people. Violence increased at home as well. In Chicago, on April 27, an estimated seven thousand students assembled at Grant Park, where a series of speakers addressed them on the war. The students were then to march to the Civic Center for an assembly. As the students began to walk down Columbus Drive, however, they were harassed by an overzealous police force. When they finally reached the Civic Center, the marchers found the plaza roped off, and, once again, the marchers were taunted by policemen. A Mundelein freshman, roughed up by one of the police officers, was briefly hospitalized. It was not surprising then that in the spring of 1968 Mundelein students joined a nationwide boycott of classes in protest against the war. The Mundelein administration wisely left the decision to teach or not to teach in the hands of each faculty member. Those who joined the boycott had to handle the difficult problem of assigning grades, especially to graduating seniors. The science faculty refused to cancel classes despite the anger it aroused among some students. Their argument was a good one. Lab classes, especially, were of utmost importance to those students going on in the field of science, and, particularly, into medical school.

Both Northland and Coffey were affected by the war. In Northland, however, the tension was lessened because students spent more time in their apartments than in the floor lounges, so pro- and antiwar positions were not aired so publicly. The situation in Coffey was more serious because the structure of the hall was such that students lived more in community and knew their neighbors more intimately. One floor had a particularly difficult situation.

Three very well-liked upperclassmen were dating West Point cadets. A fourth was the daughter of a United States Army general. The latter, a serious student, cut her pre-Thanksgiving classes each year in order to join her parents out east for the annual Army-Navy game. Preholiday absence from class could play havoc with one's grades, but for this student, it was well worth the sacrifice. For these women the antiwar movement was especially painful. Their graduating West Point boyfriends were probably headed for Vietnam. They were also deeply offended by students who asked them how it felt to be dating killers. For others, especially seniors, the war might mean the draft and Vietnam for a loved one. I spent some sad hours with a student whose fiancé was planning to emigrate to Canada. Fortunately for these young people, there was an unofficial adviser on the Loyola campus who counseled young men on what it meant to be a "conscientious objector" and the serious ramifications of choosing such a course.

Ordinarily, I think a person in authority should maintain a public position of neutrality. I was unable to assume such a stance when the issue was a moral one. I attended teach-ins, marched in protests, and allowed students to sprawl on the floor of my office at night, venting their outrage against the killing fields of Vietnam as seen on the nightly news. Aware of the resentment of students who supported the war, I urged them to invite a Fort Sheridan officer to address the resident population on the conduct of the war and to respond to the rumors concerning the brutality of our soldiers. Such a presentation, I argued, would be a learning experience for all of us. We were an academic community educated to arrive at truth through the examination of evidence and not by morning headlines or a ten-minute television piece. They agreed but did not follow through on what I think would have been an excellent opportunity for dialogue worthy of intelligent young women.

Certainly, there were some who gave lip service to the war protest but who were actually enjoying freedom from classes and an unusually beautiful spring, which provided a glorious opportunity for an early start on a summer tan. Others were so passionately involved that they turned the first floor of Gannon into a "war room" complete with Vietnam maps tracing the war's movements. One group in particular seemed to epitomize what serious young Americans on many campuses were about. They were knowledgeable about American foreign policy in East Asia and they questioned it. They disagreed with the fatuous saying that the Vietnamese would "rather be dead than Red." It was Mundelein's good fortune to have on the faculty a nationally known sociologist, Dr. Russell Barta, who gave a great deal of time to dialoguing with these students, keeping the discussions on an even keel, keeping emotions under control. In the early days of the boycott when feelings were running high, he stayed with the group throughout the night.

In the midst of the turmoil of these days there were some less serious moments. On an evening when the student leaders had planned a neighborhood peace walk, I met a freshman as I was leaving the building to join the walk. On impulse, I asked if she were going. After a brief hesitation, she decided to join me, remarking as we joined the marchers crossing Sheridan and heading down Winthrop Avenue that she felt people were carrying war activities to extremes. Her words were prophetic. Walking single file and close to the buildings as we had been instructed, she became the recipient of a pail full of water from some apartment dweller carrying things to extremes. Her sister marchers were so sympathetic about her sodden state that I think she enjoyed her fifteen minutes of fame and bore me no ill will for her unexpected role in the antiwar movement.

Some Chicagoans and suburbanites who drove north on Sheridan Road each evening around five o'clock may remember a gathering of Mundelein girls standing at the road's curve near the college. They held a huge, long banner that urged the drivers to toot twice if they opposed the war. The nightly loud and enthusiastic honking response was repaid by appreciative waves and shouts from the sign holders.

I count the years I was privileged to live among Mundelein students as among the most rewarding and grace-filled years of my life as a religious. Satisfying because they saw fit to use me as counselor, friend, and, at times, as a tolerated "Mrs. Full-Charge." Grace-filled because living alone among them, I gained confidence that my job was a worthwhile one and that, at this point in my religious life, this was where I belonged. Over the years I had evolved from my "drawbridge" mentality to an appreciation of and trust in my student officers' wisdom as they eased me from the position of benevolent despot to honorary chairman of the board. In the closing months of my regime, resident officers were presenting to the administration their demand for a "no hours" policy for seniors. Although I was secretly relieved that the new policy would not be implemented on my watch, I was pleased to note their praise of the current "hours" policy as they presented a cogent and well-stated argument in favor of extended freedoms.

Had Sister Ann Ida acceded to my plea in 1962 that managing a resident program was not among my competencies, I would have missed having a front-row center seat at the drama of the revolutionary 1960s as lived with over a thousand Mundelein students under my jurisdiction. It was a great show—and we were both audience and actors. Their response to a decade that ran the gamut from racial confrontations to war, changing sexual mores and the challenges of a modernizing church, kept me in a constant dialogue with myself. I learned much from them and have reason to believe the feeling was mutual. Even in our disagreements, at times concerning serious moral positions, we continued to respect and genuinely love each other. Putting together some vignettes of these years has only renewed my feelings of gratitude for my Coffey Hall years, despite my early inauspicious dealings with the laundry agent.

Endnotes

1. Editorial, *The Skyscraper,* 16 November 1966, Mundelein College Archives (MCA), Gannon Center for Women and Leadership, Loyola University Chicago.

2. U.S. National Advisory Commission on Civil Disorders. *Report of the National Advisory Commission of Civil Disorders* (Washington, D.C.: Government Printing Office, 1968). This document was popularly known as "The Kerner Report."

3. Editorial, *The Skyscraper,* 4 October 1968, MCA.

The Golden Age of Mundelein College: A Memoir, 1962–1969

Norbert Hruby

(left to right) Norbert Hruby, vice president for institutional development, Sister Mary Ann Ida Gannon, B.V.M., president of the college, and Sister Mary Ignatia Griffin, B.V.M.

When, in 1962, the University of Chicago closed its University College (where I was associate dean, serving under the brilliant, but erratic, Dean Maurice F. X. Donohue), I was offered a seat in the Harper Library on the main campus, at full pay, until something else opened up. I thanked the university administration for this left-handed vote of confidence, but I began to look elsewhere. Dan Cahill, an old friend from my days at Loyola, wanted me to meet Sister Mary Ann Ida Gannon, B.V.M., the dynamic young president of Mundelein College, for whom he had worked before going to the Illlinois Institute of Technology. She interviewed me. We came to an understanding. She offered me a vice presidency. I accepted. That was in April. I was to report on July 1.

On my second day in office at Mundelein, I received a phone call from Al Bland, onetime program director at WBBM in Chicago. (I had produced award-winning radio programs for him when I was director of broadcasting at the University of Chicago.) Now the manager of WLW-TV, the Crossley flagship in Cincinnati, he asked me to direct his documentary-film unit. Four months earlier it would have seemed a dream job—a well-financed version of what I had once hoped to do at WTTW in Chicago and had tried to do on a shoestring at Loyola University. But I had made my commitment to Sister Ann Ida. There was no looking back—for which I thank God!

Change was in the air. The Second Vatican Council had begun. Pope John XXIII had indeed brought a breath of fresh air into the Roman Catholic Church. There was hope that there would really be aggiornamento in that ancient institution. There was a Catholic in the White House. Feminism was in the air (Betty Friedan's and Simone de Beauvoir's books were best-sellers). All things seemed possible.

The mother general of the B.V.M.'s and her chief assistant were women of great vision. They saw in Sister Ann Ida a woman who would give enlightened, courageous leadership to their college in Chicago.

Sister Ann Ida had begun the transformation of the college by sending off several young sister-members of the faculty to the best universities in the country to get their doctorates. And she was carrying on from her earlier work in sister formation to make the B.V.M.'s at Mundelein strong, independent women. I recall with delight a scene I stumbled into one day that first summer. Sister Ann Ida had two young sisters across the desk from her. She was lecturing them on freedom, ending with the peroration, as she tapped on the desk, "Sisters, you must be free!" The two young ones dutifully answered, "Yes, Sister."

My full title was vice president for development. This suggested to everyone at Mundelein that I was there to raise money for the college. So as I interviewed the members of the faculty and administration individually, they opened their hearts to me, telling me their fondest dreams of what they could do if only the college had more money. I didn't tell them that my definition of development (and, by agreement, Sister Ann Ida's) differed from theirs. We took development to mean the restructuring of the college, from top to bottom, by analysis and synthesis, based on the conviction that, given a truly "relevant" college (the buzzword in those days), ways and means would be found to effect the changes—or, just possibly, new programs might even be created that would pay for themselves and support the institutional budget.

Those interviews had convinced me that Mundelein had a strong faculty and a dedicated, competent administration, ready to be unleashed. And I had brought with me, from University College at the University of Chicago, Maurice Donohue's concept of an institutional self-study process that could release the pent-up creative energy at Mundelein.

When I outlined for the Mundelein community that process, which was to proceed inductively through analysis to arrive at a new vision of the institution, the faculty and administration were intrigued. Literally everyone in the college community was to be involved.

Key components of the Institutional Analysis, as the process was designated, were the following:

1. searching questionnaires to be administered to each of the major constituencies of the college—faculty, administration, students, alumnae, and even the husbands of alumnae—anonymously

2. study groups, each made up of faculty members, administrators, and some students, to inquire in depth into the governance, the curriculum, the library, even the parietal rules, etc.—and to apply the questionnaire responses to those functions of the college—with the understanding that no one having administrative responsibility for a college function could serve on the study group dealing with that function (e.g., the librarian could not be in the study group evaluating the library, but she would serve as a resource person to that study group)

3. an advisory committee of eminent educators and scholars, drawn from the best universities in the country, whose responsibility was not to tell us how to redesign the college, but to react to the reports of the study groups—in effect, to second-guess the internal thinking of the college community. After all, a major desired outcome of the Institutional Analysis was to create a sense of ownership throughout the college community.

Sister Ann Ida, being ultimately responsible for every function of the college, was thereby excluded from serving on any of the study groups. Her responsibility was to provide the resources for the Institutional Analysis and stay out of the process. To her great credit, she was willing to step back and watch the process change her institution from the bottom up!

Robert Hassenger, a very bright, ambitious young instructor in the psychology department, was assigned to help me design the questionnaires—the key research instruments of the Institutional Analysis. Together, he and I designed the following instruments: (1) an 800-item multiple-choice student questionnaire (which would require at least five or six hours to answer), (2) a 350-item faculty/administrator questionnaire, plus several items from the student questionnaire for purposes of comparison, and (3) a 150-item alumnae questionnaire with a supplementary 50-item questionnaire for husbands.

These instruments, which were intended to elicit judgmental perceptions (hence the need for the anonymity of the respondents) as well as facts, were designed to be computerized and cross-tabulated.

Mundelein, having no computer capability, had to find support outside the college. Sister Ann Ida found just the man in an advertising executive, who was as much enchanted with her as he was with our project. Little did he realize what he was getting his staff into. Literally thousands of responses had to be transferred onto old-fashioned punch cards that could then be electronically processed into meaningful statistics. (I hope he got a major tax-break for that major gift-in-kind to this little Catholic college!)

Classes were called off for a whole day so that faculty, students, and staff would respond to their respective questionnaires—followed by a party. Exhausted but excited, the students were delighted to have their opinions taken seriously, not a common occurrence in the early 1960s. The faculty and staff, even the skeptics, had become fully involved.

Meanwhile the study groups were developing their agendas, waiting for the computerized results of the questionnaires, and worrying about the reaction their preliminary reports were to receive during the first visit of the high-powered advisory committee that I had recruited. The committee was composed of Marston Morse, the great mathematician and onetime colleague of Albert Einstein at the Institute for Advanced Study at Princeton; George Shuster, former president of Hunter College and then executive assistant to Father Hesburgh at Notre Dame; Bernice Brown Cronkhite, dean of students at Radcliffe College; and my good friend Joseph Sittler, Lutheran theologian at the University of Chicago.

When they came to the Mundelein campus for the first of three widely spaced visits, they were a sensation. They met in a closed session with the students. When they emerged, I asked Joe Sittler how it had gone. "On the whole," he said, "they were quite charitable." That was all any of our distinguished guests would say!

As the Institutional Analysis went on, week after week, month after month, the seriousness of the project became increasingly evident. The computerized questionnaire results were studied and restudied by the study groups. The comments of the advisory committee were taken to heart. Research studies were read and discussed. There was no way that Mundelein could ever revert to its former way of doing things. Old duchies were being shaken, old fiefdoms were being toppled. New leaders emerged. It was a quiet revolution.

I recall a wonderful cartoon in *The Skyscraper,* the student newspaper—a very feminine "skyscraper" lying on a couch—the caption: "Mundelein undergoing analysis."

The key question—Does this college deserve to exist?—was confronted and tentatively answered in the affirmative.

When the Institutional Analysis finally ended in 1963, at the same time that Vatican II was in full swing, a renewed—no, a *new* institution emerged. The Mundelein community, along with every other Catholic institution in the country, was sobered by the death of Pope John XXIII and by the assassination of President Kennedy, but the college had a new lease on life, and buoyed by the confidence of having faced itself honestly—it survived.

Change was everywhere, even in the convent. Most of the B.V.M. sisters exchanged their traditional religious habit for secular dress. Gone were the cigar-box headdress and the black gabardine sheath. "Sister Emily's Boutique" on the thirteenth floor of the Skyscraper was well stocked with fashionable attire, much of it contributed to the community by wealthy Jewish women who were intrigued by the ecumenical, social, and educational experiments going on at 6363 North Sheridan Road.

At the same time they changed their appearance, many of the sisters changed their names—or, rather, they reverted to their baptismal names. So it was that on the first day of the fall semester in 1965, when the students returned to campus, they were met by faculty women who looked familiar, but so different. The students would address their professors, "Sister?" hoping they got it right. (Several Jewish and Protestant women on the faculty took to wearing tags, stating simply, "I am *not* a sister!")

These changes were more than symbolic. They were the visible commitment to the post–Vatican II Catholic world inspired by that great, good man Pope John XXIII.

I recall the first time I addressed the B.V.M. faculty members. I opened with, "Ladies." There was a twittering in the audience. "You're not 'ladies'?" I asked. There was outright laughter. I took that to mean they now accepted the fact that sisters were also ladies. Ladies—and great women! I came to appreciate religious women as the true feminists, separated from their progressive sisters primarily by the issue of abortion.

One of the significant proposals to come out of the Institutional Analysis was a core curriculum—not the kind of core devised by Columbia University or the University of Chicago in Robert M. Hutchins's time, but a core arrived at through the introspection of faculty members and administrators. The questions we asked ourselves were these: "What are the gaps in my own education?" "What should I have been required to study to make me a better-educated, more well-rounded person?"

The resultant core was an interesting gathering of great disciplinary variety. Not too surprisingly, I suppose, it never really took hold because the conservative members of the faculty, the minority who had doubted the wisdom of the Institutional Analysis from the beginning, managed to sabotage it by persuading their students that they shouldn't have to study subjects they didn't like.

Word of Mundelein's institutional self-study began to spread in the world of American higher education (where Mundelein had indeed been one of those "invisible colleges" that troubled Alexander Astin and other students of private liberal-arts colleges). The college's courageous self-analysis was recognized as a model response to an educational culture going through radical change.

I was invited to design and administer self-studies for other colleges. I was even asked to adapt the Mundelein process for use in "renewal" studies of religious congregations to fulfill a mandate from Vatican II. With help from Bob Hassenger, I ran such studies for the Servites, the Viatorians, and the Tacoma Dominican sisters. (I even spent time at 6363.)

A significant consequence of the Institutional Analysis was the Mundelein Degree Completion Program, designed for mature women who had dropped out of school years ago. I was interviewed on WGN radio and described the program we had in mind. Before I was off the air, the WGN switchboard had fifty calls! We had struck gold!

Mundelein was among the first, if not *the* first, college in the United States to offer this kind of program exclusively for women. With the women's movement blossoming, the timing was perfect—not just for our new cohort of students but for several members of the faculty, who found these new-old students better, brighter, and more dedicated than many of the students of traditional age. Women who had literally flunked out of college fifteen or twenty years before became straight-A students! In fact, these older women were known to the younger students as the D.A.R.'s—the damned average raisers!

Once the Institutional Analysis was completed and the Degree Completion Program launched in 1965, I spent my time teaching an occasional drama course and doing research on the new culture we had created at Mundelein. The presence of older women in the Mundelein classrooms, laboratories, and studios was, at that time, a phenomenon. I was curious to see how the younger and older women related to each other, what difference their shared experiences made in their lives.

The results were fascinating. Younger students, once they got used to the idea of older women in their classes, learned to respect them, then like them, and finally enjoy them. It certainly strengthened the younger students in their commitment to getting their degrees now rather than having to return years later as these older dropouts were doing.

The younger students also reported a new understanding of their own mothers. The older students discovered some important truths about their daughters' generation. Not too surprisingly, those younger students who resented the older women in their classes were also those who gave every indication of having bad relationships with their mothers. All of the younger students, however, found one kind of older student ridiculous—the overage teenybopper!

My teaching experience at Mundelein, limited as it was, was nonetheless fascinating. When *Death of a Salesman* was the play under study in my Degree-Completion course, I swear half the women in the class were married to Willy Loman. The discussion became very intense. When I offered the same course for the younger students, they didn't understand the play at all. How could they? But when I taught O'Neill's Nietzschean play, *Lazarus Laughed,* to the younger students (on Holy Thursday afternoon, the day before Easter vacation began!), they stayed for an hour after class to continue the discussion.

Three years after the completion of the Institutional Analysis, I did a longitudinal study based on the original student questionnaire. The girls who had been freshmen at the time were now seniors. I wanted to administer the same questionnaire to them to see what difference, if any, a Mundelein education had made to them.

Because the questionnaire had been administered anonymously, the problem was to identify a student's freshman responses so that they could be compared with that student's senior responses. We laid out all of the original questionnaires and invited the seniors to find theirs, note its number, and use that number to identify their senior questionnaire.

The seniors, looking for their freshman questionnaires, were outside my closed office door. As they read what they had thought and felt as freshmen, they would burst into laughter. I knew then and there that we would get significant results. And indeed we did! There was powerful evidence that their three years at Mundelein had made profound changes in them. Obviously, they were more mature, but more than that, their attitudes and opinions and perceptions were significantly different—the difference that could have come only from their study and life as students at this dynamic little Catholic women's college. We could take comfort that all the time, anxiety, and energy invested in the Institutional Analysis had not been in vain.

After six or seven years at Mundelein, I was getting restless. I was approaching fifty, and if I were ever going to make a move, the time to do so was fast approaching. I had had wonderful experiences at Mundelein. Sister Ann Ida had given me total freedom to do what I pleased, and she seemed satisfied with the work I had done. I had made new and had strengthened old friendships at the college, notably with Sister Mary Ignatia Griffin, the brilliant academic dean; Russ Barta, professor of sociology; and Dan Cahill (who had come back to Mundelein to be its *genuine* vice president for development)—all three had left. I also became close friends with Katharine Byrne, the empathic, insightful director/counselor of the Degree Completion Program, and a whole squadron of B.V.M.'s: Sisters Cecilia and Donatus and Assisium and . . . the list is long and distinguished. (I won't try to complete it for fear of omitting good friends. Isn't it interesting that I remember them by the religious names they bore when I first knew them?)

But by 1968, frankly, I was tired of being number two, the perennial bridesmaid. I had worked hard to support Ray Sheriff at Loyola's business school. I had worked even harder to support Maurice Donohue at the University of Chicago. And I had helped Sister Ann Ida save Mundelein, at least for the time being, from its more or less inevitable eventual merger with Loyola. But now I wanted a college of my own—to see if I could really make it when there was no one to pass the buck to.

One day I got a phone call from Eugene Kennedy, whom I had known slightly at Loyola years before. He was now on the staff of Aquinas College in Grand Rapids, Michigan. Aquinas was looking for a president. Would I like to have him submit my name? The answer was, "Of course."

And so, blessed with the rich experience I had gained at Mundelein and Chicago and Loyola, I became the second president of Aquinas College, which I served until my retirement in 1986. Many of the good things that happened in Grand Rapids had been tested and developed in Rogers Park and Hyde Park. I shall always be grateful.

The Progressive Bunch, 1969–1979:
An Interview with David Orr

Elizabeth Fraterrigo

In the 1960s and 1970s the United States' involvement in Vietnam, the civil rights and women's movements' strident calls for racial and gender equality, and a growing youth counterculture embroiled American society. The social upheaval so often referred to in historical shorthand as simply "the Sixties" swept through Mundelein College, as well. Many faculty and students at the small Catholic women's school on Chicago's lakeshore embraced both the conflicts and energy of this period. Their attempts to face its challenges and opportunities took many forms: an experimental degree program emerged, in part, from the countercultural milieu of the era; another program made higher education available to older women balancing familial and work responsibilities; and a controversial campuswide strike took place in opposition to the Vietnam War. Many members of the Mundelein community sought to bring vital, contemporary issues into the classroom, as well as to extend the educational experience beyond the boundaries of the campus. At a time of great social flux, Mundelein College continued to adapt to meet the evolving needs and interests of its students.

David Orr, who served on the faculty of the history department from 1969 to 1979, played a key role in the development of several innovative courses and programs at Mundelein. All of them sought to broaden the educational experience for both teacher and student by investigating alternative approaches to learning. The Experimental College that Orr helped start, for example, allowed students to undertake a self-styled course of study that might include independent research, apprenticeships, work, travel or other pursuits outside a classroom setting. He also helped found the Weekend College in Residence, which enabled Mundelein to increase its enrollment while providing returning students with a focused, intensive learning experience. The City in Crisis summer course, through its use of site visits and guest lectures, gave students a chance to explore social and political conflict in the city, using Chicago as both case study and classroom.

Deeply immersed in the energy and political consciousness of the era, Orr was both educator and activist during his years at Mundelein. He was well placed to recall the culture of Mundelein College as well as its ongoing efforts to meet the needs of its students during a period marked by social turmoil and change. Through his teaching, administrative, advisory, and activist roles, Orr experienced the many worlds of the Mundelein community. He offers an interesting perspective of a young man teaching at a Catholic women's college in the 1960s and 1970s. Orr has served as Cook County clerk since 1990. The following interview took place in his office in November 1999.

Orr grew up in the western suburbs of Chicago, Illinois. In 1966, he graduated from Simpson College, a small, liberal arts school in Iowa. He continued his education at Case Western Reserve in Cleveland, Ohio, where he earned a master of arts degree in American Studies in 1968. He left graduate school to teach at Notre Dame College in the Cleveland area. Prior to taking this job, Orr spent two summers teaching American history in the Upward Bound program at Mundelein College.

I came home to the Chicago area each summer I was in graduate school, which is very relevant to Mundelein because my connection to Mundelein was all accidental. I was finishing my first year of graduate school in Cleveland, which would have been May 1967. I was looking for a summer job. I heard about the Upward Bound program, which was a federally funded program, kind of like the equivalent of Head Start for high school age kids. I applied to various places in Cleveland for Upward Bound, but I couldn't get a job there. Someone said to me, "Well, why don't you apply for Upward Bound in Chicago, because that's where you're from?" So I did. I applied several places, and I got this letter back from one of the nuns at Mundelein. I didn't know Mundelein from a hole in the wall.

It was a very interesting letter. I don't remember if it came from Sister Kathleen O'Brien or Sister Margaret Thornton, but it was from one of the sisters in the history department who worked with Upward Bound. I thought I would be like a counselor, one of the graduate kids who worked with the students. But the letter came back: "We looked at your resume, and we see you've had a lot of American history. We're looking for someone who could teach American history to fifty or sixty high-risk young girls from the ghetto," so to speak. You know, you're a twenty-one-year-old kid trying to come up with creative ideas to teach history in a way that would be more meaningful than the stuff you'd been getting, because I had some great professors who were very boring, I guess. I wrote back, and they hired me sight unseen.

So my first experience with Mundelein was not as a college teacher but through this other program that was taking place there. I did that in the summers of 1967, 1968, and 1969. That was a marvelous experience. The kids were wonderful. The nuns who organized it at Mundelein were what I'd call kind of a progressive bunch who were willing to experiment. You know, when you're taking maybe a sixteen-year-old kid from the ghetto, from where most of their classmates would never go on to college and so forth, how do you make them more interested in whether or not Abraham Lincoln did this or that? But we had the ability to experiment. We weren't caught up with a lot of red tape, which was a big problem for most teachers in public schools. I remember one class in which we were trying to get across what eyewitness testimony was. It had something to do with the American history experience. Three students from another class came into our room and basically tore up the room intentionally. They came in and picked up some chalk and erasers and threw them. They actually pushed— this was all women now—a couple of their colleagues. I mean, not a fist-fight, but they were probably in and out of the room in less than twenty seconds. Then, we asked the people who were in the classroom to identify who had done it. And, of course, what was interesting now, what was historically valuable, is that they couldn't. They misidentified even racially— they misidentified black for white—and so the lesson was that people could go to their death for a misidentification or something. I'm just giving you an example.

Upward Bound was a good experience because it was a whole experience. It wasn't just some people who came together once a week for three hours. It was every day, fairly intense. You were teacher, counselor, advisor, everything. I remember that first year in 1967, they had this big trip at the end of the summer for the kids. We all went along, too—the faculty and about twenty or thirty Mundelein students who served as tutor/counselors. The kids lived in the dorm with the college women, who were like advisors. That summer we finished up by going to Washington, D.C., where the kids actually got to meet with Robert Kennedy. It was the year before he was assassinated.

Orr spent three summers working with the Upward Bound program at Mundelein. After teaching for a year at Notre Dame College in Ohio, he joined the history faculty at Mundelein College in autumn 1969. Orr discussed those whom he saw as the "progressive bunch" and described both the emphasis on teaching at Mundelein and his work with the City in Crisis summer course.

Upward Bound was my first experience at Mundelein, which was so good because my teaching at Notre Dame College in Cleveland had been with a very conservative, almost right-wing, reactionary group of sisters. It did not leave a good impression on me. So to have the experience with the B.V.M.'s for someone who actually wasn't Catholic and did not have the breadth of knowledge about nuns or Catholics or whatever—it was very good for me to see these Kathleen O'Briens and Margaret Thorntons and the others who participated in this program.

I think particularly in terms of the sisters, a lot of the folks around the Weekend College—Mary Griffin, who has passed away, and Mary DeCock—were interested in what you might call progressive educational theory. How do you achieve the substance that is necessary? How do you make sure that students have a certain knowledge of content in a subject area so they can succeed? But progressive education also tries to deal, I guess, a little more with experimental and motivational techniques.

Mundelein, long before I got there, was always experimenting. When I first came in 1969, I was teaching History I and History II and we had sixty or seventy people in the classroom, and the faculty experimented with team teaching. I think one of the reasons Mundelein was known to be a good college with generally good faculty was because they took teaching seriously. There wasn't the pressure to publish. I'm sure there's more of that today, particularly because it's part of Loyola University Chicago. And there's something to that. In my view, it's very valuable for the faculty to have the time to study more in their own field and learn, but good teaching is every bit as valuable. In fact, in some cases it's more valuable to students than the individual scholarship of the professor.

There were so many great things at Mundelein. It's hard to say which were the greatest, but the City in Crisis course was a wonderful experience for me. What made it so successful—and by that I mean that most students learned a lot and they loved it—was that it was more intense. It was not just getting together for three hours, because there are different ways to teach. A really brilliant lecturer can offer an awful lot to students, you know, even if it's a one-hour segment. But the most real education goes way beyond that. Real education is befriending students; it's knowing someone to whom you could actually say: "I care about you, you're a good person, but you really have to pay attention to this because you just don't get it." You develop a certain level of personal relationship. Most learning is more than just memorizing dates and stuff; it's deeper. It's "how do I come to make decisions about life?" In some ways, real learning is personal.

Getting back to the City in Crisis, the program was unique in the sense that it had this intense all-morning session, which in some cases led to two or three in the afternoon. Quite a few of the students could stick around since this was their only class and they were getting six hours of credit. It was a summer program that met every day of the week from 9:00 A.M. to 12:00 P.M. But in many cases because people were available and I was available, it continued. So you might have class in the morning and then go have lunch and keep talking. The idea was experiential, you know, the "city in crisis"—let's get to see it. We also would have many guests, including John Stroger, who's now the county-board president, and Howard Saffold from the Afro-American Patrolmen's League. We went to Cook County Jail. We went to Chicago City Council meetings. In fact, we were there when Mayor [Richard J.] Daley made his famous "son speech" [in which Daley defended giving the city's insurance business to one of his sons], and there was almost a big riot in the city council. He was very angry at young people and sat and stared at us for hours, being so angry at youth in general. That was the day Dick Simpson challenged him on the floor of the city council. I believe that was 1969.

We went to all these places, met with community organizers, went to community group meetings. And the students had to analyze all these experiences—what people said, different opinions, and so forth. We did that for just about ten summers. What made it special was that it was experiential and they had more time. And the camaraderie that developed among the students every year was fascinating because in many cases you had older students in their thirties and forties, and younger students, even a spattering of males. The class of 1975 had these fascinating young men, and a relationship developed between them and a group of thirty-five to forty-year-old women in terms of just the exchanging of ideas. Anyway, it was a fun program. People learned a lot. And it was great for me to learn about politics in the city.

In 1970 Orr participated in Mundelein's Conference on Curriculum, or Con-Cur. The conference allowed faculty to evaluate the curriculum and generate ideas for new programs.

I think the goal of Con-Cur was to review the curriculum and try to make changes. What is the best thing we can teach and the best way to go about teaching it? We were trying to think about who the students were in the early 1970s. I was involved in a lot of that, and, again, it was a positive experience. Con-Cur is another example of people who were so committed to education, and particularly teaching, that they would take the extra time to debate these pedagogical ideas. There were always differing views. I came to Mundelein wearing a goatee when I was twenty-four years old but looked about eighteen. Many of my students looked older than me, so I'm sure many of the faculty felt, "Who is this hippie kid who knows nothing?" I talked earlier about nuns who were progressive. But people like Bill Hill and Mike Fortune—a lot of the folks like that—were also 100 percent committed. We were paid very little at Mundelein. I started at $6,000 in the fall of 1969. But it didn't matter what these people got paid. It didn't matter how many committees they had to sit on or how many classes they had to teach, which took them away from the personal research they would have liked to do. They were willing to do it. Con-Cur was just another example of that.

One of the things to emerge from the Conference on Curriculum was the Experimental College, also known as Mandala. The program, founded in 1970, encouraged students to play an active role in shaping their own course of study and evaluating the work of others. Mandala students pursued a variety of work, research, and other activities outside a traditional classroom environment. They earned their degrees not through the accumulation of course credit, but through the overall evaluation of their program by the students and faculty who together comprised the Mandala membership. Orr reflected on the cultural setting within which the Experimental College was founded, as well as on the goals of this alternative program.

Just think of this. It's 1969, 1970, 1971. It's partly a reflection of the sixties. You've got students who are saying: "Why do I have to take these particular courses, or take them in this particular order? I can learn better if you just let me do some of these things. Or maybe the focus shouldn't be on grades." It's the kind of thing that poor students use all the time to try and get out of work. But at this time at Mundelein, what you really had were good students who were on the edge of adulthood. Progressivism or even radicalism, all of this swirled around them—the civil rights movement, the Vietnam War, all the youthful energy created by all that, including the youthful disappointments over all the horrible things that were happening in the late 1960s. All that had been building. The countercultural element to it was important.

David Crosby in the English faculty was kind of the ringleader and I was his sidekick. I really can't remember if there were many other faculty involved directly. I think it tended to be mostly us. I'm probably insulting some others who played a less dramatic role. The goal of the Experimental College was, Can we achieve the same, or ideally, better, level of education with some measurement of what a student is learning and do so without the focus on grades and "you've got to go to this particular classroom" or whatever? Again, none of that's totally unique because there are very traditional professors who say, "I don't care if you come into my lectures. If you can pass the test, fine."

But it also placed a much greater burden on the students. I think they came to realize that. Freedom is a very, very difficult thing, and most of us, while we say we want it, would love to have people make our decisions for us. For all the students, that was a real challenge. For many of the students who were very capable, it was a really great experience. For others, it was a real struggle because, "If I don't have to necessarily go to that class or if I don't have to do it this way, I've got to decide for myself how I'm going to achieve these ends." That's tough. A wonderful opportunity, but very, very tough.

The Experimental College allowed students to create their own plan in consultation with their colleagues—their fellow students and the faculty, which I think was mostly Crosby and me. That's what was so difficult. In other words, we weren't saying, "Well just don't go to class." It was more like, "How are you going to achieve your goals? How are you going to become knowledgeable so that you *could* be passing these tests? So that you really *could* know about twentieth-century U.S. history?" for example. It was kind of like independent study and tutorials. The students would set some of their own goals, they would devise projects, and they would have to present them to the whole group—their peers as well as faculty—and the group would offer collective criticism. The students would also bring in other faculty outside the Experimental College, because maybe one of them was working with Mary Griffin in the English department. So Mary Griffin would be brought into this analysis.

One of the most exciting things took place at the end of each term. They would have to put on these schoolwide demonstrations. One of the students was an artist, so obviously her final presentation was artwork. Others were English majors, so they presented something they had written. Others were social-studies or social-science students who had done some sort of experiment. The final presentations put a lot of pressure on them. Again, the goal was for people to set their own agenda, with criticism from caring individuals—their colleagues in this experiment, as well as the faculty.

It was the kind of thing that worked particularly well for some of the students who had a good grounding. I think it was more difficult for freshmen to join, who wouldn't quite admit it—some might have joined because maybe they wanted to be cool. Some of the students had a hard time because they would give us excuses, like "I want to set my own agenda, blah, blah, blah," but in some cases, they were just trying to avoid facing up to the fact that maybe, for instance, they didn't write well enough.

The difference between Mandala and traditional degree programs was that you had a smaller collective group that you could deal with in a freer atmosphere. You didn't have to necessarily meet at nine-thirty in the morning. You could all meet at four in the afternoon and go for two hours, or whatever. It was a good experiment. I think it worked with most students.

I'd love to know how these students turned out and what many of them actually felt about it. I think most of them would have good feelings. Some would have mixed feelings. Some might say, "Well, I know I learned some things, but I might have been better off if I had been in a more rigid situation." Most of us realize that real education is some blend of creativity and finding your own direction, as well as just good, old-fashioned, "Hey, I want to listen to this professor because I know I could learn a lot just listening to him."

Orr discussed the perception of the Experimental College students by those in the more mainstream curriculum, along with the controversy surrounding a student strike following the U.S. invasion of Cambodia and the killing of four students at Kent State University by National Guardsmen in May 1970.

I guess I have no way of knowing how others felt about the Experimental College. Was it perceived as a radical experiment? You've got to understand, it's the early 1970s, it's a countercultural time. Crosby is a long-haired, full-bearded professor. Always seen as, you might say, a maverick at Mundelein, for lots of different reasons. I was very young. I guess my hair was much longer then, though not as long as Crosby's. But you had that and some students who were more free-spirited. So I guess there was some sense of people thinking, you know, "What the heck are they doing there?" Some with envy, some with disdain. But I don't remember much criticism. If there was a lot of thought about it I wasn't fully aware of it. I wouldn't be surprised if what I'm describing was less a reaction to "Is someone really learning this or not?" It maybe had more to do with "Who is this group that sits out on the lawn looking like a bunch of hippies?" That probably affected thought more than the quality of someone's project or the work they were actually doing.

The 1970 campus strike was, for me, a very exciting time. I came full time to Mundelein in the fall of 1969. That's when many campuses were really getting active in terms of the Vietnam War. One of the things that was so wonderful at Mundelein, both for students as well as for faculty like me, was that we all had our fights, but it was a learning community. The value of that was that people in academics—and the people that I like—believe in the value of discourse, the value of intellectual debate. Yet in many places in our society, in our politics, and in many cases our universities, there is a paucity of real debate. People are as cowardly there as they are in other places. So to have this full-fledged debate among students and faculty: "Should we do this? Should we have a strike? Wait a second, if we have a strike, that's not fair to the ones who are going to graduate. Well, but on the other hand, at a time like this when people are dying and they shouldn't be, we've got to change the rules."

The campus was full of debates like this. I remember all sorts of situations concluded with tears, with people just legitimately trying to struggle. For some of the students whom I got to know, and still am familiar with, this was a big part of their lives. Nancy Zak, who graduated in 1970 and who I'm still in touch with, was one of the leaders. I even think we had a spy on campus. Some guy who was always trying to push the envelope. I think many of us felt that he was really a setup, trying to create a problem.

But the campus was alive. I would never say that all the things that were done were right, but it was a very dramatic time. Many people look at the 1960s or some of these elements, and I just don't think they have a proper historical perspective. Sure, there were people that maybe went along with the demonstrations because they just wanted to go along. You know, it was the thing to do. But the nice thing about Mundelein, particularly with this whole strike situation, was that a very legitimate debate took place. It's hard with hindsight to know what's the right side. Do you actually more or less shut down the university to accomplish your purpose? Or is it better to keep things going? At Mundelein, there were choices, and there was debate. There were a lot of angry and upset people, a lot of experiences like that, and again, this was my first year there.

In fact, there was a very dramatic group, mostly Loyola students, who were very talented actors and actresses, and I remember about that time they were performing *Viet Rock,* which was an antiwar play. Sometime during the spring of 1970, one of the cast members had to leave. They were doing performances at Old Orchard, or Mill Run Theater, or something, for one final weekend. So they asked me to join them. And I did.

I didn't have a clue. I was extremely uptight. These were very free-spirited juniors and seniors, you know. The hard thing for me since I was a twenty-four-year-old single male with all these women around—I think sometimes you needed to put up these walls. That's partly a contradiction of what I've been saying, because I really believe you've got to be personal, but you still had these walls. With my friends, I might let loose and be a character, but with students, you had these walls. So being with this group that was very free spirited, participating in this play, in which the men were only dressed to the waist ... It was a theater in the round, and I had very few lines. The one line I had was profanity. But it fit in with the whole culture of that time.

Things simmered down, but the strike had lasting implications. There were repercussions from it. But I look at the positive side—that people struggled legitimately, honestly, with what to do, and they all got through it one way or another. Probably most activists felt it was a valuable time in their life. As for some of the students who felt, "Hey, what the heck is going on?"—whether they'd look back with hindsight and say "Well, it was legitimate intellectual discussion" or "It was just a bunch of crap," I don't know. But it was a very intriguing time.

With regard to the faculty and administration view of campus protest and the strike, you always had a mixed bag there. But even those people that I might have differed with or fought with or argued with, I respected them. I was a young kid who was caught up in this stuff, and more willing to rock the boat than others. Sister Ann Ida Gannon, for example, who was a wonderful president and prime mover—I'm sure Ann Ida thought at times, "My God, who is this crazy kid?" We sometimes fought over the years over political things, but I respect her, and I hope she respects me. I think that's what I'd say about it. That it was an open, intellectual debate in which I give the school and I give the B.V.M.'s credit.

Because they were on the edge, as a group. Some might have been much more conservative philosophically or politically than others, but remember, this is a place not only with all these things I've mentioned going on. This is also a place where the B.V.M.'s are coming out of habit. This is a place where they're standing forward on many things. There's the whole issue of choice. Remember, this is before *Roe v. Wade.* There were women seeking abortions and there were faculty counseling them. This was a place, right or wrong, I think, where you just had a lot of people with humanitarian values committed to education. So it doesn't matter whether somebody was right or wrong, or whether or not somebody was more liberal or conservative. Even though we fought about these things, there was a respect that I really appreciate, whether it came from more traditional sisters or more progressive ones.

Orr was one of five faculty members involved in the establishment in 1974 of the Weekend College in Residence at Mundelein, a program for returning students. It was primarily designed to meet the needs of women seeking a college education as they balanced multiple responsibilities, including marriage, family, work, and school.

We put together a curriculum we thought would be relevant for returning students. We're talking about a certain population of people who were going back to school. Mostly women, but not all, who . . . let me put it like this. I read a book with this title in it, and it always struck me as who these students were, particularly in the first few years of the Weekend College. We knew we were looking for people who in many cases had jobs, and in a sense they had a "hidden wound." The hidden wound was they didn't think they were as good as they should be—either how they viewed themselves or how they thought others viewed them—because they didn't have that college degree. It's easy to say, "Well, you're the same person, you just haven't finished all this coursework." But there was this hidden wound, which partly led to the tremendous energy and commitment these students had compared to some of the eighteen-year-olds who thought, "Hey, I'm here because I've got to be here."

So the Weekend College was partly geared toward knowing these people needed a lot in a short amount of time. They didn't have a lot of time for school. They would not listen to a lot of irrelevant stories from faculty or from classmates. They want to study and learn. They want a different experience. They're thirty-six, they've got jobs, and they've got kids. So the program was geared toward recognizing that to be successful in the Weekend College, students would have to do a lot on their own. The bottom line was we had to arrange the curriculum in order to give the students a certain amount of content in a limited amount of time. There was a lot of debate over this. Yet they had to do more than a normal student would do because there was less class time, and they had less free time than the average younger student anyway. So we were trying to consider the whole student.

Mundelein was having enrollment problems like every small school at the time. Because of this, the powers that be had to say, "Well, you folks over here, we may not always want to listen to you, but if you can come up with something, we'll listen now." See what I'm getting at? They say, "Okay, here's a chance for you crazy folks"—Mary Griffin and Mary DeCock—and so there was an opportunity for us. Because, as I've said, we were these people who were always plotting, Is there a way that we can do some educational experiment that works? This was a very practical one and a financially successful one for the school. Mary Griffin was our primary researcher, and we knew that there had been this weekend college experience, but never a Weekend College in Residence. This was the element that we added.

In a sense it was revolutionary, because many of these returning female students were married. Leave hubby with the kids for the weekend. What the hell? Let's have a little equity here. Their class time had to be jammed into a weekend. They didn't have a lot of time, so we added the residence part. Because why should they be spending hours going back and forth between a Friday-night class and home? The residence aspect was a very popular thing and very intriguing, too, because many of these women had kids.

The Weekend College was a total experience that fit perfectly with the times, too, because people wanted to move more quickly. Why should these talented people take seven years to get through college? See, you had to break down the barriers where everybody has to do it the same way. Bull! If they can achieve the level of knowledge sufficient to someone justifiably getting a degree, why not let them do it in a different way if we believe they're learning? We clearly believed they did learn, at least most of them. It was just very exciting. These people were hungry. They were hungry for the recognition. Many of them, frankly, were a lot more talented than most of the B.A.'s I knew. But they had this wound, and they wanted to prove something to themselves and others.

In his role as faculty-advisor to students in the Weekend College, Orr sometimes encountered women grappling with issues of marriage and family, and observed the rapport that developed among the students in residence.

One of the most interesting students I had in the first year was a woman who was a very talented writer. I lost touch with her. I think she went on to write some things. She's been published. She left her three kids. She left them. In fact, I think one of her books or essays that she was working on at the time was "What do I say to my children, as to why I had to leave?" Of course, this was exceptional but that was just someone in that first group. But that whole issue of marriage and family often came up. There's always tension in terms of how close one can be, how far one can go in terms of discussing things with another person. I think many people at that time were ripe to discuss things. I didn't see many inhibitions on the part of women who were dealing with the male faculty. Dan Vaillancourt, Bill Hill, and I think all of us experienced the whole thing. Not only "How can I get through this, how do I learn this, how do I study that?" but also if there were other issues that affected Weekend College students, they came up. Because it was an atmosphere in which that was okay. Yes, there was a lot of that. That's why I think it's important to remember there are all these other social elements going on. Did it start in 1974? The women's movement was beginning to pick up steam. There were women who would bring that into it. You know, like the spouse having to take care of the kids while she was there.

I just saw so many positive things. I'm sure there was also the negative. I think the students built a lot of friendships. They were probably less interested, at that age, in recognition or approval from their classmates. I saw a lot of very good relationships develop, some of them lasting. I think they basically got along well because they had this collective goal, to learn and learn fast. They were serious about it.

During his time at Mundelein, Orr designed and taught many courses that examined subjects often overlooked in American history. He talked about how such courses as Movements in Welfare Capitalism and Radicalism in the U.S. related to the world outside the classroom.

When I started at Mundelein, we had History I and History II. When you're teaching courses like that, you decide which things out of all this history you're going to talk about. And part of what's going on at this time is that women, or African Americans, or later Latinos, are saying "Wait a minute, we're not very much a part of History I and II." There's always this revisionism stuff going on, if you want to call it that. Always different approaches. So I tried to look at some of the things that aren't discussed as much: labor in American history or welfare capitalism as another way to look at economic systems more carefully than we have.

I think a lot of it reflects a desire on my part to learn more about teaching. There was a lot of experimentation. I laugh about it. I team taught a course called History of Evil—I think that was the title—with Bill Hill. All these educational experiments are not easy. It's not an easy thing to team teach something. "Oh, my God, my colleagues are going to know how much I don't know about everything." You know, faculty are very weird that way. As much as they know or don't know, they always feel like they should know more. But that was a great experience. I got a kick out of the fact that I actually taught a course where religion credit was received.

In 1979 Orr left his position as assistant professor at Mundelein College to run for alderman of Chicago's Forty-ninth Ward (Rogers Park). He was reelected to city council in 1983 and 1987. In spring 1987 Mayor Harold Washington appointed him vice mayor. Following Washington's death on November 25, 1987, Orr served as interim mayor of Chicago. In 1990 Orr was elected Cook County clerk, a position to which he has been reelected twice. Orr sees a link between his work as both educator and activist at Mundelein and his later political career.

I got politically involved with what you might call the antimachine progressive forces that led to my meeting a lot of people in Rogers Park. Again, at Mundelein, the culture was good to me, because in 1974 I was campaign manager for a good friend of mine, Mike Kreloff, when he ran for alderman, and I think I had a limited teaching schedule because of that. Plus, it was the beginning of the Weekend College that fall, come to think of it. It must have been a pretty crazy time. I think it all fits well. I think to the extent that people either liked my teaching or respected it, the ones who probably appreciated it most were students who also saw a value in activism beyond the classroom, in which you did a little of what you preached. That probably was an attractive quality.

I became gradually more and more involved on the political front, until I just decided I'd become the candidate. Once I did that, I had to make the decision that I would be a full-time alderman, which means I couldn't keep up my full-time job at Mundelein. I had to give up tenure, which was . . . I had to fight very hard for tenure so that was not an easy decision, but that's just the way it had to be. I think that toward the mid- to late seventies I was feeling like "This is really good, but I need something more than just full-time teaching."

I always felt the academic world was valuable because it forces you to think through where you are. It forces you to learn. In order to teach you have to learn. I miss some of these great experiences I've had at Mundelein. I really did have a good time. I was very lucky to have that kind of environment at twenty-four, to step into that. It was, in some ways, kind of an ideal situation for me, because I was interested in all these education experiments, as well as history and politics. It served me well.

"Damned Average Raisers": The Continuing Education Program

Marianne M. Littau

A hallmark idea from Mundelein's two-year self-study was the need for innovative higher-education programs for adult women—those who were beyond the traditional college age. Mundelein's administrators were aware of this possibility even as they began the self-study in 1962. Dr. Norbert Hruby, vice president for development and the driving force behind the study, had been associate dean at University College, the University of Chicago's continuing education program. Sister Mary Ann Ida Gannon, president, had been a member of the Illinois Commission on the Status of Women in the early 1960s and in that capacity had come in contact with hundreds of women who called for more avenues for women to reenter college. The self-study crystallized and localized this need because it surveyed women who had begun their education at Mundelein but never completed it. Fully 69 percent of the 185 former students who responded said they would be interested in a program for returning students if one were offered.[1]

When the self-study recommendations were published in spring 1964, the Committee on Organization of the College stated "that Mundelein institute a degree completion program for the benefit of that large number of former Mundelein students (and other ex-alumnae of other colleges and universities) who did not earn degrees. We see this program as being implemented by a newly created division of continuing education."[2]

The Committee on Counseling affirmed this recommendation: "Mundelein College should explore quickly and in depth the various programs that other colleges and universities are adopting for the continuing education of their alumnae. . . . Counseling programs should play a vital and integral part in this aspect of higher education."[3]

The implementation of these recommendations began in October 1964, with the formation of the Committee on Continuing Education.[4] With Dr. Hruby as its chair, the committee examined the model provided by the relatively new Division of Continuing Education at Sarah Lawrence College. The committee ultimately emphasized a strong counseling program and grappled with the curricular and teaching requirements of such a program as well as with the issue of credit for life experience.

The committee's design came to life with the first recruitment brochure for fall 1965. Targeted generally at women over the age of twenty-six, it stressed the availability of counseling and introduced a series of seminars offered one day a week from 10:00 A.M. until 2:00 P.M. The seminar content followed the Basic Studies curriculum that emerged from the self-study. Thus, the committee maintained the college's new curriculum but altered the format and schedule. The planners also recognized that some enrollees might be more advanced than the seminar level and therefore could transition immediately into Mundelein's "regular" course offerings. In March 1965 Dr. Hruby was appointed administrative head of the program; he then hired Katharine Byrne as counselor and instructor for the program. (Byrne ultimately became the second director in fall 1969, when Hruby left Mundelein.) The Degree Completion Program (DCP) became a reality.

Who were these first DCP students in fall 1965? The charter group included 108 students ranging in age from twenty-one to sixty-five; 23 had no previous college background while the remainder had about two years. Their reasons for enrolling ranged from personal development (37 women) to career development other than teaching (28 women) and fulfilling a lifelong ambition (19 women). They came from the city and suburbs, and about 20 percent had attended Mundelein previously.[5] The program had no counterpart in the Chicago area or in the Midwest. Indicative of this is the fact that Kendall College, Wheaton College, Barat College, Loyola University Chicago, and DePaul University agreed to give Mundelein the names of their former students for recruitment purposes.[6] This willingness to share soon changed as other schools began to recognize the advantages of having such a program.

The average DCP student in 1965 was a forty-one-year-old married woman with three children. Many were active in their communities, had attended noncredit courses, or were members of book discussion groups. A few were business or professional women who had simply never completed their degrees.[7] In spite of these credentials, Mundelein wanted further assurance of their likelihood of success and so it tested each potential student, using the Ohio State Psychological Test to measure their vocabulary and reading skills.

Dr. Hruby's acceptance letter to each student indicated some of the uncertainty the administration and faculty must have felt as they opened the doors to this new group of students:

Your acceptance is, in effect, provisional for one academic year, during
which time it will be established whether or not you are capable of
carrying the burden you have assumed. Clearly this is not a question
of intelligence; rather it is a question of motivation, time, and energy.
As of now we believe that you have offered satisfactory evidence of your
intentions; we hope that your present high purpose and enthusiasm
will be sustained. [In a draft, the final clause read "it remains to be seen
how it will work out."][8]

But succeed they did! Of the initial 108 students who each registered for about one and one-half courses, 102 completed the term successfully.[9] Slightly over one hundred students were enrolled in the initial three seminars: Contemporary Drama (taught by Dr. Hruby), Natural Science, and Fine Arts; forty-one DCP students were enrolled in twenty-nine courses with the traditional-age Mundelein students.[10] Even in this first term, the DCP students cemented their reputation among traditional-age students, as reported by a DCP student in a local newspaper article: "The girls call us the D.A.R.'s (Damned Average Raisers) and I'm proud of it."[11]

In winter 1966 eighty-two DCP students returned for their second term and were joined by ten new students. Most of the others from the initial fall term indicated they would return for spring term.[12] In subsequent years the program continued to grow as more women heard about it from friends or through the many stories that appeared in city and suburban papers. By 1968 the program had graduated its first thirteen students. By fall 1968, 216 students were registered for 352 courses.[13] By fall 1976, enrollment was 330 students.[14]

As the original planners anticipated, the college had to resolve the issue of whether to grant credit for life experience. Dr. Hruby was aware that Brooklyn College in its Special Baccalaureate Degree Program for Adults had addressed this thorny issue. With that program as a guideline, in fall 1967 Mundelein began offering CARE–Crediting of Academically Relevant Experience. A DCP student seeking such credit petitioned a designated departmental faculty member and provided rigorous demonstration that a prior experience had approximately the same outcomes as an academic course. Students who were successful in articulating their cases paid an administrative charge for recognition of this credit. Through 1969 some 135 courses were certified, about 4 percent of the total number of courses taken by DCP students.[15] Thus, while the number of courses actually awarded through this program was relatively small, CARE itself was revolutionary since it signaled an openness to nontraditional forms and avenues of learning.

Under the continuing-education umbrella, specialized programs were developed to appeal to particular student segments. For example, in 1966 the Division of Continuing Education and Mundelein's education department offered DCP for teachers in response to an archdiocesan mandate that parochial school teachers had to have received degrees by a specified date. In the early 1970s, under the guidance of Sister Susan Rink, B.V.M., the program's third director, the division worked with the biology department to evaluate nursing-school transcripts for CARE credits, thus enabling registered nurses to return to college to earn a bachelor's degree. In the mid-1970s the program worked with the National Association of Bank Women (NABW) to create an intensive management program for women working in the banking field.

The Division of Continuing Education represented impressive accomplishments. Mundelein College was the first in the Midwest to offer such an innovative program designed specifically for women who had not completed their degrees. During its life, about one thousand women earned degrees through the Division of Continuing Education[16]; countless others were challenged and enriched by the courses they chose to take. The soul of the program, though, was in the collective stories of these women. They represented a range of ages and a variety of religious, racial, and ethnic backgrounds. They shared a common desire to pursue education seriously and to devote a significant amount of time and money to themselves. Some were clearly focused on a career choice, while others began without a specific direction and allowed the education experience to help shape their future. Many were not oriented toward careers but simply wanted to earn a degree for their own personal satisfaction. Most had the support of their husbands and children, as witnessed by the many happy family scenes at each year's graduation. Others came and persevered in spite of the obstacles placed in their paths by families who just couldn't understand what this new interest was all about. Still others gained new respect from their children who were genuinely proud of their mothers' achievements. I particularly remember a sixty-five-year-old returning student whose adopted son provided her with a personal scholarship because he had benefited from her respect for and appreciation of education.

As the fourth director of the program from 1974 to 1978, I had the great pleasure of interviewing and working with several hundred of these students. I recall clearly the anxiety and fear that many felt over coming back to college. While the women's voices and stories were unique, their questions were fundamentally the same. Can I succeed? How will I learn to study again? How will I do this and continue to support my husband and children? Many had the added burden of having a less-than-stellar college history. Low and failing grades on earlier transcripts were not uncommon, as these women had been focused on other goals back then. But as a general rule, these returning adult students succeeded admirably and surprised themselves with their new-found seriousness of purpose. They were better-than-average performers and highly motivated students. In addition, they were superb teachers themselves. I learned many important life lessons from them—an eagerness to accept new challenges, an openness to new experiences regardless of age, and a willingness to continue learning whether in formal or informal settings.

Just as times changed in 1965 with the founding of this remarkable pro-gram, change continued through the mid and late 1970s. Specifically, many colleges—both two- and four-year, public and private—began offering inno-vative programs for returning students. Also, more and more women were returning to the workforce, decreasing the demand for a daytime program. Mundelein itself responded to these changing circumstances with another innovative program, Weekend College. In spring 1978 Mundelein's executive team decided to centralize the admissions and counseling functions of its three major programs (traditional-age students, continuing education, and Weekend College). This transition was successfully completed in fall 1978. Adult day-students continued to be recruited and educated at Mundelein, but there was no longer a separate continuing education program whose task it was to recruit, counsel, advise, and plan a distinct curriculum for a returning adult population.

The continuing education program grew from a need for creative, sup-portive avenues for adult women in higher education. The program flourished because it met this need admirably, providing a challenging, but warm, proving ground for these students. But just as our country in the 1960s and 1970s witnessed the expansion of women's roles and the active presence of women in the mainstream in all walks of life, so too did Mundelein. These changes signalled the end of Mundelein's continuing education program. It was no longer needed precisely because it had succeeded.

Endnotes

1. Norbert J. Hruby, memorandum to the Committee on Continuing Education, "General Orientation of the Committee on Continuing Education," 30 December 1964, 5. This document and all subsequent documents are from the Mundelein College Archives (MCA), Gannon Center for Women and Leadership, Loyola University Chicago.

2. Ibid, 1.

3. Ibid, 2.

4. The initial committee members were Sister Mary Ann Ida Gannon, Russell Barta, Sister Mary Donald McNeil, Sister Mary Ignatia Griffin, Betty Matula, and James Richards. According to spring 1965 memos, James Richards was replaced by Sister Mary Cecilia Bodman and Sister Mary Marina Kennelly.

5. Norbert J. Hruby, memorandum to faculty and administrators, "The Arithmetic of the Degree Completion Program, Fall Term 1965," 29 October 1965, 1, 3.

6. ———, memorandum to the Committee on Continuing Education, "Progress Report on Degree Completion Program," 8 June 1965, 2.

7. ———, memorandum to faculty and administrators, 29 October 1965, 1, 3.

8. ———, draft and final version of acceptance letter, summer 1965, 1.

9. ———, "Report to the Faculty on the Achievement of Students in the Degree Completion Program, Fall Term 1965," 7 January 1966, 1.

10. ———, memorandum to faculty and administrators, 29 October 1965, 5.

11. Debby Rankin, "Freshmen Fresh from Kitchen," *Chicago Daily News,* 20 December 1965.

12. Norbert J. Hruby, "Report to the Faculty on the Achievement of Students in the Degree Completion Program, Fall Term 1965," 1.

13. ———, memorandum to faculty and administration, "The Arithmetic of the Degree Completion Program, Fall 1968," 17 December 1968, 1, 4.

14. ———, "Fall 1976 Enrollment Reports through the Summer," undated, 1.

15. Katharine Byrne, "Report to Faculty Senate," 14 October 1969, 1.

16. ———, "Continuing Education Graduates," undated, 1.

The Joy of Learning, 1987–1994

Tomi Shimojima

Man's mind, stretched to a new idea,
never returns to its original dimension.
OLIVER WENDELL HOLMES

Dreams can come and go, some to be realized, others abandoned. For those who are determined and focused, dreams can be fulfilled in a relatively short time. Where life goals or circumstances change along the way, some people may set aside earlier dreams to be replaced by new ones. There are those, however, for whom the pressures of career and family demands preclude the luxury of chasing after dreams, at least for a while. Such dreams will lie dormant for many years, only to resurface later, much like a persistent itch. A dream delayed but later realized can sometimes be sweeter in its fulfillment. My dream was to go to college and this was the way it happened for me.

My husband, George, and I had often discussed what we would like to do when we retired from our respective careers in the summer of 1985. Travel was an attractive option, something we had greatly enjoyed over our many years together. Another was to go to school; his wish was to pursue graduate study, mine to begin undergraduate courses. But mainly we hoped to enjoy the freedom that was ours, and the first eight months of retirement were delightful as we enjoyed excursions, theaters, musical events, and exotic new foods at fine restaurants.

Life sometimes works in unpredictable ways. George and I were not destined to have the joy of spending many more golden days together. My husband became ill, was diagnosed with cancer of the liver and pancreas, and died four days after the first anniversary of our retirement. I found solace in volunteer work at Edgewater Library, where I catalogued new books and patched torn ones to prepare them for shelving. Working in the library's back room gave me quiet time to think, and for a year I reflected on the direction my life should take.

As I deliberated seriously on the possibility of pursuing my earlier dream of returning to school, I thought of enrolling at Mundelein's Weekend College about which I had read and heard many good reports. Mundelein was a small liberal arts college for women, and since it was located near my home, it appeared to be an ideal choice. As I discussed this with my daughter, Anne, I mentioned that it might take me ten years to complete my studies, a long time indeed. Anne's reply was that ten years would pass whether I decided to go to school or not, and that this should not keep me from doing something I had long wished for. With her encouragement I was ready to start working on my dream, although not without some trepidation. I met with Sister Jean Dolores Schmidt, Mundelein's capable admissions counselor, in a conference that I will always remember. If I had any misgivings about my new venture, they were soon alleviated. Sister Jean spoke to me as if a sixty-seven year old returning to school were a common occurrence. I took the English and math tests for evaluation, wrote an essay as required, and was duly accepted.

After a fifty-year absence, I benefitted from Mundelein's core curriculum as a reorientation to classroom study. Courses in English, history, science, mathematics, psychology, philosophy, theology, fine arts, and languages (as well as advanced extensions of these courses) greatly challenged me. Within the various disciplines, I particularly enjoyed the following: Science and Human Values, Contemporary Ethical Issues, Twentieth Century Art, Asian American History, Art of Listening to Music, Theology of Faith, Marxism and Communism, and Sociological Perspectives. A genuine interest in their students' welfare, both academically and spiritually, was a gift the B.V.M. sisters gave in generous measure. They were available for conferences and counseling and were truly dedicated to see that students did well. In my own case, the help I most appreciated over the years were the suggestions, questions, and comments (often quite numerous) that were handwritten by professors on the essays I submitted. From these marginal notes, I learned that term papers should be well researched, carefully thought through, and written with clarity. This was a constant challenge for me. Mundelein College's endeavor to have students write clear, reasoned, and well-articulated papers helped to improve my writing skills, and I am grateful for that.

My favorite subject was philosophy, which became my major. I admired the ethics and wisdom of the Greek philosophers Socrates, Plato, and Aristotle. The philosophies of Aquinas, Descartes, Kant, James, Locke, Dewey, Mill, and Camus, to name just a few, introduced me to theories and values that were new to me. I could not always agree with the rationale inherent in the views of certain philosophers, but I realized that I could be open-minded about others' divergent thoughts and ideals. In the end, I began to trust my own intrinsic values as to which view I was free to accept or reject.

Because of my own situation as a returning adult student, I became interested in the motivations of others. What had brought my classmates to study at Mundelein's Weekend College? Because most were working men and women in their thirties, forties, and fifties, I surmised that they were in class for career-enhancement purposes. I decided to pursue this subject for a sociology term paper titled "The Adult Learner on Campus." I conducted a small survey among fifteen of my weekend classmates and asked their reasons for being at Mundelein. Because the survey covered only a small group of women, it could not be gauged as representative or conclusive for all adult students. Still, I was surprised that the reason most frequently given for attendance was not, as I initially believed, a wish for workplace promotions, but rather "personal enrichment and learning." I also asked another question, "What were one or two of the best aspects of your experience at school?" The answers were gratifying. Below are excerpts from the women's responses:

- Stretching my talents, exploring my abilities, and savoring my accomplishments

- Finding that I can do things that I had never realized before

- Learning so much more than I had anticipated because each subject shoots off into something else

- Exposure to extraordinary faculty, students, and unlimited resources

- Knowing that I can still learn and be open to new ideas at my age

- My age and life experience have given me an edge in my theology classes

- I am more motivated at age forty-four than anyone could be at twenty

It may well be that each of the respondents had come, in one way or another, to embrace the thinking expressed in the words of Oliver Wendell Holmes, first chief justice of the United States Supreme Court. With the learning of new ideas the mind stretches and grows, an exercise that continues at all age levels.

From my Mundelein professors, I learned that there are two purposes in learning. First, we seek to learn for its own sake, that is, to acquire knowledge. The mind is a powerful tool; learning promotes growing and that is good. Second, we apply knowledge gained in a practical or humanitarian cause. In this way, we can help to enrich the lives of others, and this provides meaning and purpose to our own lives. And so I became increasingly sensitive to ways in which I might help others.

Acting at a personal level, one-on-one on behalf of others, is the way I work best. I have joined two service-oriented groups at my church, Christ Church of Chicago. One group is called the Outreach Ministry. Patterned after the Stephen's Ministry, members of this group volunteer to befriend congregational members who, through illness, loneliness, or depression, are in need of compassionate care. Among those I have befriended is one whom I remember well. Ill with ovarian cancer, my friend needed someone to drive her to chemotherapy treatments at the University of Chicago Medical Center. The wait at the medical center was always very long and she was grateful to have me sit with her. I cooked meals for her and as we shared them together, she talked and I listened. When she died two years later, I felt that I had lost a dear friend. I now befriend a ninety-four-year-old widow who is homebound in a senior citizens' home. Her physical needs are provided for by the home so she manages fairly well. But her two grown children live in faraway states, and she appreciates the companionship from my visits, conversations, flowers, and the occasional favorite delicacy.

Another group I have joined is called the Bereavement Ministry. For those who have undergone the death of a loved one, the compassion and understanding of someone who has been through such a loss can be especially helpful. With the pastor, we help those who are at their saddest to plan funeral or memorial services. During this most traumatic and difficult time, the families are faced with many issues, and so we assist in any way we can. Later, we continue to maintain contact with the family to see that they are managing well. Within our congregation, the increasing number of deaths in recent years points to the need for this ministry. My involvement in the outreach and bereavement ministries is the result of the lessons I learned (sometimes indirectly) at Mundelein about caring and sharing.

My Mundelein education has brought me a new sense of personal accomplishment and self-worth. I now serve as president of the women's fellowship at my church, where I hope to be a good leader and discharge my duties with fairness and good judgment.

In May 1994 I was awarded a bachelor of arts degree, magna cum laude, from Mundelein College. I was then seventy-four years of age. It had not taken me ten years to fulfill my special dream; the seven years of study had actually seemed quite short.

I am indebted to the good sisters who taught me, encouraged me, and served as my friends during my studies at Mundelein. As educators, they have enriched the lives of countless numbers of students who will be able, in turn, to contribute to the well-being of others. My gratitude goes to Sisters Jean Dolores Schmidt (counselor), Joan Frances Crowley (history), Ann Harrington (history), Judith Dewell (music), Mary DeCock (theology), Marina Kennelly (chemistry), and Katharine Forsyth (mathematics).

To the four outstanding professors of philosophy who nurtured my love for this subject and challenged me as I studied and learned, I extend my very warmest affection: Sister Louise French and Professors Dan Vaillancourt, Thomas O'Brochta, and Richard Westley. It is from them that I have learned my greatest lesson, the need to be an authentic person. To each and all, I express my deeply felt *Arigato*.

Reinventing Mundelein:
Birthing the Weekend College, 1974

Mary Griffin

As I think back to its unlikely beginnings, one thing is clear: the Weekend College in Residence (WEC) was a team effort—from its inception to its realization. So it can't boast a single author. Nor did it spring "full-panoplied from the brow of Jove"! It really was a horse created by a committee, and it had all the endearing characteristics of a baby elephant.

Across the years, a few facts remain clear:

1. In spring of 1974 traditional enrollments at Mundelein College were seriously dwindling. (In 1964 Mundelein boasted 1,167 full-time undergraduate students; in 1974 there were 740.) Whatever the reasons for this precipitous decline (that's another country!), the college had to find a new population or close its doors.

2. The notion of a Weekend College in Residence was fresh, original, and enormously attractive.

3. There was a small nucleus of creative faculty willing to take the plunge—to spend (unpaid) a summer of ten-hour days designing the curriculum, recruiting the students, and planning the initial courses so that the WEC could be launched the following fall.

4. The college president and the board of trustees were willing to grant us limited seed money to launch the project.

5. We had a prize-winning New York advertising firm eager to take the plunge with us and back us all the way.

As a matter of fact, it was from Jane Trahey (then president of Trahey Advertising and a Mundelein College trustee) that I first heard the words "weekend college." It would prove to be the most spectacular of her innumerable gifts to Mundelein.

It was a May evening. I was at my desk in the Learning Resource Center (locally termed "the Lurk") when my phone rang. It was Jane. She had just left a trustees' meeting at Seton Junior College in New Jersey. They were trying something new, she said—offering classes on the weekend. No special program, just an effort to accommodate working students, primarily nurses. "It's an interesting idea," she mused, "a weekend college."

When I put down the phone, I felt like a character in a cartoon strip with an electric lightbulb glowing in my mind: Mundelein's Weekend College had just been conceived! As a former dean, I knew that bringing it to an early, if not premature, birth would be a tricky business. But for us, the *Titanic* was listing. Speed was imperative.

If this idea were to have a chance at all, it couldn't go through the tortuous business of curriculum committees and faculty debate. It would have to be seen as an experimental concept—one that could bypass the usual byzantine decision making of academia and (with approval of the trustees) go into action the following September. How to get such a notion into the academic consciousness?

My chance came the following Thursday when Dean Susan Rink, B.V.M., challenged the faculty to come up with some new ideas to expand admissions. Two or three ideas surfaced. I suggested a weekend college experiment. Susan was game. "Anyone interested in exploring that one, see Mary Griffin after we adjourn."

Outside my office there gathered a small group of intrigued faculty. I took one glance and relaxed. They comprised what I privately thought were some of the most original and successful teachers in the college. And the range of experience was great. Recently appointed to the philosophy department, Dan Vaillancourt was the youngest. David Orr (presently in his third term as Cook County clerk) was a popular young teacher of history. Mary DeCock (then chair of the graduate program in religious studies) was a shrewd faculty leader and sought-after teacher. Bill Hill was a seasoned popular instructor in religious studies whose courses on the Holocaust had gained him a wide following. (He would go on to become the first and enormously successful director of the Weekend College in Residence when it was launched the following September.) No one ever imagined that this would prove to be the most original and enduring program the college would launch since its own inception.

Once the board of trustees gave this group the go-ahead, we formed ourselves into a planning committee and launched into one of the most strenuous and productive summers of our lives. Ten-hour days were de rigueur. I remember standing at the corner of Winthrop and Loyola one July night arguing heatedly with Dan, Bill, and Mary DeCock. It was nearing midnight and we were far from agreeing on how to structure the introductory course we all

The faculty team that designed the Weekend College in Residence program
included (left to right) Mary DeCock, B.V.M., Daniel Vaillancourt,
Mary Griffin, William Hill, and David Orr.

agreed every entering student would have to take. "Ok," Bill said, as he and
Dan backed off. "You two design it. We'll critique it."

In the long run, it turned out to be the cornerstone of the WEC Strategies
for Learning—the required first course for all entering students. Everyone had
a hand in designing it. And everyone had a chance to teach in this unique first
course that launched every student who entered the WEC. The first students
were all ninety-eight registrants who made up the charter class. Eventually,
Strategies held two hundred entering students and enlisted eighteen faculty
people! It was unique to Mundelein and probably one of the most satisfying
(if demanding) teaching experiences any of us ever had.

Why this required course? Because of the broad diversity of students we
were confronting. We had planned to start with a modest pilot group of thirty-
five students. But the response to the Trahey advertising campaign in the *Chicago
Sun-Times* was so overwhelming that we upped the figure to one hundred.

Were they carefully selected? Indeed. Applicants had to be at least twenty-
six years old—men or women. They had to submit academic resumes and to
undergo a screening interview with Bill Hill. It was thus that we found our

new student body. For the most part, they came from the business world—
every layer of it. They were sales managers, postal workers, real-estate brokers,
accountants, company vice presidents, company secretaries. We even had a
miner who commuted from Pittsburgh who was determined to go to law
school and had to finish his degree.

We found that WEC candidates came from Indiana and Wisconsin as
well as Illinois and Pennsylvania. Madeline Kennelly flew in from Glendale,
California, every third weekend and kept her interior-design clients happy
between times. Whatever their origins or work patterns, they had one goal in
common—they wanted a college degree. Weekend College was the first viable
alternative to a debilitating night-school routine. They said frankly that they
just couldn't hack nine years of night classes.

A lot of these students were married. It was tough getting to class MWF
nights from 7:00 P.M.–10:00 P.M. Some held down executive jobs. They had to
travel. Their travel plans sometimes were hostage to unscheduled meetings.
They felt that they were in a pressure cooker. Planning around a weekend
schedule that tied up only five out of thirteen weekends looked like a god-
send. The weekend format not only left them time for their work lives. It gave
them time for their families.

From the point of view of faculty, the easing of time constraints was perhaps
just as attractive—and for many of the same reasons. But one major reason
proved to be that the WEC format actually made for enthusiasm about learning! True—the new time structure meant that every single class meeting had
to be redesigned. (Who can give, let alone sit through, three hours of lecture?)
WEC led to the most interactive teaching any of us had ever engaged in. It
meant that you could assign the whole of *Mrs. Dalloway*, not just the first
chapter! Because most classes met at two- or three-weekend intervals, there
was real time in between to do the heavy reading most college courses demand.

Moreover, this was a Weekend College in Residence. Once a class was
over, there was time to grab a beer or a coffee and hash it all over with fellow
classmates and/or instructors before you wandered up to your dorm room.
(One married student admitted that her husband was a bit envious as she
packed her weekend bag for a stint on campus. And she admitted, "I sometimes feel like I'm heading for a weekend with a lover!")

Whatever the circumstances of their various lives, WEC students claimed
that learning was not just a weekend affair. It was a whole new intellectual and
social experience. On any given weekend, about one third of the students were
staying on campus and reveling in a library that stayed open until midnight.

Juanita Shepherd, mother of three, gave the credit to her husband. "He gives me the entire weekend to study, to write papers, to have a pizza with my pals on campus. I've already had two job promotions. Mundelein's Weekend College has changed my life."

Carmen Springate stressed the intellectual stimulation. She moaned that she was about to graduate and couldn't think what she'd do with herself. "I'm already looking around for a graduate program. [Weekend College is] the perfect solution for people with careers."

But before we had graduates, we had applicants. And evaluating academic credits was essential. Some had never gone beyond high school. Many had finished thirty to sixty hours of college work. A few were close to completing degree requirements. A handful were eligible for "life experience credit." (Carl Hirsch brought in an armload of prize-winning novels for young readers he had published over the years. He got the equivalent of English Comp II. Actually, he could have taught the course!)

And before we had any applicants at all, we had to break the news to Chicagoland that we were launching a brand-new experimental college. Mundelein wasn't without experience in this regard. Back in the 1960s Norb Hruby had brought to campus one of the first continuing-education programs for adult women. Esther Rauschenbush did it first at Sarah Lawrence. Mundelein stood on those shoulders and designed its own version here. Most of us had taught in the program and had learned something about teaching adults.

But the problems facing the WEC planning committee were unique. First, it was to be coed. Second, the age range would be far broader. Third, we had to design a brand-new curriculum, one that would reflect the liberal-arts commitment of the college but not duplicate the entire range of traditional majors. It was clear that the program would have to be interdisciplinary and frequently team taught.

Through June and July, we divided up the jobs and worked against what often seemed an impossible deadline. Trahey Advertising launched an eye-stopping print campaign in Chicago's *Tribune* and *Sun-Times* newspapers, along with large-scale posters at the El stops and outside Coffey Hall. Radio talk shows featured whomever was available. The trustees came up with startup funds. We set up phone banks to reach personnel directors in Chicago businesses and learned to our immense satisfaction that lots of corporations had already established tuition-reimbursement programs for employees who wanted to go back to school. Bill Hill's phone began to ring. And admission interviews were underway.

At night we routinely shaped ourselves into a think tank and worked out the details of the curriculum. We looked at who our prospective students were and tried to design a curriculum relevant to their lives: personal lives, work lives, lives as Chicago citizens. We came up with three interdisciplinary areas of general studies and labeled them

- Personal Universe—courses in humanities: philosophy, literature, languages, theology, history, science (nonlab)

- Community Life—courses in social sciences: sociology, history, psychology, economics

- Business World—courses in economics, mathematics, accounting, finance, marketing

To enable students to move skillfully among these areas were courses in communication skills: writing, analytical-critical reading, research skills. Faculty who had long taught these courses in the daytime program were encouraged to rethink them and redesign them for adult students. There wasn't a rush to fill these slots. No one was eager to teach on weekends along with regular weekday courses. There was, in fact, a good deal of criticism from faculty who claimed it wasn't possible to cover a semester of course work in five three-hour time slots. The lack of enthusiasm for weekend teaching was a major hurdle. I remember discussing this problem with Gerda Lerner, founder of the women's studies program at Sarah Lawrence and one of a series of lecturers Jane Trahey sponsored to launch the Weekend College. "Don't worry about it," she told us. "When weekday courses are getting thin and they're looking for majors, those faculty people will be coming to you!" she prophesied.

And she was right. Those who scoffed did eventually come to stay! The problem was that they wanted to bring their traditional majors right along with them. They found a new audience and found them so challenging that they redesigned their majors to fit them. So the single WEC curriculum was eventually eroded. For WEC students turned out to have a hankering for majors that would get them into graduate school. And they wanted a graduate program in liberal studies that would lead to a respectable master's degree in liberal studies. (By 1983 the Mundelein Master of Liberal Studies program had been designed and successfully launched. It was the second such program after the Johns Hopkins program in Baltimore. Today, it is available at most of the top universities across the country.)

But if departmental pressures eventually displaced the original three interdisciplinary majors, other innovations survived and continued to enrich weekend learning:

- Blocks of time for course meetings—e.g., two-and-one-half- or three-and-one-half-hour time slots on Friday nights and on Saturdays and Sundays

- Advance assignments mailed out to incoming students and grace periods at end of term to allow for completion of long papers/projects

- Independent-study options for students whose work lives took them out of town for extended periods

- Dialogical styles of teaching to engage adult interactive learning

- Telephone consultations to replace office hours (today, we have the boon of e-mail!)

- Recognition of life experience credit as a valid substitute for formal course work

- Saturday office hours for registrar, bursar, dean, advisors, et al.

- Scholarships and financial aid to the full ability of the college as a supplement to tuition reimbursement plans

Teaching WEC courses is unquestionably demanding. Faculty quickly discover that there's no way you can lecture successfully for two and one-half hours! There has to be real variety: in-class discussion, use of graphic materials, student presentations/critiques of papers, guest lecturers, etc. Yet time is of the essence. One can't dictate assignments. These have to be photocopied and handed out or mailed out. Papers must be ready, graded, and returned at the following class meeting if not sooner. When you have only five meetings, every minute counts. There's no question that teaching in the Weekend College was brisk, superbly well-prepared, and demanding. And the feedback was stimulating! There's something about teaching child psychology to a group of young parents!

When T. S. Eliot was establishing himself as a poet in London back in the 1920s, he held down a full-time job in a bank to support himself and his young wife. He had tried teaching in a boys' prep school but gave it up after one semester. He said he couldn't stand beating history into the heads of fourteen year olds! But just then the Workman's Education Bill was passed. It covered courses for adults. In a two-year stint, Eliot took his students from Beowulf to TSE! He taught every Monday night from 6:30 to 9:00. (And Vivienne complained that he spent all day Saturday and Sunday preparing his lecture!) Eliot said that nothing in his experience at Harvard had ever been so stimulating, so satisfying. These working adults, he wrote, were the most intensely interested, highly motivated students he had met in his lifetime. Those of us lucky enough to teach in the Weekend College knew that Mundelein's adult students were blood brothers and sisters to Eliot's!

David Orr was careful to point out that some of our prospective students might be shy about returning to college since their last formal education some ten or even thirty years earlier. He stressed the need for community building among students. (Eventually, dorm living and Saturday-night conversations at the local pubs on Broadway met this need beyond our concerns!)

Mary argued successfully for the need of a common introductory academic experience, as well. To this end, we created Strategies for Learning— the one required course all students took and all instructors taught. It proved to be the glue that bound us all together and launched WEC students into their respective major concentrations.

Strategies for Learning was designed as a team-taught orientation course for adults returning to college. Its primary goal was to prime them for independent learning. The so-called banking concept of education was dead (the teacher deposits, the student withdraws). Today, computer skills would head the list. At the time, it included

- Reflective Learning (autobiographical writing)
- Reading Skills (Mortimer Adler's *How to Read a Book*)
- Research Skills (developing a hypothesis and a thesis, collecting evidence, using the library, etc.)
- Critical Skills (writing analytical/critical essays)
- Creative Response (reacting to music, photography, art, etc.)

What we had intuitively stumbled on was a common educational philosophy shared by faculty (there to stimulate, prod) and students (there to learn actively).

The key to the success of Strategies was that this common introductory course was a course about how we learn. It was taken by all entering students and team taught by all faculty. Within two years there came an opening night in the fall semester when 270 new students expectantly faced twenty WEC faculty members in Galvin Hall. It was the teaching experience of a lifetime! Before the evening was over, everyone had done an initial skimming of Freud's *Civilization and Its Discontents* (a la Adler) and gone off in twos and threes to the library, the dorm, or the local pub to hash out their reactions. The following Sunday morning when we reassembled, there would be an in-depth discussion of the book as a whole (presumably read in toto)! This was a far cry from dragging out a discussion in MWF fifty-minute periods. It is exhilarating to deal with a writer's work as a whole—for teachers as well as students.

I think now that the success of Strategies was that this common first course was a course about learning. (Initially, students all took a learning-skills test and discovered their own learning orientation. That initial discovery was an eye opener. We all have learning proclivities. But we need to master styles that don't come naturally.) The philosophy of education underlying Strategies set the pattern for all WEC courses. They were designed to be experience-based, egalitarian, and interactive, with lecture kept to a minimum.

It seems to me now that, without labeling it as such, we had developed a feminist model of learning. It assumed that everyone who can profit from it has a right to an education, everyone has a right to a schedule that offers classes when students are free to attend, and everyone has a right to a residential experience with their fellow students.

Thus was Mundelein's Weekend College in Residence. It was the teaching experience of a lifetime!

We weren't the first to put college courses on the weekend. C. W. Post College on Long Island gets that credit. And Seton Junior College in New Jersey was experimenting with weekend courses for nurses. Much later we learned that the University of Houston was routinely scheduling class meetings on the weekend. But Mundelein was the first to design a new interdisciplinary program radically different in content and format from its traditional undergraduate program—residential in intent and directed by a separate faculty with the authority to custom-tailor its curriculum, course requirements, and degree specifications. What we came up with was a college within a college, truly experimental and self-regulating. Its goal was to meet the unique needs of a rapidly growing segment of college students—working adults, both men and women who, for one reason for another, had never finished college but couldn't face a lifetime of night classes. Our survey indicated that there was an intellectual curiosity out there. And that intellectual hunger deserved a second chance. Today, so many college and universities offer weekend programs on the undergraduate and graduate levels that they no longer seem novel. Back in 1974, it was a brand-new idea.

It turned out to be the most cost-effective undergraduate degree we could hope for. And it used everything its innovative faculty had learned since Norb

Hruby had created the Adult Degree Program for Women back in 1965. It had the support of a courageous (or desperate?) college president, Ann Ida Gannon, B.V.M., to give us the go-ahead, and an encouraging board of trustees to hand us a $10,000 startup fund. Neither was to be disappointed.

Someone once likened changing a college curriculum to digging up a graveyard. We were lucky. We had nothing to change; we had everything to create! And we went about it quite pragmatically . . .

[The above essay is the unfinished first draft of Mary Griffin's memoir for this publication.]

The College on the Curve, 1967–1997

Michael Fortune

In 1967 I decided, after almost two decades of teaching at a university in north-central Wisconsin, that it was time to travel. This was not to be a little trip, but a voyage of no return. The northern Midwest winters had taken their toll on my psyche, which threatened to leave me. I drew a red line across the thirty-fifth parallel, which served as the northern limits of my focal point. Having grown up close to the Atlantic Ocean, I decided to give preference to a community on either seaboard. I enrolled at the placement bureau at the University of Wisconsin and waited to see if some school in an ocean-bordering community with a mild climate would be interested. Before long, listings of interested schools appeared weekly in my mailbox. One such university in Southern California seemed to fit the bill. I contacted the school and was interviewed at the Modern Language Association convention. I was offered a contract and decided to accept the position. Surprised at how smoothly it all went, I began preparing for my northern exodus when I hit a snag that I hadn't expected.

My daughters, who had gone along with the idea, decided they wanted to finish school in Wisconsin before leaving. This would mean that I'd see them only at Christmas and Easter, which I could not imagine doing. I decided to postpone any move until my daughters graduated, when there arrived an inquiry from Mundelein College. While it was neither in a warm area nor on either coast, it was in Chicago, the home of the Art Institute, Chicago Symphony Orchestra, and Civic Opera, which would help compensate for the rigors of winter. Another compensation was its location on the coast of the largest inland sea (a.k.a. the Great Lakes) in the world. And, most important, I could make it home in just over four hours. But what kind of school was it?

I had shared my curiosity about Mundelein with a few colleagues, one of whom showed me an article in Columbia University's magazine, *Columbia Today*, listing the top three Catholic institutions of higher education, one of which was Mundelein. Michael Novak, the Catholic theologian, with whom I had dinner a few evenings later, described it as one of the most exciting schools he had ever visited. He added that his sister was a student there. I contacted the school and arranged for an interview when my mounting interest dissolved upon learning that it was not only a women's college but that it

were an adjunct member of a spiritual order. Was this, I wondered, what Paul described as the "something special" about the school?

Although the campus was limited in size, there was nothing parochial about Mundelein. I often wondered what the thousands of motorists who passed the school every day thought about this little women's college. Were they aware of the internationally renowned scholars, theologians, artists, writers, and politicians who addressed students and faculty in McCormick Lounge? Several years later, the artist Ivan Albright, to whom we gave an honorary degree, said to me, "I never realized all the great things that go on in this place." One event that caught my attention was an internal film festival sponsored by the French department. Sister Mary St. Irene Branchaud, B.V.M., chairperson of the department, had brochures on each film and its history, cast, and director available at the door. Discussions of each film were conducted after its showing. Word spread around Rogers Park, and scores of outsiders attended the event, featuring the works of Bergman, Fellini, Kurosawa, Truffaut, Visconti, Antonioni, Eisenstein, Pudovkin, Rhomer, Satyajit Ray, and other directors who would never be shown at the Granada, a nearby movie theater.

Another reason militated against parochialism: the B.V.M.'s had been following closely the events in Rome. In response to the Second Vatican Council, they began to redefine what it meant to be a nun. Questions of identity led to a reassessment of the role of "religious" life in every respect, including the wearing of the traditional habit. Both faculty and sister students were asking themselves whether they would be of greater use to humanity outside the order. This had a profound effect on me. I had never met any group of humans who had so sincere a dedication to their purpose and the courage to change if their assessment of that purpose dictated one. I thought of Saints Teresa of Ávila, Hildegard of Bingen, and Mother Theresa Benedicta (nee Edith Stein), who made similar decisions. My view of sisters changed dramatically as I listened to several who shared their concerns with me and later told me that they decided to leave the order. I became sensitive to the offensive attitude of the lay world toward nuns and was especially appalled by Hollywood's portrayal of sisters. Was I any different, I asked myself, just a few months earlier?

The classes I had taught prior to coming to Mundelein were for the most part male oriented. It made little difference if women outnumbered the men. The texts were written by males, anthologies were arranged primarily by males, and I, the instructor, was a male. How would they feel about a male instructor when the majority of their education had been provided by nuns and laywomen? What kind of focus would an all-female class adopt? I was sensitive to these issues as I entered my first class. To my surprise, the students accepted me immediately. I left the first meeting impressed with the level of interest the students showed and looked forward to an exciting term. There was a slight detour that I did not anticipate, due to what I later realized was based on a sexist attitude toward the student body.

In my classes at a coeducational institution, I was invariably asked by one or two males about the relevance to their professional future of my course in Greco-Roman literature. The typical question was, "What does Homer's *Iliad* have to do with engineering?" or "Since I'm going to be a doctor [or lawyer, etc.], why should I have to read the *Aeneid*?" Now, I figured, because my classes consisted of women only, I would not be forced to justify the course or a specific selection. I assumed that the students would either enter teaching or get married. I was wrong.

At the beginning of the second meeting a scholastic said she had read the assignment and concluded that nothing could be more irrelevant than the *Iliad* in a world of global suffering. She did acknowledge the satisfaction of reading Homer's epic at one's leisure, but that leisure was a luxury we could least afford in a world crying out for justice, peace, and understanding. Her question had nothing to do with a career; it required a moral, not economic, justification for the course. I was delighted by the question, for it would lead directly to the core of Homer's great poem. I asked her to ask the same question of the author. She provided a focus for the entire class. Collectively, we observed Homer exploring issues of honor, violence, society, and personal commitment. We followed carefully the Greeks debating the rationale of continuing a war in which their honor was at stake. At the time America was exploring the possible negotiation of an honorable withdrawal from Vietnam. Questions dealing with the general disapproval of Agamemnon as a person with a respect for the office he held paralleled similar questions regarding Richard Nixon. Literary style was not ignored, for in order to understand the time of Homer beyond the range of war, we paid special attention to the epic similes and such symbols as the shield of Achilles to see the parallels between that world and ours. Several students regretted leaving the *Iliad* to go to the next selection.

It wasn't long before I realized the class was not unusual for Mundelein. I witnessed the same seriousness in the two other classes I taught that term. Nearly every student came to my office to discuss other texts they might read to supplement the required books and class discussions. Three students asked whether they could come to my office to discuss authors not included in a given course. One student asked whether I would be willing to discuss with her a list of Russian writers that she compiled that paralleled another course she was taking. She later attended the University of Wisconsin as a Woodrow Wilson fellow.

Before long, crocuses and jonquils popped up around Coffey Hall to inform me that I had made it through that winter. I was stunned by how oblivious I had become to the waning cold. I was going through a period of self-discovery. I always believed I was totally free of any bias regarding race, gender, or religious conviction. The surprise I felt over the positive experiences I had at this college led me to question that belief. I realized that I had anticipated less and, I concluded, that I expected less because my students were women. I didn't want to accept this. Some of my best students at the university were women, so why should I be surprised at the high level of student performance at Mundelein? Further reflection led me to recall an incident that occurred before I came to Mundelein.

Sometime in the 1950s a book was published on marriage in which the author suggested that because college graduates earned three times that of high school graduates, a college was a good place for women in search of husbands. While recognizing some validity in that statement, I believed that the primary purpose of most of the women I met was to get an education. There were several who married before graduation; in some of these cases, the woman left school to support her husband's education.

I recall one exceptionally bright woman at the university who dropped out to work in the registrar's office and support her husband. I had him in two classes in which he struggled to perform on an adequate level. I occasionally ran into her in the library and found her doing work in the area of her husband's concentration. His grades improved dramatically. Obviously, her husband was her top priority. This, I reasoned, could not happen at Mundelein where future husbands were not available. A Mundelein student would never allow anything, or anyone, to get between her and the degree she sought. I concluded that the presence of men, if they were permitted to attend classes, would have no effect. In the winter of 1969 I was forced to revise my thinking.

That year Mundelein entered an agreement with Loyola University Chicago to permit its students to take six credits from the other institution. Four men entered my class in medieval and Renaissance literature. I welcomed what I assumed would be a more "normal" situation in which men and women would coexist as they do in the "real" world. The first two sessions were dominated by the males. They didn't deliberately take over the discussions; the women merely sat quietly and made no attempt to speak as they had previously. The third session was a repetition of the first two, even though two of the men drew erroneous conclusions from the material we read. I asked a few of the women to remain after class.

"What's going on?" I asked. None of the women spoke. "You have ceased speaking. Why?" They said nothing. "If one of you had made some of the statements I heard in this class, you would have annihilated her. It surely can't be the presence of men."

"Of course it is," said one of the most brilliant students I have ever taught.

"But I'm a man. You wouldn't have accepted those comments from me."

"You're the teacher," she said.

I began calling on several women during class sessions and eventually the women held their own. It wasn't my intent to favor one gender over the other, but rather to provide the opportunity for each to complement the other and develop mutual respect. I felt relief in believing that the class now reflected the real world. Yet I was unable to dismiss the incident from my mind. Did women really yield to men in discussions of ideas? I found myself eavesdropping on couples in sundry places and before long realized that the students were invariably correct. It never was a direct confrontation between the two sexes; no difference was openly admitted.

I concluded that among most couples, regardless of the social level, a subtle understanding of the subordinate role of women lay at the base of their relationships.

This was especially evident one evening as I was leaving a theater. Two men who were walking beside me seemed to be having an argument about the film we had just seen. Having paid little attention to them, I had no idea of the source of their disagreement. Finally, one of the men became angry and said derisively, "You think like a woman!" I said nothing, but I wanted to invite him to any one of my classes to learn how a woman thinks. As I drove home I became increasingly angry, mostly with myself for being oblivious to the truth. I recalled a colleague once saying, "Heaven protect me from an intellectual woman."

Other similar statements or events from the past came to mind. The truth was there all the time. Had I been too dense to see it? I considered myself totally devoid of any sexual bias. At no time would I ever have endorsed my colleague's view. I forget my response; I probably shrugged it off. Because of my experience with the students and nuns at Mundelein, I would have taken issue with him. I had grown to care deeply for these remarkable women and could only imagine the pain they experienced in not being as accepted as their male counterparts. I realized how cheated the fathers, brothers, and husbands were by the pressures that kept their wives, sisters, and mothers from revealing their true selves. I concluded that it was up to women to demand equal acceptance for the situation to change, and it was up to males to assist their efforts wherever possible. I resolved to combat sexism, in part by replacing texts with few or no women writers with paperback copies of writers of both sexes.

Many older women students were enrolled in the Degree Completion Program, created for those who postponed their education due to work, marriage, and family responsibilities. For the most part, these women attended seminars designed exclusively for them. I taught several of these classes and discovered a feeling of excitement exuded by these women, who were picking up pieces of their lives and sharing them with fellow students. The dramas of their own lives were often reflected in their perspectives on the works we studied in a class I taught on modern drama. I found a wisdom born of their contact with the real world.

One woman, who was forced by her lawyer husband to give up her children, wrote one of the best papers I ever read on the dilemma faced by Medea in Euripides' tragedy. When several of these women began taking courses with the younger students, a general tension could at times be felt as the older students unconsciously threatened to dominate class discussions. When this was brought into the open, the older students backed off a bit, and both groups grew to appreciate each other's perspective and the experiences from which they arose. A certain bonding resulted as both articulated the female experience from different ends of the spectrum. Often, the younger students began to understand their mothers, and older students their daughters, because of the exchanges of perspectives.

One morning, a woman in her early forties entered my office to inquire about the possibility of earning a degree in English. She had some reservations because of what she called her "advanced age." I assured her that age was no barrier, as we had several students much older than she.

"And a lot more who are less than half my age," she said with a broad smile. "Promise me you won't laugh if I told you I intend to enroll." I laughed. "That's not good for an old lady's morale." She laughed.

"I didn't intend to laugh. It's just the way you put it," I said.

"In spite of your discouraging response," she said, "I intend to enroll. After all," she added, "a woman's reach should exceed her grasp, or what's a heaven for?"

"Nice line," I said.

"Browning liked it when he first heard it," she said.

"Browning who?" I asked.

"Oh, you're funny. I suppose you need a sense of humor to chair an English department. Is that your real name? Fortune?"

"It is."

"That's a good omen."

"Why?"

"Better than the misfortune of being told I couldn't get my degree. I definitely came to the right place. Oh, by the way. Call me 'Duckie.' Why are you laughing?"

"I'm sorry. I've never met a Duckie."

"Well, you have now. And you're not likely to forget her. Am I bold or what?"

Duckie Matthews explained that her name was given to her by children with whom she worked. She had dropped out of college to support her husband while he worked on his undergraduate degree and went on to graduate from law school. She worked as a retailer before she wrote several plays for children. She was now on the staff at WTTW, a PBS station in Chicago, where she produced and directed some of her work with children. After reviewing her work, I told her she would be able to earn a major in English and graduate within two years. She was thrilled and informed me she would take a year of education courses to attain her ultimate goal in life: teaching in the primary grades.

"I told my kids that one day I'll have my own students who will be like eggs, and Duckie will watch them hatch before her eyes. They decided that we'd call my class Hatch Heaven, and when they grow up they'll send their kids there so I can watch them hatch." I imagined the fun she had with children. She had no children of her own. Her husband convinced her to wait for a family until he was established in a profession. Before leaving my office, she paused at the door and asked, "Did you ever feel that you had just turned a corner?"

"Yes," I answered. "In fact, just recently when I came to this place." She nodded with a smile and left.

Duckie did well that term. She was popular, especially with the younger students with whom she would invariably be seen in the cafeteria. Her laughter was infectious. She did not appear for registration for the following term and finally came to my office to announce she was turning another corner. She explained that her husband was being transferred to Italy and that she was again forced to put her education on hold. She would be out of the country for at least five years and expressed excitement at having found a position teaching English in Italy.

That was in the spring of 1972, prior to my taking a sabbatical for two years. I returned in the fall of 1974, when one afternoon I heard a voice call out, "My God, it's you!" It was Duckie. I noticed her step was a bit slower than I had remembered it as she approached me. We went to the cafeteria, where over a cup of coffee I asked whether she had turned the corner. "My husband did," she answered. "The bloke met a younger woman." When I expressed my sadness, she said, "I look at it this way. Hatch Heaven is just around the corner."

I saw her regularly. She got her job back with the children's theater. Each time I met her, she shared a new comic anecdote involving her children. Her laughter was as loud as ever, but if one looked closely, her eyes had lost a bit of their sparkle. Obviously, I thought, it would take her much longer than she expected to get over the shock of what had occurred in Italy. She registered that summer to complete her major and enrolled in student teaching for the fall. I suggested that she slow down and take one course. "I don't have the time, my dear," she said.

"You have plenty of time," I assured her. "According to Browning, 'The year's at the spring, the day's at the morn.'"

"Browning who?" she asked. We laughed. She wished me a happy summer. "I'll see you when you get back."

When I returned, I noticed her name was not listed among those of my advisees. I went to the registrar's office and asked Sister Frances Shea if the error could be corrected. There was no error, she informed me. Duckie had died of uterine cancer in early August. Noticing my inability to continue the conversation, she added, "Duckie never expected to return."

"Then, why did she sign up for two courses?" I asked. "Had she rested over the summer, she might still be with us."

"She should have died eight months earlier," said Frances. "School is what probably kept her going."

"And I told her she looked tired. Why didn't she say something?"

"She told me she didn't have the heart."

Duckie had the heart. And the mind. And the soul that touched everyone who came her way. She never got her classroom, but she taught me much about being overcome but never defeated.

I shake my head and smile when I recall a comment made by one of my colleagues at the university just prior to my coming to Mundelein. "I'll tell you what Mundelein is," he said. "It's a finishing school for young women."

Nothing ever seemed finished at that college. Faculty and students were constantly changing to meet the challenges that came from Vatican II and the turmoil of the 1960s and 1970s without diminishing the quality of the curriculum. The reality of war was brought to our doorstep with the murder of several nuns in Central America. Speakers, a few of whom were denied a hearing on other campuses, appeared in the McCormick Lounge to discuss national and international issues. Mandala, an experimental college, was set up to explore alternative modes for learning and offer a degree. Individual lives changed. Many B.V.M.'s left to explore other avenues for serving the universe. Sister Mary Ignatia left the order and went south to teach at a black college in Mississippi for three years. One faculty member, David Orr, was elected to the Chicago City Council with the support of many students and faculty and was largely responsible for the present code of ethics eventually adopted by the council.

The college introduced a variety of new programs, including the topical major, and liberal studies. One student just out of high school requested a major in gerontology. At the time there was no major in gerontology, so she entered Mundelein to pursue that goal under the auspices of liberal studies. By combining courses from the departments of science, literature, and social studies, the school was able to create a concentration for her. She is now one of the leading gerontologists in the nation.

A Japanese American youth, who was a member of that first class of men I taught, pursued a liberal studies major with a concentration in playwriting. He went on to win honors at the Yale School of Drama and eventually win an Emmy for a drama he wrote. He went on to serve as story editor and producer for an award-winning television series.

Mundelein went on to establish one of the first weekend colleges in the nation along with a graduate program in Christian spirituality and a master of arts in liberal studies. All of these were instrumental in Mundelein being designated almost annually as one of the top ten colleges of its class in the nation.

It was hardly a finishing school.

When I took that sabbatical back in 1972, I returned to the University of Wisconsin, Stevens Point to chair the department of foreign languages and establish a program in comparative literature. A teacher of Russian, who had just arrived from the University of Oklahoma, had few students in his classes, two of which were canceled. He asked how he could become better known and begin to build his program in Russian. I suggested that, along with offering public lectures on Russian culture and literature, he offer a course in the comparative literature department on one or more Russian writers. He showed me a syllabus of a course he taught in translation at Oklahoma.

That afternoon I advertised the course throughout the university. The following morning my phone rang constantly as several department chairpersons and members of the faculty senate accused me of subverting academic protocol. I was told the course had to be approved by the curriculum committee, the academic council, and, eventually, the board of regents, a procedure that would take at least two years. I removed the course and the teacher took on some administrative assignments until he became better known. I had no idea when that occurred. I didn't stay. I missed the spirit of people like Sister Therese Avila, B.V.M.

One afternoon in the spring of 1970, Sister Therese, chairperson of the Spanish department, stopped at the table where a member of the French department and I were having lunch. She said that she had just finished teaching *El burlador de Sevilla* and suggested that the three of us offer a course in Don Juan. As she elaborated on her idea, we began to think what each of us could bring to the course. Before we left the table, we agreed to teach the course. Eventually, we also involved the departments of music and psychology to discuss *Don Giovanni* and Don Juan, respectively, as archetype. My contribution was Byron's comic masterpiece *Don Juan* and Pushkin's *Eugene Onegin* in translation. The entire class attended the Lyric Opera's performance of Mozart's opera. The course was an outstanding success. This was the first of many team-taught courses in which I participated (Impressionism, Surrealism, Asian Art, and Film and Literature, to mention a few). When possible, we made use of the city's museums and music facilities.

I remained at Mundelein for thirty years. Geographical climate could never replace the intellectual climate I found at Mundelein. The friendship I established with several members of the faculty and student body provided me with greater warmth than I could ever find a thousand miles south of Chicago. It was that warmth which, born of a feminine energy, Paul Friedman and I detected the first day I set foot on the campus.

Recently, I drove by the campus and discovered that the city had expanded the curve that fronted the campus. The curve seemed to me to be the perfect metaphor for Mundelein. I thought of Duckie Matthews and her turning points. Mundelein has turned another corner and now serves as the school of adult learning for Loyola University Chicago. The school has come up with another innovative program for students age fifty-five and older called the Emeritus Connection in which I participate from time to time. I am certain there will be other turns as time warrants. As I drove past the two angels out in front of the main entrance and headed west along Devon Avenue, I recalled Paul Friedman's comment.

"There's something special about that school."

Mundelein College: Catholic Substance, Ecumenical Ethos, 1976–1991

Stephen A. Schmidt

"Dr. Schmidt, I think God sent you here."

It was a cold, windy, gray wintry day that January 15, 1976, when I first stepped on the campus of Mundelein College. I was on my way to teach an evening course for the Institute of Pastoral Studies at Loyola University Chicago, just north of Mundelein College. At the time, I was on a semester leave from Concordia Teachers College in River Forest, Illinois, a leave insisted upon by the president of that same institution. Concordia was in political and intellectual chaos. As a school of the Lutheran Church, Missouri Synod, the college experienced radical academic cleansing as part of the dramatic right-wing "takeover" of all fourteen Concordias throughout the United States.

I was at the center of the conflict at the River Forest Concordia and was viewed as the faculty leader and the most vocal critic. I spoke and wrote publicly against the blatant Biblicism and political fundamentalism of the new administration, never giving much thought to the serious implications of such behavior. I was removed as chairperson of the education department. My course books were under constant scrutiny; they were too filled with biblical criticism, too "liberal," too open to the whole world of historical scholarship. No longer could I preach in chapel, and false doctrine charges were filed against me with the board of control. The last attempt to silence my efforts at dissent was to offer me, with a clear administrative directive, a semester's leave, with the proviso that I neither publish nor speak publicly about affairs at Concordia during my time of academic exile. I agreed, thinking that my violent, hostile dreams about the president might diminish and that perhaps I might find some other teaching position while on leave.

So, that January evening I was on my way to my first class at the Institute of Pastoral Studies, Loyola University Chicago. Jerry O'Leary, the director of IPS, and I had studied together at Union Seminary and Columbia University in New York, and he knew of my difficult circumstances, so he offered me this interesting diversion. With a couple of hours on my hands before class time, I turned into the parking circle of Mundelein College. I had heard of Mundelein often, from Jerry and many other Catholic religious educators, and particularly about its strong program in religious education. It was common knowledge that Mundelein College had one of the finest religious-education media-library centers in the Chicago metropolitan area. So I ventured for the first time in my life onto this small but well-known college campus.

The building identification was clear, marking a wonderful stone mansion right on Lake Michigan's shore the "Mundelein Center for Religious Education." I walked quietly into a space quite unlike any I had experienced at Concordia, or for that matter at any other college or university. The floors were dark wood, the furniture gracious; the lights were dim, and the walls, lined with bookshelves, were all filled with books and religious-education curricular materials. One of the lamps appeared to be a Tiffany, and the massive staircase to the second floor led to a stunning stained-glass window, which also looked as though it had come from a Tiffany gallery. I walked slowly up to the second floor and found more books lining still more walls, as well as two large rooms that appeared to be classrooms. The setting was peaceful and the center empty. Apparently no classes were being held at this time, I had seen no one since entering the building. I slowly began to explore this marvelous collection.

While sitting on the floor, completely fixed on this ecumenical collection of materials, I suddenly felt a firm tap on my shoulder. "I am sorry. I don't think I know you, and I understand from Sister Rose, the receptionist, that you did not identify yourself when you entered. I suspect you are welcome here, but we do appreciate knowing who is browsing in the library." I turned to face a tall, thin, almost frail-looking woman with dark eyes fixed pointedly on my being. She smiled, but I felt I owed her an explanation as well as some kind of apology. I had not seen the receptionist, I told her, and I had never been on this campus before.

I explained that I was to teach that evening at IPS and had just dropped by to see the religious-education collection, which I had heard so much about from colleagues in the profession. I told her my name and something of my recent professional history—that I taught at Concordia, preparing teachers for Lutheran parishes; that my particular discipline was religious education, or practical theology; and that I was at a difficult juncture in my professional life. I showed her my faculty identification to assure her that I was truthful. She began to smile. "Well, I am Sister Carol Frances Jegen, the chairperson of graduate religious studies at Mundelein. My mother was a Lutheran until she married my father, and I have followed the recent press releases about the conflict within your church body, the Lutheran Church, Missouri Synod. Why don't you come into my office and tell me more about your school, your church, and your own teaching. Would you have time to do that?"

Of course I had time. And the experience was more like catharsis or confession than a careful rehearsal of the events in my own religious family of origin and ministry. My story was long and detailed. I explained the sectarian circumstances of Lutheranism in the United States at that time; I shared my anxiety and fear about my own teaching position; I told her that I had been searching for another teaching position for the past year, but had found none.

Sister Jegen listened while I talked about my fears, my anxiety about the future, my frustrations, my sadness, and my anger. Then she thoughtfully took off her glasses, looked me straight in the eye, smiled gently and said, "Dr. Schmidt, I think God sent you here." My response was halting, confused, a little amused, slightly embarrassed, and not a little uncomfortable. I knew few nuns, I knew little of the Catholic world, and I surely lacked any sense of ever knowing the immediate will of God in my life. In fact, I suspect I would have labeled such a sentiment, were it mine, "a theology of glory, not a theology of cross." Luther was suspicious of such direct unmediated knowing, and I was Lutheran! I didn't know what to say, so mumbled something like, "I'm sorry, what do you mean?"

She then asked if I knew that Mundelein was searching for a religious educator and that the school was in the last stages of that search but had not yet made a final decision. She was sure that I was the very person meant to fill that position. I knew nothing of the available position; I had heard nothing of the search. She asked, "Would you consider teaching young women in a Catholic women's college?" I stumbled and groped for a response. Yes, of course, I would consider such an offer; and yes, I liked women; and yes, perhaps this possibility was an answer to my prayers. All the while, I had a deep suspicion that this was some kind of unreal late wintry afternoon apparition. I didn't say much more. "Would you send me your CV tomorrow? And will you pray about this possibility, as I will?" She took my home phone number and address and walked me to the door of the center. She smiled and thanked me for a very interesting conversation. I walked into the darkness and to my class at Loyola. I can't remember anything about that particular class period.

When I arrived home late that night, my wife, "Gick" (Hildegarde), met me at the door and told me that I had received a phone call from some sister at Mundelein College, asking me to bring nine copies of my vita to Mundelein the next day. The sister had also asked if I would be able to stay a few hours for an interview with the religious studies department about a position in religious education. Gick had no idea of what had transpired. Nor had I!

Gick and I talked late into the night, wondering about the strange, mystical, unlikely, absolutely uncommon series of events. The next day I arrived early afternoon at Mundelein's Piper Hall, delivered my CV copies and spent the afternoon in the library reading until the meeting at 4:00 P.M. I entered a room of complete strangers, except for Sister Carol Frances. Most were women, but there were three men present as well. They proceeded to engage me with serious academic questions, with questions of faith, and with questions about my professional background. The conversation was animated. I thought I had little to lose, so I relaxed and brashly did my best to answer their queries, to ask my own, and then to leave with a strange sense of wonder and hope. I knew that academic positions were not acquired this way. I realized that in the complete unconventional nature of this strange series of events, I could hardly hope for such an offer. I slept fitfully.

The next morning, early, the phone rang. It was Sister Carol Frances Jegen and Sister Mary Donahey, respective chairpersons of the graduate and undergraduate religious studies departments. They called to inform me that the departments had reached a decision. They were offering me the position of associate professor in religious studies. My particular teaching emphasis would be in religious education and practical theology. I can't remember my exact words. But I told them that I was delighted, surprised, and that I would give "prayerful" consideration to their offer. I put the phone on the hook, called Gick and our children, and told them of the phone call. I didn't yet know whether God sent me to Mundelein. What I did know is that I would take the offer. I would teach in this "strange" small Catholic women's college, and I firmly believed that this acceptance was to be but the beginning of something deeply transforming in my life, my work, my theology, my family, and my person. Little did I realize how true those early sentiments were.

A Woman's World

If it was true that God sent me to Mundelein, then it follows that God surely must be a woman. I entered a whole new universe of meaning. I thought I knew something of women—I had been married for twenty years, had three daughters, and had taught both women and men for the past twenty years. But Mundelein was not the world I knew.

Here, all of my superiors were women: the department chairpersons, the dean, and the president. It was a new reality to work in a world where women were in control. Women were the leaders of the college, they were the founders, they were most of the teachers, and they were the significant colleagues. One did not engage them with charm, nor win arguments by tone of voice or volume. Here was a community of mutual discourse. Our department meetings took hours. I remember after my first year, I asked the department members if they ever voted on an issue. We had not that entire academic year. "No," they told me, "we seek consensus." Consensus takes time, especially among academics, and more particularly among the B.V.M. sisters. I had come with the misguided notion that sisters all thought the same, that they would never argue among themselves, and certainly would not do so in public. Instead, I found feisty, adversarial, strong-minded and strong-willed women who deliberated with passion, reason, and conviction. Consensus came slowly. Democracy was disarmingly difficult. On bad days I almost longed for one simple decision to be made by some dean or president. On those nights, I deserved and had terrible dreams, dreams of control and intimidation. I was back at Concordia. And the next day, I always rejoiced in my good fortune! Messy, long, difficult, and endless meetings. But we reached consensus.

These recollections are surely not documentable; they are I believe, still true. I remember often fearing my thoughts at Concordia. There, I wondered and worried about the wrong questions. I had experienced the humiliation of raising a "wrong question" a time or two and bore the internalized fear of sometimes risking my convictions. Here, at Mundelein, there was no wrong question. The typical response, both emotional and intellectual, was an encouragement to explore the question.

My world of biases turned upside down. I had always thought Catholics were doctrinaire, that they were of one mind, that there was a dogmatic and doctrinal unity that was as legalistic as my own tradition. Here, I experienced a Catholic substance of openness and inquiry. Here, women deeply committed to the Catholic faith questioned every aspect of that same tradition. Here, I learned something of the universality and diversity of what it meant to be "catholic." And, here, I experienced a freedom of thought, a vibrant intellectual debate about all things Catholic and most things patriarchal.

Here, I learned to know my first intellectual stirrings of feminist thought. Many of my courses were team taught with my female colleagues. Gifted feminist colleagues confronted me daily, monthly, and, finally, yearly. And I was challenged and changed. Whether I ever really understood, or whether I really "got it," is not a judgment I can make. What I did understand was a profound new experience of relationships with colleagues. Women here talked the talk and walked the walk.

Relationality was the way we experienced collegiality. Talk was the way to meaning and understanding. And conflict was the sure sign of truthful conversation. Endless meetings, endless talk, endless questions, endless debates, and endless interaction. No voice was silenced. No person was made to feel less human than any other because of opinion or training. Here, honest academic relationships were the analogue of academic freedom.

Yes, there were times of discomfort. Certainly, there were times I felt threatened, but only by ideas, not by administrative dictum. The man's world was always in question, and I came slowly to appreciate the question, and less and less to feel guilty about being a man. I, too, had experienced the same patriarchal reality. And gradually I began to know the full meaning of self-criticism and gender honesty. Again, I am not a good judge of my personal changes. My wife and daughters continue to tell me I've only begun to understand, and they regret that Mundelein is not still part of my ongoing world of being. I understand a little of their meaning. A woman's world is not the totality of the real world, but for a time—a small, historical, brief moment—Mundelein College in Chicago was the real world: a world of promise, of hope, of equality, of freedom of thought, of affirming the wholeness of all of the experience of being human. I will not forget that time.

On Being Lutheran in a Catholic World

Paul Tillich, a contemporary neo-Lutheran, distinguishes between Roman Catholicism and classical Protestantism on the basis of what he calls the Protestant principle. Essentially, Tillich argues that the distinctiveness of Protestant theology is that it is "against the identification of our ultimate concern with any creation of the church, including the biblical writings."[1] So there is within Protestantism a self/institutional critical process that engages all religious language, concepts, practices, dogma, doctrine, theology, as well as rules and ritual. To be true to Protestantism is to be prophetic.

There is however a second theological principal of equal importance for Protestantism, according to Tillich. That is the ideal of Catholic substance. Whatever metaphor one chooses—tradition, doctrine, dogma, canon law, liturgy, sacramentality, credal confessions—all these are the "substance" of any form of Christianity. There is a spiritual content to the faith, and that content ("presence" according to Tillich), remains fairly secure in Roman Catholicism. Though Protestants are critical of much of the hierarchical structure of the

Roman church, most agree that there is a continuity of "substance" to the Catholic tradition: "The concrete embodiment of the spiritual presence."[2]

When I began to teach at Mundelein, I brought with me these Protestant biases. I expected to experience a monolithic theological tradition. I thought there would be little theological disagreement among my Catholic colleagues. I was initially scrupulous about my course preparation and cautious about exercising my Protestant principle. Words of criticism were rare, my language was cautious, and usually my critical words were nuanced by introductory words of apology. Perhaps I did not understand, or maybe I was incorrect. I muted my Protestant principle and exalted the Catholic substance of Roman Catholicism, illustrating current trends in my own Lutheran tradition, which pointed to a renewal of "substance," especially around the spiritual reality of liturgy, sacramental theology, and biblical studies.

What I learned in my early years at Mundelein was something about the "Protestant principle" of my Catholic colleagues and the diversity and theological debate about the "substance" of Catholicism. I found my religious studies colleagues deeply divided about matters theological. I was soon to learn something of the energy and passion of Catholic feminist theology and its radical critique of the church, particularly around matters of ecclesiastical control and male dominance. The entire "substance" of the tradition was under critical question. And my Catholic peers were hardly cautious about their opinions.

I thought, before I taught at Mundelein, that surely the sisters would represent a common view, theologically and in matters of the tradition. Yet my religious colleagues enjoined the most heated debates in the religious studies department. Here, Catholic women scholars were critical of each other and unabashed about their disagreement. Here, the principle I thought I brought to Mundelein was practiced with far more integrity than within my own Lutheran tradition. Here, everything seemed turned on end. I found myself caught off guard by the diversity and the "Protestant" style of Catholic theological conversation. Here was a place where any question was received. Here was a community of academic freedom that I had not experienced in my own tradition. Here, there was serious theological disagreement among colleagues, yet deep respect and openness to the unresolved issue.

And there were other theological surprises, all deeply personal and both difficult and corrective in my own life. Some were embarrassing, and most were filled with wonderful humor and joy. I learned much of the commonality of our traditions. There was little to disagree about in much of the "substance." Scripture scholarship and instruction at Mundelein was the same as within the Protestant world. Some of my colleagues had studied with Lutheran Scripture scholars; there was a commonality of method in matters of biblical exegesis.

During those early years, I regularly team taught with several of my religious-education colleagues. Rarely would we surface significant theological differences. Each semester I was invited by Sister Joan Frances Crowley to address her world history class on the Reformation. These events were always wonderfully affirming. I would try to present my own tradition with charm and gentleness. But the discussions were always honest, searching, revealing, and instructive. I learned that young Catholics were as misinformed about Protestants as Protestants were of Catholics. But as to serious matters of disagreement regarding the "substance" of the faith, there were few, and these usually related to hermeneutics, the interpretation, rather than to dogma.

Where were the differences, if not in the formal doctrinal documents of the traditions? They were in the Catholic ethos, where spirituality abounds and forms those who share that ethos, in the being and doing, not primarily the thinking and knowing. I found them usually by surprise—in liturgical worship experiences, in Eucharistic liturgies, and in the daily practice of being Catholic. I remember one of my first Eucharist services; Gick had joined me. The music, we both agreed, was awful—guitars, soft uninspiring voices, mistaken chords. The "ethos" of Eucharist was quiet, subdued, serious, and "different" to our ears and our experience. We went to receive communion together. I had asked and was assured by my colleagues that we were welcome at the table and we felt comfortable attending. We were seated toward the back of the chapel. After we received the wafer, we walked slowly to partake of the cup. There was no wine. So we returned silently to our pews. Gick whispered in my ear, "I feel awful, we did not receive any wine. We have not had real communion."

I waited until after the service to assure her that Luther himself had no serious question on this communion practice. In fact, early in the Reformation he always informed his pastors to introduce the cup "pastorally" after time, to instruct the parish on the reception of both species, and never to destroy a troubled conscience. Yes, we really had Eucharist. But I did not confess to Gick, neither that day nor any since, my own personal discomfort with the experience.

Recently we attended a wonderful Catholic wedding of one of Gick's staff at Dominican University. The Eucharist was served only in one species. Neither of us commented, neither felt strange, and we both knew we had been changed, each in Catholic academic settings, each slowly growing accustomed to the most difficult ecumenical reality, matters of sacramental ritual, the "substance" of the faith. We are what we do, and slowly we have become more and more Catholic in our practice, and gradually our bodies responded with the peace of familiarity.

I taught at Mundelein until 1991, when the college was joined to Loyola University Chicago. I think I now better understand just a few of the continuing (substance) issues between my own religious tradition and that of Catholicism. I am of the absolute firm conviction that Catholicism is anthropologically more positive than my own religious tradition. I continue to argue that point with my Catholic colleagues, insisting they have lost Augustinian and Pauline insights about evil and sin; indeed, I sometimes use the metaphor *antinomian* to describe Catholic anthropology. My Catholic colleagues insist I am stuck in dark Reformation shadows and they contend that the reality of life is much more positive. On this issue, I remain in tension. I would want to argue that "original sin" is the most persuasive theology of human experience.

The second theological issue, which does indeed continue to divide our traditions, has to do with the institutional structure of Catholicism. Roman Catholicism is theologically structured hierarchically and continues to be controlled by male clergy. I believe Lutherans are more Catholic in this part of our "substance" than my Catholic colleagues.

Finally, Catholicism has the richest and most developed liturgical tradition within Christendom. Yet at Mundelein I experienced a "dumbing down" of the wonderful musical heritage of the church. I was disenchanted with guitars and popular "religious" music. I continue to worship at Catholic parishes today, never hearing the great chants of the church, rarely hearing any serious organ accompaniment, and hardly ever experiencing a serious liturgical choral tradition. I believe Lutherans do worship better . . . or at least more musically.

I am, on the other hand, equally convinced that Catholics render aspects of the "substance" with far more integrity than do most Protestants. Those differences were apparent at Mundelein. There is a serious public theology of social responsibility in the Catholic Church. Catholics continue to engage the larger culture with a substantive tradition of social teaching in matters of life and death, war, and justice. Secondly, Catholics, I am sure, pray better. I continue to be changed when I pray with Catholic Christians. They can sit in stillness for long minutes. They can practice meditation and prayer with honesty and obvious blessing. The "spirituality" of the Catholic "substance" remains unknown to Protestants. I envy Catholic piety, and slowly, I have learned to sit for a "few" minutes in silence . . . after twenty-three years of teaching at Mundelein and Loyola. I will probably never risk a long retreat. I retreat back to my lesser "substance" of communal prayer and a serious effort at living with some sense of Catholic integrity. I claim to be Catholic in the Lutheran rite because of my new self-understanding of Catholic substance and the prophetic posture of the Christian tradition.

And how has my thinking about Catholic "substance" changed because of my years of teaching at Mundelein? I have learned that there is no uniform American Catholic consensus about the "substance" of being Catholic. I have learned, however, the awesome power of Catholic spiritual presence. American Catholics are often more "Protestant" than Protestants. They are more serious about public policy. They are finally, deeply committed to this institution called Roman Catholic, and they exercise that commitment with regular, informed, scholarly critique.

Academic Creativity: Feminist Praxis

When I arrived at Mundelein, the graduate religious studies program already had a long and important history. Sister Jegen was perhaps most responsible for the creativity of the program. Each student took courses in seven separate discipline areas: theology, social sciences, literature, the arts, psychology, religious education, and Scripture. Each discipline was responsible for integrating the religious component of that aspect of human knowledge. As one might imagine, our faculty meetings were long and conflicted. We worked from different paradigms of reality. What held the strong liberal arts–religious studies curriculum together was the firm conviction that human life was about a partnership of meaning. This is surely a cherished feminist understanding.

I doubt that Sister Carol Francis Jegen would have thought of herself as a feminist in 1975. I suspect, however, that this model of learning was of feminist essence: shared insights, mutual conversation, partnerships in truthing, corporate energy instead of individual male thought. In contemporary feminist thought, this model is akin to that of a "midwife." I believe, to this very day, that the M.A. program in religious studies at Mundelein was one of the most creative curriculum structures in theological education during this period. Here was no ecclesiastical dominance, no theological arrogance, no appeal to authority or even the Catholic tradition; rather the unique spiral process of several academic disciplines working together to understand the nature of the religious phenomena.

The next few paragraphs contain the most biased of my memories. These reflections are not about historical accuracy; they are about my interpretation of that history. Some of the feminist unity of the department faltered with the introduction of a new spirituality program brought to Mundelein in the late 1970s. When Matthew Fox came to Mundelein in 1979, I was director of the graduate religious studies program. So my memories are both those of administrator and teacher. Matt initiated his first creation-centered spirituality program at Mundelein College and from the beginning of that program followed several years filled with tension, debate, conflict, energy, and spirited opinion. Fox was a strong, unique, dominant presence in his program and in the graduate religious studies department. Here was a different spirit, one of personal charismatic leadership, one of a single-minded and narrowly conceived course of study, and one of absolute male dominance. Within three years, Matthew took his center to California, an environment better suited to his style and leadership. Matt was a spiritual guru. He disallowed any critique of his central ideas, arguing that the church suffered a long history of "fall-redemption" thought. He believed his notions about spirituality deserved equal time without analysis or critique. I once challenged Matt to an open debate about the creation-centered tradition and the "fall-redemption" heritage of the church. He refused to participate. Academic debate about spiritualities was not permitted in his center.

My favorite creative story from this brief program diversion has to do with the heart of Catholic substance, the Mass. Matt was celebrating the end of a semester with his students. They were invited to his home for this occasion. After a wonderful meal and a long evening, they began the celebration of Mass. Matt had at that time a dog, his loyal companion. Somehow, as the bread was being shared, one of the students gave some to Matt's dog. I am not sure to this day if Matt even saw the event, but the story circulated throughout the department. I leave to your imagination the kinds of results that followed. Matt left Mundelein the next academic year.

With Matt's departure, the graduate program developed its own spirituality sequence, one centered more directly in feminist thought, yet strongly dialogical because of the diverse nature of the department. The program continued until Mundelein joined Loyola. By the time of the merger, the women's spirituality program was taught at extension settings in Peoria, Joliet, and on campus. Team taught and structured as a weekend pattern, the program grew in numbers and reputation. It did "fly" in Peoria, for a number of years, until the advent of Bishop John J. Myers.

His view of church and ministry was not the same as Mundelein's. The decision to discontinue our relationship was mutual, both on the part of the new bishop and on the part of Mundelein/Loyola.

A few final words need to be said about the Mundelein Center for Religious Education library. This collection of religious-education materials served as the single media center for the Chicago Archdiocese for decades. It was part of the early vision of Carol Frances. After the merger with Loyola, the materials were officially turned over to the archdiocese to become the Jegen Center for Religious Education. I believe this development was an appropriate decision, keeping the center and many Mundelein influences alive for decades to come.

Critical Personal Passages: A Compassionate Catholicism

Leaving Concordia was a difficult decision for me. Yet I knew it was not just a matter of necessity. I suspected that it was a wonderful opportunity, and most assuredly a challenge to grow and expand my theological horizons. I did not have the same clarity about calling and place as did Carol Frances, not in those early years. There was deep grief over the loss of my own tradition. Several Concordia colleagues died in the immediate years following the conflict that took place there. I know one can make no claim for a simple equation of stress and loss to sickness and disease. Yet I know as well that this loss, this act of carefully destroying probably the best intellectual community among all the fourteen Concordias, took a personal toll on me and on many of my colleagues. During those early years, I could not bring myself to walk on Concordia's campus, even though I passed it each day on my way to Mundelein. "My" school no longer existed; there was a kind of death.

But death entered my experience in a more personal way shortly after coming to Mundelein. My mother died suddenly of a stroke November 11, 1977. She and I were engaged in a spirited discussion about our family, our roots, our family history, and our mother-son relationship. For several years, I continued to "argue" with her about issues of our family life, especially about memories of childhood. She would become angry and "matriarchal." Her style of debate was always one of silence when losing. So many of our conversations during those years ended with her silence. I would continue to talk, and Mom would smile or frown and simply not respond, thus ending the conversation.

In the fall of 1977 my mother took my aging father to my sister's home in New Orleans. There I am sure she planned to die, knowing my sister would be present to take care of my father. After my mother's stroke, my sister found directions for her funeral in her purse—choice of hymns, text, and pallbearers. My last discussion with my mother occurred in a New Orleans hospital. I talked and held her hand, and she adopted her customary role of silence. But this time, her silence was involuntary; she was comatose. I left her with a warm embrace, told her how much I loved her, and how radical I was finding this end of our debate. I held her hand and felt a small, slight squeeze. I flew back to Chicago, and upon arrival at home, my daughter met me at the door. "Dad, Grandma just died." I knew I had lost the argument.

Mundelein colleagues knew nothing of our mother-son conflict. What they knew was that my mother had died, and they knew about comfort, hospitality, and simple shared love and compassion. Letters came from my colleagues. I suspect no Schmidt relative was ever blessed with so many prayers. And I remembered my father's insight about Catholics when he told us as youngsters, "When Catholics pray, they really mean it; they do what they say. Don't assume the same truth when Lutherans tell you they will pray for you." The Mundelein community prayed for my mother. She experienced part of the "Catholic substance." And so, too, my own family and myself. I was touched by another part of authentic Catholic spirituality, the straightforward sharing of the hope of the resurrection in act and word, in hugs, and care-full conversation. Mundelein was important in my soul care. But this care was not exceptional; it was expected within the Catholic ethos. I felt home. I felt Catholic.

Ten months after my mother's death, I experienced my first serious personal health crisis. Early September 1978 I entered Loyola Medical Center for emergency abdominal surgery. I had Crohn's disease, a miserable, chronic intestinal inflammatory disease without cure. My doctors told me that I needed to resign as director of the graduate religious studies program. My professional upward mobility ended. I loved to teach, so the decision was not difficult.

During that time, my peers were helpful and always supportive. I was encouraged to do what I needed to do for my health. Colleagues taught my courses during my absence; there was no pressure to return to my work until I was ready. I was back teaching in two weeks and happy to be there.

Six weeks later, October 18, our youngest daughter, Ruth, then sixteen, was brutally raped. The events of those days are as clear in my mind today as when they occurred. It was the most difficult period in our family's history. We had no guide for our feelings and actions. We lived each day afterward in terror and with constant care and concern for Ruth. We prayed together, we talked endlessly. Our son wrote his sister a song, one we still cherish and rarely sing. Our friends responded with love and care. Our closest friends spent the next day with us, just to listen and hold us close. Ruth and her new boyfriend sat that day on our porch steps, holding hands, crying, and talking. Evenings and nights were the most difficult. Gick held our family together. Night after night she would sit with Ruth, hours on end, listening, holding, simply being with her. Nighttime dreams were times of sadness and pain. I was filled with hate, anger, terror, love, hope, and a deep sense of guilt. I, too, was a man.

Mundelein sisters and some male colleagues sent cards, called frequently, and continued to accept my feelings and expressions of rage and despair. One male colleague drove from Evanston to our home the night after the rape. He met me at the door, gave me a card, a long hug, and simply expressed his concern and care for our family. Cards continued to come. Prayers were said on Ruth's behalf.

These next few sentences may not be true to reality; they are true to what I remember. Several of my closest male Concordia colleagues did not call in the next few weeks. Later I asked them why and expressed my disappointment and rage at their absence. One, in a candid response, answered: "Steve, I simply did not have anything to say. I could not call you, I didn't know what to do." This friend, a Lutheran pastor, is still a close friend. What I think I learned most clearly in those early years after the rape is something about the separate worlds of women and men. I could not enter my daughter's world, as my wife could. For months Ruth could not hug or even touch me. The most difficult emotional issues related to Ruth's rape were about my inability to protect my daughter, and my own recognition about my maleness.

That event changed me for life. Feminism was no longer an academic discipline or the response of angry women. Feminism was about my daughter's life, her reality, her world. Now the insights of women were insights I needed to know. Now the agenda of women was my agenda, in a very personal way. Now Mundelein, a college for women, had a far more significant meaning in my life. Since that October evening, my life has radically changed. I shall never forget. And I continue to grow in understanding and appreciation in the struggle for justice and love between women and men.[3]

My teaching has changed since that event. The bibliography I use is now always inclusive. I listen differently. I attend to woman's issues radically differently. I take women seriously in a way I never did before. The experience of Ruth's rape and the response of my colleagues at Mundelein have changed my life, my teaching, and surely my marriage.

November 29, 1998, Ruth gave birth to her first child, Noah. The birth has brought healing and joy to our whole family. Noah is for us a sign of hope and promise. Ruth's body, once violated, became the womb of promise. Noah is, I think, our family's sign of healing. God forgets not her own and brings Noah into life. Noah is a child of love and compassion. And compassion begets justice and justice creates hope for Ruth, our family, and this aging grandfather. Mundelein has been part of that self-understanding, and I am grateful.

Lost, Love's Labor

Mundelein College merged with Loyola University Chicago in 1991. It is not my intent, nor am I able, to make informed judgments about the reasons for the merger. What I want to do is simply acknowledge the personal pain and sense of loss I felt when that decision was reached. Twice in my academic/ministerial vocation I have experienced a significant personal loss of vocational place. My ministry ended abruptly when I left Concordia. My ministry at Mundelein ended equally abruptly. Both colleges were schools where I had deep connections. Both of my vocational tasks, training Lutheran teachers and Catholic religious educators, were labors of love. Both experiences of closure were filled with sadness and pain. Each experience nudged me into a time of personal reflection upon my life goals, my vocational decisions, and my faith commitments.

My sense about the Christian life is caught in the metaphor of journey. My understanding of the Christian faith journey is that it is largely uncharted. And I believe deeply that the task of prayer is not so much about asking God for the desires of my heart as about asking God for the will of God's heart for my life. So these difficult endings in my vocational journey were disconcerting and difficult. They were also times of honest reflection upon what God might indeed be doing with my life. And I am back to Paul Tillich.

Tillich's strong emphasis upon "ambiguity" as the essential metaphor of the Christian life is appropriate soul care when I become too self-centered and self-absorbed about my "lost love's labors." Protestantism values too highly, Tillich argues, the blessings of labor. The scriptural testimony is less enthusiastic. Labor can be curse as well as blessing, can divert us from our own creative development. So work, like all of life, is bordered by ambiguity. That which gives meaning also creates the boundaries of our limitations.[4] Faith finally calls us out to the journey, to a new place, to another time, to a final meaning, a *telos* of hope against hope. "Dr. Schmidt, I think God sent you here" almost feels true. But where next? That is more difficult. To that hope and that goal, I continue to turn again and again with the eyes of faith, always seeing "through a glass darkly." So I continue my journey, glad for the Mundelein oasis, a place of healing water, great fun, wonderful colleagues, gifted students, and an abundance of hope. And I will be forever grateful!

Endnotes

1. Paul Tillich, *Systematic Theology,* vol. 1 (Chicago: University of Chicago Press, 1951), 37, 227.

2. Ibid., vol. 3, 243.

3. See the articles "After the Fact: To Speak of Rape" by Ruth Schmidt and my own response, "To Speak of Rape: A Father's Experience," *Christian Century,* Chicago, 6–13 January 1993.

4. Tillich, *Systematic Theology,* vol. 3, 50–110.

Reminiscences of a Mundelein Junkie

David Block

Circa 1975

"You're going to Mundelein? Isn't that a women's college?"

"It isn't just for women anymore. Mundelein has a weekend program that's coeducational."

(Puzzled look, followed by a nod of acceptance).

Later That Year

The required course is called Strategies for Learning. The course title leads everybody to wonder about it. We are taught that our experiences outside the classroom mean something. Our impressions, our feelings, our experiences all count in the learning process. A cross section of Mundelein's finest faculty put their hearts into showing us that our brains can take it all in from any direction. Reading is not the only vehicle for learning; listening counts, as does experimenting, feeling, exploring, working, relating, and imagining.

Not bad.

People speak of going to "a lurk" to study. I wonder what's lurking where? I learn that lurk is a pronunciation of LRC (Learning Resource Center), and I'm assured that nothing's lurking behind a corner.

In the meantime, another world exists a few yards away. The students are all women. They take physical education, religion classes, and they giggle a lot. Almost none of them venture into the world of the Weekend College at this early date. Almost all of us in the weekend program work at our day jobs to make a living. Never, I think, will these two schools known as Mundelein ever have much in common. The young women are nameless bodies that we pass in the library or the halls.

Circa 1977

By now, I have made one or two good friends among the working Weekend College group, but I still feel like a commuter. I am male. I go home to my wife instead of staying on campus Friday and Saturday nights, so my Mundelein gives me diversification—via the classroom and my studies—not socially.

The Holocaust in Film and Words. I thought I knew something about the subject before I walked into this class.

Wrong.

Professor Bill Hill helps us walk with Elie Wiesel, Victor Frankl, and millions of murdered human beings. One or two teenage women from the weekday college, the "other Mundelein," begin to cry uncontrollably at what they learn and see on the screen. I am shamed by my own poker face in the presence of this exposition of evil. These young women are teaching me to cry, too. The walls between the two Mundeleins, weekend and weekday, begin to crumble for me at that second.

From the depths of the Holocaust, I move into Professor Mary Griffin's world of literature. The transition, all within fifteen minutes each Saturday, is almost too great to manage. I have leapt from the basest manifestations of evil up to the highest forms of imagination and optimism in less than an hour. Mary Griffin smiles, encourages, prods, accepts, smiles some more, and waxes eloquent. She uses excerpts from the poets as her tools of illumination. She treats each student as valuable. I am deeply in love, and I vow never to miss one of her class offerings.

Over in music class, Sister Louise Szkodzinski blends the Byrds, Mozart, and Dave Brubeck into a piercing listening experience. The music room is in the Skyscraper, and young female students are everywhere. I feel like an interloper. I cannot figure out where to sit in the cafeteria. So I sit alone. But the moment I walk back into the classroom, I am home again.

Circa 1978

I shift upward into a state of overload. A psychology course. A business course. Two courses in Russian literature at the same time, with a reading load that destroys my ability to sleep. Yet I cannot pull myself away from Raskolnikov or Eugene Onegin. I am overdosing on the blend of working and going to school, and I become depressed. I know that I can't do it all. I shut down. My son is born in February. I can't do it all. I just can't. I talk to Professor Bill Hill about it. Bill offers to help arrange a scholarship.

No, I have to do this on my terms. My money. My timetable.

I leave Mundelein. I am, I think, a permanent college sophomore.

Circa 1987

A new marriage, a new family, and a business doing well enough to send me anywhere I want to go. I am missing something, though. I go to a poetry reading and realize that I need to hear more. I need to study this subject. I need fiction. I need a classroom. Where can I go?

I walk back into Mundelein. Sister Jean Dolores greets me as if I have never left.

I want to find poetry, Sister Jean. I want to develop my philosophy of life. Just aim me in the right direction.

Nonsense, says Sister Jean. You're going to finish your degree, David.

Have you ever tried to argue with Sister Jean Dolores?

The world of Mundelein has changed upon my reentry into its atmosphere. The weekend classes now have plenty of day students picking up extra credit hours. The giggles that I used to hear only in the halls or in the cafeteria now come into the classroom. My life is about to change.

The insularity of the Weekend College in Residence yields to the reality of Mundelein College and the Sisters of Charity of the Blessed Virgin Mary. Often, I am the only male in my classes.

And what classes they are! Mary Griffin has barely aged, but she has left administrative duties behind and brings all her energy to teaching. I take every class she offers, plunging into Faulkner and Gwendolyn Brooks with an enthusiasm I never realized I possess.

I am thirty-five years old, I'm going to college for the fun of it, and I realize that it's time to enjoy my teachers. Dr. Mike Fortune takes time after mythology class to talk about life. Mary Griffin offers a poignant moment during career counseling. And Bill Hill seems to design his curriculum specifically to whet my appetite for learning. Dr. Tony Gramza and Bill blend quantum physics and environmental studies into a bigger success than they think. But the best is yet to come.

I have begun to study with some of the day pupils. I feel like a real college student.

Circa 1989

By now, my improved writing skills have begun to show up in my business accomplishments. School is feeding me. I am feeding my company. Life feels good.

I am approaching graduation in about two years, so I choose my courses carefully.

Vietnam. Hmm. Why not?

Professor Bill Hill has recruited Achilles Fischer, a Vietnam veteran, to help plan the class. Bill assigns a brilliantly designed bibliography for us to read on our own time and discuss in class. He supplements this with film. And after class we adjourn to Achilles' home in Rogers Park.

Each Saturday, a different Vietnam veteran comes to the house to recount his or her memories. One man, now a Sunday school teacher, recounts his role in Operation Phoenix. It had been his job to infiltrate and befriend members of the Viet Cong. After befriending them, he had them killed.

He seems to look to us for some type of forgiveness. (Fortunately, he is not the first veteran from whom we have heard a horror story. Two weeks ago, a vet brought his Zippo lighter so we could see what he used to burn down Vietnamese thatch huts).

We do not need to forgive the Sunday school teacher. By now, after weeks of studying and listening, we know that Lyndon Johnson's ego had dictated that he just wasn't going to let that damn Ho Chi Minh beat him. We know that soldiers follow orders as a matter of survival. We know that the "combat mentality" is so different from our own that we dare not judge its players. The Sunday school teacher had been murdering civilians because the guy at the top had lost his reason and his advisors were too weak to stand up to him and because Washington had forced a combat mentality upon him without clearly identifying the real enemy.

So we do not treat the Sunday school teacher like a murderer. We treat him like one of us. He begins to trust that we aren't patronizing him, and we realize that this course has become such a powerful experience that we can now speak with eyewitnesses to history without sounding naive.

But how, if we forgive the Sunday school teacher who shot his best friend in the head, can we not forgive the Nazis and other killers? Bill helps us see that the guard in Auschwitz exists in all of us, only scantly removed from exploding into evil under the right circumstances.

Meanwhile, back at the Skyscraper, I sit in class with the day students twice a week while Sister Joan Frances Crowley and Professor Dan Vaillancourt immerse us in Marxism and Communism. As we get past Marxism and into the horrors of the Stalin years, we spend some time on the Khruschev revelations of the 1950s and the betrayal and disbelief of American leftists when they realized that they had been espousing loyalty to a mass murderer.

And as Sister Joan Frances speaks of those days, I realize that she must have been one those true believers. She, personally, had to go through the letdown of discovering that a sadistic tyrant had exploited the principles that she thought would lead to a fairer world. As I watch her eyes, I see history before me. And never again will I trust leaders without intensive research into their motives and actions.

Even as I listen to Sister Joan Frances bring history alive, some of the teenage young women next to me are whispering to each other about their boyfriends, engagements, and social lives.

Dan Vaillancourt speaks next. After reviewing the regional antagonisms of Uzbekistan, Tajik, Armenia, Georgia, and the rest of the Soviet Union, Dan asks us what we think will go on there in the future. I raise my hand. "It can't last," I say. Dan looks somber. (A year later, the Berlin Wall falls and the Soviet Union disintegrates).

The class ends. The younger women in the room can't wait to talk with each other. I wish the class hadn't ended.

Over in Dr. Brooks Bouson's classroom, I sit with twenty other students discussing a book by Margaret Atwood. I am the only male in the room, and the other students tolerate my enthusiasm although yielding subtle clues that what's going on here is, really, a female thing. I wouldn't understand.

They are right. One of Atwood's characters, Joan Foster, reminisces about her overweight childhood. (For a recital, the ballet teacher has taken the fat girl and let her stand on stage as, essentially, a prop, where she draws tremendous applause for her courage. Joan, the prop, hears her mother's faint and damning praise, but retreats into her own world in desperate pain.)

Dr. Bouson asks everybody in the class whether they feel that their parents really, truly understood their feelings about their self-images. Only two women out of twenty raise their hands affirmatively. I am awestruck. What else don't I know about the world of women?

The instructor gives me an opening—a chance to write a précis on a classic feminist reader-response essay by Patrocino Schweickart. I take the assignment.

Another Mundelein-generated awakening. I quickly come to see that almost everything I have ever read can be seen through a feminist view that forces the reader to notice that the heroes are male, the enablers are female, and that the literature game has been rigged for more centuries than one can count.

Dr. Bouson gives me an A on my précis. I have never felt prouder in receiving a letter grade in my life, and the Schweickart essay becomes one of the guiding forces in my dealings with women.

Circa 1990

As I approach the end of my long trek toward a college degree, I reach out in search of new course directions. From the time I was five years old, I was convinced I could not draw. So I sign up for Professor Pat Hernes' art course.

In order to get through this course, I need to learn to see. Not easy for one who gets by on analysis and wit. But I try. And I struggle.

I decide to draw the Yamaha music synthesizer sitting in my son's room, but I keep losing the discipline to commit to paper what I really see with my eyes. I continue to draw what I think a synthesizer will look like rather than simply mirroring what's in front of me. I take a week off work to draw. I scream, I cry, I tear up dozens of sheets of paper, and I break down as the old, rusty right side of my brain tries to activate itself after years of lethargy and neglect.

I survive the assignments and prepare for the final project—a self-portrait.

The night before I plan to begin painting my own face, I climb into bed. My sleeping wife reaches out to give me a hug. And she pokes her thumb deep into my right eye.

Screaming in pain, I call a doctor in the middle of the night and get a patch. The next day, with searing pain in my eye, I go to the mirror and complete my final assignment. I produce a two-dimensional image of a man with a patch over his eye. The picture survives to this day. And Pat Hernes allowed me to pass the course.

Not far away, I dance, sing, read, and rehearse my way through a medley of Sister Frances Dolan's music courses. When I get older, I want to be like her. In fact, I want to be like her right now.

The rumor that Mundelein might not continue as a women's college evolves into an eventuality. Loyola is probably going to take over.

My first response is to scan the real estate. This looks like a sensible merger of assets. But when I settle into Mary Griffin's class, Mary interrupts the routine to allow some of the women to ventilate on the subject of women's education and Mundelein as an institution.

The women speak of the safety they find with each other. The absence of men allows some of them to raise their hands without feeling like they have to compete for the instructors' attention. It changes the way they dress, their tone of voice, and their freedom to love one another as friends.

My heart goes out to the women who will never have a chance to know this type of experience in Chicago.

I am almost forty years old and about to receive my first undergraduate degree. At my mother's request, I go through the final Mundelein graduation ceremony. As Loyola moves in to take over, I breathe and take in the sensitivity that has touched my spirit through this place.

I walk with women barely twenty years of age to receive a certificate from an institution that was built for them. I feel lucky. I think that we males were few enough not to have spoiled the atmosphere while the school was alive as an independent institution, although it still seems strange to think that our anatomical differences should be enough to change the learning environment.

I do not have the memories of a great social life, multiple lifetime friendships, dormitory pillow fights, nor any of the "normal" events associated with youthful undergraduate living. Mine was the Mundelein of the working man and woman, where the Granville El stop meant the beginning of an intellectual adventure.

While I attended my final classes at Mundelein, my stepson was going through his junior year at Amherst College, one of the most exclusive liberal arts schools in the world. I took the time to visit and attend some of his classes with him. I was dumfounded to see that my work at Mundelein had brought me to an intellectual level equal to that of Amherst. The classes there were no better and no worse than those at Mundelein; I had been taught by the best in the business.

But it was the education of women, and not the education of those such as I, which had led to Mundelein's founding. Women's education suffered most from the school's closing. I cherish the equality under the law that allows us to break down gender barriers. But I also feel for the shy, perhaps overweight woman in the back of the class who doesn't feel safe enough to come out of her cocoon in the company of warrior personalities.

I know one thing. I didn't intimidate all the women in the school. One day, I decided to take the small elevator near the cafeteria to get back to class after a break. I neglected to push the right button, and before I knew it I found myself on the top floor looking squarely at a group of B.V.M. sisters waiting to go down from their residence. They were startled to see me.

I said to them, "Bet you don't get too many Jewish guys up here."

They all broke up. And their laughter was the sound of grace.

Epilogue, circa 1999

"Where did you go to college?"

"Mundelein."

"Wasn't that a women's college?"

Yes. It was.

Moving West of Raynor, or "What's a Good Lutheran Girl Like You Doing at a Catholic Graduate School Like This?" 1985–1990

Nancy Bartels

> *When a woman turns forty,*
> *she does one of three things:*
> *gets a Cuisinart, takes a lover,*
> *or goes back to school.*
> CONTEMPORARY AMERICAN PROVERB

On June 11, 1990, a bright, warm, late spring day, an accident of the alphabet put me at the head of the procession of graduates into the hall at Mundelein College. The scene was typical of graduations everywhere: proud, excited families and equally excited graduates, usually trying to be too worldly wise and sophisticated to show it; slightly bored faculty (how many of these ceremonies had they attended after all?); and curious onlookers, momentarily caught up in yet another odd bit of street theater on Sheridan Road. The pocket cameras and the hugs were everywhere, and for a brief moment, everything seemed possible to this group of people.

A year later, the scene was, I imagine, somewhat different. Then it would be the last class ever to graduate from an independent Mundelein. What had begun sixty years earlier with such promise and hope was coming to an end, a victim of changing times, customs, and economics.

Still, that afternoon in 1990, all that was ahead. At the time, the moment was all celebratory and full of anticipation, and the only thing on my mind, beyond getting through the procession without disgracing myself, was a private joke. I found myself wondering, as I slipped into my rented master's cowl for probably the only time in my life, what Cardinal Mundelein and Sister Justitia Coffey would think, assuming they knew, of the woman leading the procession of graduates.

Surely I was not what they had in mind when they struggled and wheeled and dealed to get a college for young women in Chicago. Their dream was to provide a place where young Catholic women could study the liberal arts and prepare for careers without the danger to their faith inherent in such secular— or even nominally Protestant—institutions such as the University of Chicago. A worthy dream, no doubt, but I don't think a woman like me was really part of their vision—one no longer quite young, already launched on a more-or-less satisfying career, divorced, painfully representative of the sins, failings, and anxieties of women of my age and class in fin de siècle America, and, probably worst of all, a spiritual daughter of the man who shattered forever the unity of the Western Christian Church, Martin Luther.

What would the cardinal and Sister Justitia make of me, I wondered. And what would my own parents, mentors, and teachers, who had to the best of their ability carefully molded a "good Lutheran girl" and equipped her to get through life with that sectarian worldview in place like body armor, think of me among the papists, clutching an honors degree granted by (gasp!) the Sisters of Charity of the Blessed Virgin Mary? What could *I* have been thinking when I embarked on this journey?

The short answer is that it seemed like a good idea at the time (and still does). The longer, more honest answer is that it was, in retrospect, a logical, almost inevitable choice. In a peculiar way, contrary to the assumed expectations of the both the college's Catholic founders and my own relentlessly Lutheran forebears, coming to Mundelein was, for me, coming home.

Before I proceed, I must deliver a fair warning. Those of you hoping to find some systematic history or pedagogical analysis of the Mundelein Master of Liberal Studies (MLS) program had best look elsewhere. It's not that such an exercise is not useful or necessary; it's just that it's not one I can perform. We are all the heroines of our own stories and the center of our own universes to one degree or another, and all I can tell is my own story and Mundelein's part in it. Faculty struggles, the nuances of curriculum development, the warning signs that the end was near for the college as a whole must have been evident when I was in attendance. I didn't see them.

When I entered Mundelein in the summer of 1985, I was at a watershed in my life. I had been divorced less than a year. Both my parents were dead. True, I had an adolescent daughter, but whatever demands she made, she didn't require the constant attention a younger child would have. I felt liberated. For the first time in my life, I had no one to answer to for my actions. The only person I could really disappoint was myself. The only limitations would be self-imposed. I was free at last, and I was terrified.

So I did what the wounded and terrified always do if they can: I sought sanctuary. I went to the one place I had always felt secure and in control of my destiny—school.

By chance, I found the Mundelein MLS program in an article in the *Chicago Sun-Times* (an article illustrated with a picture of Mary Griffin standing in front of the Sullivan Center) describing the program as an example of cross-disciplinary graduate study, and I knew I wanted to be a part of it. I didn't think about what kind of school Mundelein was (I was clueless at the time), whether I could afford it (I couldn't really), whether it would be a good career move (it was ultimately irrelevant), or even about why I wanted to go or what I hoped to gain from such an experience.

Only in retrospect did the decision make sense. I needed to get back to school at that point in my life because school was the one thing that had come as naturally to me as breathing. As an eager kindergartner, I had instinctively grasped the school game and never looked back. I was good at it. It was the one place during my growing-up years when I had mastery and control. It was the one place I could be confident of my skills. In 1985, with the emotional and relational blocks of my life cut from under me, going back to where I could function was a move akin to a fox running to earth. It was a place I would be safe.

School had always been an intellectual and emotional home for me. My Lutheran upbringing, strong on knowing the Truth (the capital was always at least implied) or being able to find it from the written word, had prepared me for academia, and I was entirely at home in a religious environment, even if it wasn't my particular brand. I have never believed that the term "thinking Christian" was an oxymoron.

The Mundelein vision of interdisciplinary study was the only kind of graduate work that made sense to me. I had absolutely no interest in law, medicine, social work, education, or an MBA. Advanced work in history or English, my undergraduate majors, were equally uninviting. The truth was, I had always shied away from specialization. Somewhere in my early education, I had been entranced by the vision of the liberally educated person—one on familiar ground in a number of subjects and able to draw connections between them, engaged in an attempt to know something about everything in an ever-expanding universe of knowledge—and I have never been able to let it go. The fact that the attempt is always ultimately doomed to failure—human

knowledge expands faster than anyone can keep up with—has never both-
ered me particularly. That may be a Lutheran conceit: As with one's salvation,
the destination has already been determined; what matters is the journey.

My entrance interview was with Mary Griffin. She was calm and serene
and utterly charming (I don't ever remember her being anything else). I was
nervous and desperately trying to hide it under a blanket of witty chatter.
What I really wanted to say in that interview was, "Please, please let me in. I
know my undergraduate grades aren't as good as they could be. I know my
two years at the Lutheran seminary without a degree don't look good. I know
I haven't made a rational case for what I hope to get out of this experience, but
please, please let me in anyway. I *need* to be here."

Of course, I didn't say it. I suspect Mary Griffin knew that anyway, although
she never said she did, and I never had the nerve to ask.

All I know is that I sent for transcripts and did the requisite paperwork in
record time, tapped my savings account for the first quarter's tuition, and by
the summer of 1985, I was taking Aspects of Love from professor of philosophy Tom O'Brochta.

My instincts had been sound. Getting up to speed academically for the
first time in several years was just what I needed. The required reading, the
rigorous demands of logical writing, the salutary experience of having to argue
on my feet and either best someone or be bested in debate were all oddly healing and comforting. It was reassuring to discover that my brains had not been
turned to pudding by the multiple demands of family, failing marriage, and
job hunting. I may have been a bad wife, a less-than-perfect daughter, a
marginally competent parent, but by God, I could be a good student.

The next five years, in memory, come only as vignettes. I remember certain lectures, certain people, certain scenes. Four of us with Tom O'Brochta in
a small sixth-floor room in the Skyscraper with an overworked air conditioner,
arguing over Plato . . . learning not to study on the first floor of the Sullivan
Center because I would inevitably be drawn into the deep blue of the lake
horizon out the front windows—good for my blood pressure, bad for my
studies . . . the team-taught core courses: biologist Tony Gramza and human-
ist Bill Hill on The Fate of the Earth and artist Blanche Gallagher and writer
Mike Fortune dragging me painfully out of my Apollonian, logical thought
boxes and into the more Dionysian, or at least riskier and less ordered, world
of Jungian myth and dreams and my own psyche . . . the cool marble, furniture wax, and old-book smell of the Skyscraper in summer . . . jug wine, pizza,
and endless conversation at the little restaurant on Sheridan Road . . . the

three months my kitchen table was taken over by one after another of Frank Vodvarka's assigned art projects . . . the painful development of the requisite self-discipline to complete an independent study and the discovery of some of my limits and potential as a writer . . . and, most of all, the rush, the exhilaration, the excitement of immersing myself in this intellectual adventure and this urban intellectual community.

It was in many respects like being in love. The rest of my life seemed less important, less exciting. Mundelein on Saturdays—for the most part, the MLS program happened on Saturdays—was in Technicolor; the rest of my life was in black and white. "Real" life seemed to be happening at Mundelein. Everything else was just pausing for breath in between. Studying, getting ready for class was like preparing to meet a lover. No effort was spared; no time spent was too much. Even the boring parts (God help me, I could not learn to get excited about Jean-Paul Sartre or certain essays on *realpolitik*) were willing sacrifices one made for the beloved. The sense of belonging and affirmation that came with being part of the MLS program was payback.

It was a far different experience than my first attempt at graduate school— two years at a Lutheran seminary in the late 1970s—only a few years after the church had allowed the ordination of women. The environment as I remember it was not hostile, but not exactly welcoming either. That intellectual enterprise was also career-oriented. The assumption was we were all on the same page in terms of what we were about—preparing for a career in ministry, probably in the parish—and the curriculum was structured with that in mind. It was assumed that we would trust the knowledge of our betters as to what courses would be good for us. Spiritual and/or intellectual searching were encouraged, of course, but within the fairly limited constructs of what needed to be accomplished in a four-year program. It was perfectly all right to want to explore the thought of Christian mystics in the Middle Ages or the influence of the social gospel on Lutheran polity in the early 1900s, as long as you also got in your required courses in homiletics, worship practice, Old and New Testament theology, Greek, teaching adult Christian education, and pastoral care.

Inevitably, I suppose, we women seminarians felt we had to defend our right to be there, and as is frequently the case with feminism in my experience, we were often our own worst enemies. There was a sense that the failure of one of us would reflect badly on the rest, but rather than encouraging a helpful, ministering kind of community, that sense tended to make us judgmental of one another. "Is she pulling her weight or making it hard for the rest of us?" seemed to be the unspoken question. Doubts and struggles that we would have viewed in a first-year male student as an ordinary part of his intellectual and spiritual growth, we saw as evidence in ourselves—and in other women—of lack of "seriousness" at best and failure at worst. I don't think we ever cut ourselves or the men around us enough slack to allow for the fact that we were feeling our way along what was a new path for all of us.

In the end, after two years, I pulled out, unwilling to continue the struggle. I don't regret the decision, nor do I regard the exercise as a failure. Part of the purpose of a seminary education is to make the novice absolutely clear about the nature and cost of her call. I learned that lesson and another vital one that many of my sisters had to learn at far greater cost: One of the great lies of the feminist movement of the 1970s and 1980s was that we could, indeed were entitled to, "have it all." We can't and we weren't. Life, even for educated, liberated women, involves some hard choices. Sometimes you have to give up one good thing to get another. In the end, torn between the demands of seminary life and those of a troubled marriage and a growing daughter, I made a simple, if painful, choice. The church would survive just fine without one more conflicted and exhausted pastor. My marriage and my daughter might not prosper under my full-time attention, but they certainly would not without it.

Eight years later, Mundelein had none of that laborious sense of serious, high-minded mission and purpose, intellectual manning of the barricades, or publicly proving a point. I don't mean to imply that the program was frivolous or that we were frivolous about it. Sister Justitia's dream of preparing Catholic women for careers and intellectual lives had not been abandoned. After all, we took core course with titles like The Fate of the Earth! It was just that everyone was more *relaxed*.

At Mundelein I was the beneficiary of dues paid by two previous generations of women. They had already fought many of the hardest battles and gained a good portion of the high ground. Part of my sense of relaxation also came, no doubt, from being on home turf, so to speak, in the company of other women. Mundelein was our place by definition. While the faculty (at least as I experienced it in the MLS program) was divided about fifty-fifty along gender lines, the student body was almost 100 percent female. I do remember three or four brave males in various classes, but, for once, they were the aliens, feeling their way. And the male teachers were all veterans of the women's college experience. Whatever they may have thought at one time, they were long since over the temptation to patronize or dismiss or question one's right to be there on the basis of gender. We were the reason the college existed in the first place.

Still, as with most love affairs, there was a sense of the illicit about my time on Sheridan Road. Mundelein was not, in spite of the Technicolor weekends, "real life," or at least not my only one. My job, my home, my family, my church in the suburbs were real, too, and made their own demands. Like the faithful, if uninteresting spouse, those things also commanded my loyalty and demanded my attention and left me always with the sense of being tugged in two directions—Mundelein, where I wanted to be, and home in the suburbs, where I needed to be.

Perhaps the metaphor overstates the case. Part of the tension was an inevitable byproduct of the commuter college, I think. The life of the college goes on twenty-four hours a day, seven days a week. The people who live there and are immersed in it experience it full-time, to a good extent, it is their world. For those of us who were commuters, who came in only on weekends—and most of us in the MLS program were—the sense of community and belonging was always a much more tenuous and fragile thing. We belonged, but not in the same way. There were enormous gaps in our knowledge of the community that could never be made up in five or six hours on a weekend. We were both members of the community and visitors at the same time.

Being a long-time suburbanite commuting to the city reinforced my sense of otherness. True suburbanites make a religion of "niceness." Tidiness, cleanliness, green lawns, and conformity are commandments far more honored than the original ten. We revel in the security of owning a home whose outside façade is identical to that of 25 percent of our neighbors and that is complementary in appearance to the other three-quarters. Republicanism, "safe streets," and unlimited parking places are rampant. Save for a few enclaves, people of color and of differing cultures are neither seen nor heard. We are safe with our assumptions and our prejudices because it's easy to ignore any challenges to them.

The city is all the things suburbanites have fled from—disorder, shabbiness, an element of danger, or at the least the very real possibility that something exotic and/or unexpected may occur right before our eyes. People of different colors, cultures, and values rub our noses in their strangeness and are indifferent to our resulting discomfort. The poor, the criminal, the dysfunctional, the simply weird, and the marginally sane are free to confront us with their condition and challenge us to do something about it. Of course, poverty, criminality, and nonconformity of all sorts exist in the suburbs, too, but they're much better hidden. In the suburbs such conditions are treated like crazy relatives in the attic: We ignore them when we can and try to deal with them discreetly when we must deal with them at all.

The contrast between those two environments was jarring. I was always grateful for the long drive from the northwest suburbs east on Devon Avenue. It served as a kind of decompression chamber for me. Going west worked the same way. It gave me time to reorient myself to whichever world I was about to enter.

Another source of tension was the nature of the MLS program. Interdisciplinary Master of Liberal Studies programs are doubly suspect in the eyes of many. Inside academia, they are often viewed as "graduate school lite" because of their lack of specialization and emphasis on traditional research disciplines. Outside the university, because their utility is not readily apparent in terms of career preparation, they are suspected of being frivolous or unimportant. Inside the Mundelein community, we were committed to the idea of the liberal arts and the virtues of interdisciplinary study. Outside, I always felt as though I had to convince myself and others that I wasn't just "playing school." I stopped counting the times I explained that, while, yes, I no doubt would earn more if I got an MBA, my graduate work was not about my lifetime earnings. My explanation that the answers to some of life's crucial questions could not be organized on an Excel spreadsheet and that the purpose of the liberal arts was to address those questions was not particularly convincing to many of my friends and acquaintances.

Finally, my sense of "otherness" was reinforced by my personal awareness of being not Roman Catholic. Whatever the theological persuasion of the MLS student body (less Catholic, I suspect, than the undergraduate, but by no means Protestant or secular), the atmosphere, the worldview, the *flavor* of the institution was Roman Catholic. The faculty was full of nuns or former nuns. Many of my fellow students were crossovers from the religious studies master's program, had been Mundelein undergraduates, or had come from some other Catholic institution. The rhythm of the school year and the traditional community institutions and events reflected the church calendar. The Roman vision was the default mode of operation.

Now, I have long since abandoned some of the more arcane rigidities of the Lutheran worldview. There are times when my Protestantism teeters perilously on the brink of civil religion or downright agnosticism, but after nearly thirty years of trying, I find I cannot shed my Protestant take on the world. But there I was anyway, with my innate suspicions of Roman authority and my discomfort with what Robert Browning calls "the raree show of Peter's successor" ("Christmas Eve," line 1240), heading off on weekends to indulge in an intellectual love affair among the papists. And though I largely ignored them, the plaintive voices of long-dead pastors, teachers, and parents sometimes rang in my ears, demanding to know, "How could you?"

> *The answers one gives to life's crucial questions*
> *are never truly spontaneous. They are the embodiment*
> *of years of contextual experience, of the building*
> *of patterns in each of our lives that eventually*
> *grow to dominate our behavior.*
>
> CALEB CARR, *THE ALIENIST*

To formulate a reponse to my ancestors requires a digression. To explain why Mundelein loomed so large in my middle years I must abandon it and even the northwest suburbs of Chicago for a bit and explain what life was like for a small Lutheran girl growing up in Joliet, Illinois, in the 1950s. All unknowing, I was preparing for my five-year adventure on Sheridan Road in the late 1980s on Oakland Avenue in the 1950s. Sometimes that place seems so far removed from what my life is about now that it seems to occupy another planet. And yet, ironically, it was lessons learned there that would resonate for me forty years later at Mundelein. Some of them I would unlearn. Others would at last become clear to me. Thomas Wolfe says you can't go home again, and he's right. But what he fails to add is that, in certain crucial respects, you can never abandon it completely either.

In the 1950s Joliet was a grubby but prosperous industrial town over a hundred years old, the county seat of Will County. It had a steel mill, an arsenal, a railroad, oil refineries, and a prison. There were also many working farms not far from town, a small municipal airport, a race-car track, and several nature preserves. We were proud of our industrial muscle and defensive about the prison. What we hated most was being thought of as a suburb (a new term in those days) of Chicago. We'd been an independent city nearly as long as Chicago, long enough to have a Civil War memorial on the courthouse lawn, thank you very much, and we didn't appreciate ignorant, pushy people from north of Lockport trying to take us over.

Joliet in the 1950s was like an insect in amber. Eisenhower was always the president, the Yankees always won the World Series, Pius XII was always the pope. John Wayne—with a little help from our fathers—had won The War (the term never needed qualifiers in those days), and we lived in the greatest country in the world. Blacks were "colored people," Hispanics were "Mexicans" regardless of where they came from, and they all knew their place and stayed there. We hadn't heard of Martin Luther King Jr., and Vietnam wasn't even on the radar screen. That change was seeping into our lives with every new television set bought and every new mile of expressway laid down was something that would be seen only in retrospect. In spite of the air-raid drills in school (which we took as jokes for the most part), we felt safe, secure, and just a bit smug.

But beneath this Norman Rockwell façade, I grew up with a gnawing sense of "otherness," a feeling that my family and I were not like other people. It is a sense I carry with me to this day, and it lies at the root, I think, of the belonging/not belonging tension that was part of my Mundelein experience.

In those early days, this sense of otherness was, for the most part, just below the level of awareness, rather like a low-grade fever. Only in late adolescence, as an undergraduate, did it enter an acute phase that in part (but only in part) explains a disastrous marriage and a long emotional exile in the suburbs. I found myself craving conformity. I wanted to "pass," to be just like everybody else. Later, perhaps in part as a result of my Mundelein experience, where I found myself reenacting the role of "outsider," I made peace with the contradictions of my situation.

Geography, culture, and the accident of birth, I think, mold the outsider's temperament. It certainly was in my case.

First, the accidents of birth. I am the younger of two children, both girls. My older sister is what we called in the far less politically correct 1950s mentally retarded and physically disabled. Growing up in a family with a "special needs" child, the first thing I learned as my world widened beyond the horizons of my own front door was that my family was *not* like others, no matter how like others it may have appeared to be. The places we couldn't go and the things we couldn't do because of the needs of that "special child," the unexplained silences and unspoken (at least in my presence) understandings of the adults around me, the unmistakable looks of pity—followed by the quick looking away—from strangers when they saw our family in public: all these set me apart. They were not actually awful or necessarily terrible. I learned to live with them. But they marked me early and deeply.

Then there was the fact that I was a girl. For reasons far too complicated to explain here, I *hated* being a girl. I was sure some terrible mistake had been made and that I should have been a boy. God knows, I wanted to be one. So I became a tomboy instead and, for preference, played with the neighborhood boys until puberty raised the great divide of our maturing sexuality. I had girl-friends too, but girls' games bored me. The girls bored me. Boys had all the fun and all the adventures. To my mind, it was obvious: Boys were better. But I was never really one of them, and I was never really comfortable with the girls. Just one more place, it seemed, I didn't quite fit.

The geography and culture of my growing up further deepened and reinforced this sense of otherness I was born to.

Joliet is divided by the Des Plaines River. On the east side of town lived— then and now— "poor people" and the "coloreds" and "Mexicans." As families prospered—an easy enough thing to do in the boom days of the 1950s—they moved west, across the river, up the bluffs, and out toward the farmland. That westward migration was not a new thing. Near the river on the west side were great, rambling Victorian relics that earlier generations of prosperous citizens had occupied. But they were beginning to fall on hard times as the children and grandchildren of those early burghers moved farther west, succumbing to the lure of bigger lawns and more modern ranch houses. By the 1950s to have "made it" in Joliet was to move west of Raynor Avenue. Oakland Avenue, where I grew up, lies a secure eight blocks west of the river, but an aspiring three blocks east of Raynor. To live on Oakland in the 1950s was to be lower-middle class, to have not quite arrived.

It was that geography that gave our neighborhood its distinctive charac-ter. It was a magnet for a great many first- and second-generation immigrants, still steeped in the languages and customs of "the old country." They tended to act out the classic American immigrant conflict—clinging to their tradi-tions and rituals, while aspiring to the golden American dream that would inevitably require them to abandon those same things. Growing up, my friends and I accepted as a matter of course that the neighborhood *babushkas* listened faithfully to the "Joliet-American Yugoslav Hour," where all the news came in Slovenian, but secretly we were embarrassed. People west of Raynor, *Americans,* listened to Chuck Berry and Elvis on WJJD or the Cubs and White Sox on WGN.

Because I was part of the neighborhood, I absorbed the conflict in my bones, although mine was not an immigrant family. My father's people have been in America since the 1830s, my mother's since the 1890s. That's not quite being one of the *Mayflower* families, but it should have been more than enough to lose any immigrant insecurities. But somehow on Oakland Avenue, the order of things had been reversed. I, about as close to a "native" white

American as you could find in Joliet in 1955, was the outsider. My best girl-friend, whose father, it was said, had "sent home" to Slovenia (one never called it Yugoslavia to Mr. Reposh's face) for his wife, seemed to fit the culture of Oakland Avenue better. My girlfriend, after all, helped her mother with her English.

Then, of course, was the fact almost everyone on Oakland Avenue was Roman Catholic. My family and one across the street were Lutherans. The only other dissenters were the mysterious couple and their grown son at the end of the block who rarely spoke to anyone and whose religious identity was universally condemned in the hushed tones usually reserved for cancer patients as "not much of anything."

I owe it to the lost world of Oakland Avenue in 1955 to explain that, while we were in some respects obsessed with denomination and ethnicity, we were not given to hatred or division. Our parents seemed to have arrived at a live-and-let-live modus vivendi. Each family was careful to see that its own offspring were brought up in the correct odor of sanctity, but we were forbid-den to allow our own assured salvation to interfere with decent, neighborly relationships. My Catholic friends knew without doubt that I was damned—at least to limbo, possibly to purgatory, quite probably to hell. I was secure in the assurance that they were absolutely Wrong. I was Right and therefore saved and that was that. Besides, God would probably forgive them for think-ing otherwise. He seemed big on doing that—especially when forgiveness was required for vague sins whose implications I didn't quite understand, like tax collecting and adultery. Surely Roman Catholicism fell in the same category, I thought. Besides, God's judgment was both inscrutable and a very long time off, and meanwhile there were many summers to get through together. A good hitter or fielder could be allowed a lot of doctrinal leeway in the theological calculus of Oakland Avenue.

My cultural isolation was compounded by my father's insistence on a parochial education. Our church, St. Peter's, the oldest Lutheran parish in the city, had a small grade school. It never had more than a hundred students. Its physical plant was woefully underequipped, and I doubt its faculty would meet certification requirements today. Frankly, I have always wondered what the quid pro quo was that kept it certified then. But the Rev. Erdmann Frenk was a formidable specimen of the old *Herr Pastor* tradition and fully as capable of bending local civil authorities to his will as the most authoritarian Roman bishop. Still, whatever its failings, St. Peter's was sound on fundamentals, and I got a good basic education there.

However, going to St. Peter's meant that I attended school with none of my neighborhood friends. Most of them went to Catholic schools, either St. Joseph's or St. Raymond's. The rest went to the public school two blocks away. Only I made the six-block walk east to the limestone edifice on the bluff overlooking the river.

Going to a Lutheran day school was, if my friends' accounts of their experiences can be believed, like going to Catholic school without the uniforms or the nuns. Every day began with an hour of religious education. We were required to attend church regularly and were on the receiving end of numerous pious lectures on the evils of drinking, smoking, dancing, and the dangers of dating people of other faiths. The occasional visits from Rev. Frenk or the associate pastor, who was in real life his son, were treated like visits from God himself. (And, yes, that did lead to some interesting theological misapprehensions for the young believer, although the father/son pastoral team was not uncommon among Lutherans in those days.) We were provided with a clearly marked moral yardstick by which to measure ourselves and, although we lacked the prod of weekly confession, we were expected to use it with great regularity. If the exercise didn't mark me exactly with the "Catholic guilt" made famous by novelists and comedians, the scar is strikingly similar.

But in those days, it was the differences that made me feel apart. I was neither fish nor fowl. I shared the public-school calendar, but not its comfortable, assimilative culture. It seemed to me I had all the hassles and restrictions of a religious education without the glamour of a school uniform or the extra saints' days off.

Two other quirks of geography loom large in my childhood. In the 1950s the Diocese of Joliet began construction of St. Raymond's Cathedral. The property was three blocks from Oakland Avenue, on the east side of fabled Raynor Avenue. Rumor had it that we were now living on "cathedral property" and therefore land values would go up. (They never did, but our parents had their hopes.) As construction proceeded, the cathedral's bell tower soon came to dominate the visual landscape of the neighborhood. Lutheran or not, I was growing up almost literally in the shadow of the Roman Catholic Church.

The Romans also manned the southern border of the neighborhood. Running for three or four blocks on the southwest side of Plainfield Road was the Franciscan sisters' property. St. Francis Convent was the motherhouse of the Franciscan order of nuns that ran the College of St. Francis and St. Francis Academy (the girls' high school). Both the college and the academy buildings were there as well, and my memories are punctuated with pictures of older girls in blue wool uniforms with white blouses and dark socks walking in giggling groups past my house on the way to school and with the rarer spottings of the nuns themselves, always in parties of two or three, in white wimples and dark brown habits with rosaries dangling from their waists. They moved slowly, serenely, and for the most part silently, usually quickly disappearing behind the brick walls that surrounded the Franciscan property, a place to which I was told I must never, ever go. Ignorant Lutheran that I was, I didn't understand the domestic restrictions under which those women lived. I assumed that arcane rituals went on there that would somehow contaminate me if I got too close. Yet the convent held for me the attraction of the forbidden. Surely, I thought, all those people wouldn't stay there if something *interesting* wasn't going on.

In truth, I was secretly jealous of the St. Francis girls, all dressed alike, none of them standing out, none of them different. The nuns, with their own wonderful "uniforms," were mysterious and a bit terrifying. All of them seemed to be part of some marvelous, secret society from which I was forever banned.

One last powerful influence engendered in me that odd, conflicted sense of both belonging and not belonging on Oakland Avenue. My father bought our first television set about the time I was seven, changing my life forever just as every other American's life would be changed. For me, television strengthened my sense of otherness (as if it needed to be strengthened).

Television showed Americans in the 1950s how we were supposed to live, and life on Oakland Avenue didn't measure up. Mrs. Cleaver wore high heels and pearls to clean her house. Our moms wore tired cotton housedresses and floppy slippers. The dad on *Father Knows Best* didn't make blood sausage in the basement and yell in Slovenian at his family when he'd had too much to drink. Of course, we on Oakland Avenue knew the difference between pretend and reality, but there was always a nagging suspicion at the back of our minds that the people west of Raynor Avenue lived a lot more like the Cleavers than we did. And we all wanted to live west of Raynor.

Television tripped me up another way. Lutherans had all the important things right, of course, and Catholics didn't, but Catholics seemed to have mastered television. Bishop Sheen in his natty black cassock with the red piping got on television, and even my father grudgingly admitted that his talks were "interesting," although he profoundly disapproved of the "JMJ" scrawled at the top of the bishop's blackboard. Rev. Frenk, who was truly majestic and terrible in the pulpit of a Sunday morning, was never on television.

In those days, as now, television producers filled lots of airtime by running old movies, which I absorbed like a sponge, but there were never any Lutherans in the movies either. Movie preachers were either generic wimps like the spineless prig in *High Noon* or Roman priests, and the priests got all the good parts. Bing Crosby and Spencer Tracy never played Lutherans. How come the Catholics got all the starring roles, I wondered. What were we Lutherans, chopped kielbasa? It was disappointing and a little bewildering.

Of course, I could never *say* that. I was proud of my heritage after all. Nearly five hundred years earlier Martin Luther himself had proved that we were right and that Catholics were wrong. Catholics were okay, of course. Most of my friends were Catholic, and while novenas and confessions seemed a little odd to me, I was already enough of a freethinker to wonder if Rev. Frenk wasn't, well, overreacting on the subject. But as a Lutheran, I was beyond that stuff. I didn't need saints' days off, because I didn't pray to saints. I went right to The Top with my requests. I didn't need any pope in Rome to tell me what color skirt to wear to school. To think that Bing and Spence and Bishop Sheen and the St. Francis girls might have something I wanted would have been disloyal.

But the truth was, while life on Oakland Avenue was good and being a Lutheran was the right thing, somehow the life lived west of Raynor Avenue and, I thought, shown on television was what everybody wanted. In terms of religion, Bing and Spence got all the votes. And on Oakland Avenue in the 1950s, at least part of the time, what I wanted more than anything else was to be like everyone else and do what everyone else did.

As time went on, on the surface at least, I succeeded. I left Oakland Avenue and its immigrant mindset behind. I went on to both public and Lutheran colleges, learned to use the right forks at the right time, and to speak the language of the aspiring middle class. I lived through the 1960s and developed a shallow sophistication that allowed me to believe I had outgrown all those early conflicts. I went to church more or less regularly, I told myself, because it was "good" for my daughter and to keep the grandparents happy. It took several more years for me to realize that "passing" in the suburbs was costing me intellectually and emotionally far more than the experience was worth.

By 1985 I was primed, I suppose, for some kind of change. That the instrument of change was a Roman one was, of course, on one level pure chance, on another, the operation of the Holy Spirit. That I was open to the lessons Mundelein had to offer was, I think, a result of recognizing, at least on a subconscious level, that in coming there, I was only three blocks from home. The women of St. Francis had been there all my life. The women of Mundelein couldn't be all that different, and maybe it was time for me to see what lay on the other side of the convent wall.

> *But what went ye out for to see?*
> MATTHEW 11:8

By the time I came to Mundelein in 1985, that secure world of Oakland Avenue in the 1950s was as much gone with the wind as Margaret Mitchell's antebellum South. The 1960s had happened. Vietnam had happened. Vatican II had happened.

In one way, Vatican II was as much a seismic revolution for Protestants as it was for Catholics. The situation was analogous to one of a long-term dysfunctional marriage where one or the other of the couple suddenly reforms. The remaining party doesn't quite know how to respond and may even resent the fact that now he or she is required to reform, too. Those we had thought of as "the enemy" had suddenly changed on us. Our secure vision of "us" and "them" shattered. All those tidy comparisons that had defined my childhood were no longer valid. We were now required to examine our fellow Christians for similarities instead of differences. Our leaders—some of them anyway—suggested that finally it might be time to let go of more than four hundred years' worth of bad feelings. Few people—certainly few laypeople—cared anymore about what had been said at Augsburg or Trent in the 1500s. Most of the Lutheran parish pastors of my acquaintance were relieved to shed the burden of trying to explain to their parishioners why they *should* care. By the 1980s it was possible to do such things as sit in the congregation at Holy Name Cathedral listening to Lutheran Martin Marty preach at a service in celebration of Lutheran-Catholic dialogue. For a Lutheran woman to enroll at Mundelein College in 1985 was barely worthy of notice or comment. Why shouldn't she, after all?

By the time I metaphorically breached the convent wall by enrolling at Mundelein, the Catholic world that had so fascinated and repelled me was gone. I was now part of the club, at least as an auxiliary member, but the club had changed. Most of the nuns had abandoned their habits. Many had abandoned religious life. The Catholic Church, just like its Protestant counterparts, was reevaluating its comfortable, triumphalist view of the world. We were all under siege, from radicals within and, more seriously in my view, from a relentlessly secular culture without. Our new modern understanding of our own faith expressions and one another's was surely better, more reasonable, and more theologically sound, but we were still all wearing it like a new pair of shoes. It didn't quite fit comfortably yet. We had all, perhaps, achieved our childhood goal of moving west of Raynor Avenue, but there was the nagging suspicion abroad that in the move, we had left some important underpinnings behind.

Mundelein itself, I sensed, was struggling with a contradiction that, I suppose, contributed to its eventual demise as an independent institution. To believe that a woman is just as capable of intellectual achievement and professional accomplishment as a man is in some ways, at least, to subscribe to the belief in gender equality. That, in turn, at some point raises the question of the need for a separate educational institution for women.

The college in some respects was a victim of its own success. It had worked itself out of a job. Sister Justitia and her colleagues had dreamed of a school that would provide young Catholic women with the means to make a difference in the world. And that is just what they had done. By the 1980s the term *professional woman* was no longer an oxymoron. Women were far freer to succeed in careers and pursue professions than they had ever been. Ironically, because the wider world was a somewhat easier place for them than it had been for their grandmothers, young women no longer felt the need to segregate themselves to get a fair hearing. It was easier—and certainly more fun—for them to go to school side by side with their brothers. Furthermore, in the ecumenical post–Vatican II world, the need for a religious fortress mentality to keep the vulnerable young from outside influences was clearly not in keeping with the times. Young Catholics could presumably navigate freely among the shoals of both Protestant and secular influences. There may still be a valid, positive answer to the question What are women's colleges for? For the present at least, the answers are not powerful enough to overcome the forces pushing in the other direction.

The other contradiction apparent to me at Mundelein is one endemic at any Christian liberal arts college. Theology is no longer the queen of sciences. A modern liberal education is inevitably in some ways a secular education. Of course, a college can have a department of religion. It can operate on Christian (Catholic or Protestant) values. It can even, to a point, choose faculty to reflect those values. But if it believes in the spirit of free inquiry that is at the heart of a liberal education, matters of faith have to be presented as options, not absolutes. The college may choose not to say that above a whisper. Perhaps in its theology department the suggestion is not even breathed aloud.

But the fact remains, in the modern world, the best a Christian college can present in terms of a faith model is a recommendation, not a mandate. That's a tough place to be for any putative institutional guardian—either Protestant or Catholic—of "the one true faith."

The Master of Liberal Studies program at Mundelein reflected those tensions. It was never overtly "Catholic" or even Christian. It would have been possible to go through the entire program and never have the subject of one's personal religious life come up. One was, of course, free to pursue one's own interests in religious matters as part of the program, and many of us did, but doing so wasn't required. In my own case, I was more interested in testing my limits as a writer, and except for Core III, which explored the notion of myth in relationship to one's personality, the subject of religion was never overtly part of my studies. (Except, of course, that for good, church-obsessed Lutheran girls like me, the subject is never far below the surface.)

Still, there was something very Catholic about the enterprise that went well beyond the obvious. I saw it most clearly in the theme of the program and the core courses. The theme was the survival and quality of life of the planet itself, of civilization, of individual people. The three core courses were The Fate of the Earth and Human Responsibility: Perspectives on the Planet; Between Past and Future: Perspectives on Polity; and Love and Work: Perspectives on Person.

What I hear in that choice are echoes of the Catholic tradition, born out of the admonishment of the letter of James (James 2:17) that faith without works is dead, that faith alone (*sola fide,* the Lutheran mantra) is not enough for salvation. In Catholic tradition, nobody gets a full-ride scholarship. You have to *do* something about it. Correlatively, the core curriculum was pure Mundelein, reflecting the school's mission of making a difference in the community. Finally, and perhaps inevitably, it revealed a large dose of American pragmatism—the unshakable belief that anything can be fixed given the right combination of intelligence, hard work, faith, and optimism. It is a curriculum that a refugee from Oakland Avenue could understand—a potent combination of the faith of one's fathers and the American dream that would propel one west of Raynor Avenue.

However, as a Lutheran, I was—and remain—suspicious. It's not that Protestants in general or Lutherans in particular don't believe in social action or responsible behavior toward our neighbors or our planet, or that we ought not attempt to make the world a better place in the here and now. But the Lutheran take on the matter—and on many others—is a paradoxical one. For us, the issue of ultimate survival is in God's hands and has already been decided. Ultimately, we're doomed. In God's own time the world will end, no matter what we do, and our actions in its aid earn us no credits in the final reckoning. Our own salvation has also already been determined by means of our baptism. The contradiction lies in the fact that, having said that, we are required to live as though what we do matters anyway. We believe that everything depends on God and are called to live as though everything depends on us. That gets us to the same place as our Roman brothers and sisters in terms of action and values, but we come from a different and perhaps less intellectually direct or secure route.

But it was these very underlying contradictions of the MLS program that appealed to me. By the time I became a Mundelein student, I had more or less made my peace with the fact that I would never see the world quite the same way as other people did and that I was fated to never quite feel like I belonged. I had come rather to enjoy the role of outsider and observer. Furthermore, I had moved west of Raynor and discovered it wasn't all it was cracked up to be. It was time to regroup and rethink. As I said at the beginning of this essay, coming to Mundelein was, spiritually and intellectually, coming home.

I think the Christian church, whatever the particular form of faith expression, functions at its best as the minority report. Our job is to speak with a prophetic voice, not only for the widows, orphans, and strangers in our midst but for a value system that runs contrary to that of the dominant culture. We must ask the hard questions, such as What is your life about once you've moved west of Raynor Avenue?

The Mundelein MLS program did the same thing. It presupposed that there is more to education than professional training, that intellectual discourse has goals beyond a better job offer and a passport to consumer heaven. The MLS core theme and curriculum struck these Lutheran ears as a bit triumphalist, a bit full of hubris, a bit touchingly naive, but at its heart, it resonated for me as both theologically and intellectually sound. After all, what does it profit a woman—or a man—if she gains the whole world and loses her soul?

Still, I suppose one has to answer the question, What good was all that? And to answer that question, I would need to ask three more. Did Mundelein change me? Did it make a difference in my life? Have I, because of it, made a difference to anybody beside myself? The answers are no, yes, and I don't know.

In many respects, I came and went through Mundelein oddly untouched. I got good value for my money and effort. I think I gave good value in return. Then I left, still as much observer as participant, outsider looking in. I remain a bred-in-the-bone Lutheran, full of contradictions, both delighting in and hating the intellectual paradoxes endemic to that condition. I remain an emotional outsider. I'm still a prisoner—or perhaps, more accurately, a trustee—of Oakland Avenue, living out a love-hate relationship with life west of Raynor Avenue. At this point, barring divine intervention, that is who I am.

But yes, the MLS experience did make a difference in my life. Beyond providing the very real service of giving me a safe place to regain my emotional bearings and my self-confidence, it gave me another priceless gift. It was at Mundelein that I learned to truly like and respect other women. Here I finally learned to give myself permission to enjoy their company. I had always been jealous of men the same way I was jealous of the St. Francis girls. It seemed they knew secrets I could never know and shared a community to which I could never belong. Yet I was not totally comfortable with women either. In my mind, no matter what we as women did or accomplished, it was tainted by the fact that we were, well, women, and that perception of taint clouded my relationships.

At Mundelein, for whatever reason, I was able to shed my intellectual blinders on this issue. There I learned that women—all women—have interesting stories to tell and gifts to give, that they too can have exciting adventures, blaze trails, dream dreams, and speak important truths. It wasn't that I discovered late the simple truth that girls can do anything if they want to badly enough. What I learned at Mundelein was that liberation for a woman (or a man) comes from finding one's own path and following it, and a woman's path is no less worthy because it's not a man's.

I had always known that women saw the world differently than men. At Mundelein I learned that the different view was a gift, not a defect. I learned to stop blurring my woman's vision to try to make it more like a man's, not in an attempt to understand his point of view, but because of a secret belief that his view was the only valid one. At Mundelein, listening to other women's stories, seeing other women's work, and hearing them speak their minds, I discovered the club to which I did belong.

Why there and then and not years earlier somewhere else? I don't know. God works in mysterious ways, her wonders to perform.

These kinds of epiphanies are all well and good, of course, but Catholics and Lutherans both are required to recognize that life and its meaning are rarely, if ever, just all about us. Did the Mundelein MLS experience, filtered through me, make a difference in the world? Maybe. How would I know if it did? No one has come up to me and said, "You have changed my life" since I graduated. No one ever said that before either. Likewise, I haven't been motivated to start any world-altering projects since my days on Sheridan Road, nor have I written the Great American Novel, painted the Transcendent American Picture, or made the Ultimate American Movie that will influence generations to come.

So what good was it? That may be the wrong question.

Every woman who went through the MLS program, I suspect, went for different reasons. But I think each of us, although we might have each phrased it differently, saw that the question was not what graduate school or the liberal arts were for, but what our jobs were for, and, in the end, what our lives were for. We felt that answering those questions—or at least pursuing answers—in the end made us better at whatever job we did and, perhaps more important, made our lives more meaningful, maybe even made us better people. Or maybe not. Like the attempt to lead a Christian life, the pursuit of the answer may have been the answer in itself.

Ultimately, I'm not sure there's a way to justify a program like Mundelein's MLS—at least not in the eyes of a secular or career and specialization obsessed culture. Such a project is an act of faith, which the writer tells us is the belief in the evidence of things not seen. To my mind, the MLS program was, in theological terms, the nurture of a community that understood the decision to opt for the soul over the world, a very Christian/Catholic/Lutheran exercise that should satisfy the ghosts of Cardinal Mundelein, Sister Justitia—and Rev. Frenk, as well.

Mundelein College Baccalaureate Address, June 9, 1991

Mary Griffin

As I listened to today's scriptural readings a few moments ago, I was keenly aware—as you undoubtedly were—of their rare appropriateness to this important occasion.

The first reading, from the book of Proverbs, is part of the so-called wisdom literature, which flourished throughout the ancient East. According to the Jerusalem Bible, it had no national boundaries and was little affected by religious beliefs. Essentially the wisdom of experience, it offers us a blueprint for successful living and celebrates wisdom as a cultural achievement.

The Greek word for wisdom is *Sophia*—the feminine face of God. And it is one of the ways that Jesus himself imaged God in the New Testament. Thus Proverbs assures us, when we are in wisdom, God is at our side. God will "keep our feet clear for the journey."

> Wisdom, then, is the distillation of experience.
> It is a blueprint for the good life.
> It is an enviable cultural achievement.
> It is a reflection of the feminine face of God.

Thus does Proverbs—across the ages—speak to you, Mundelein's graduates on this day, to students who all of their days on this campus have been in pursuit of wisdom, of Sophia, of the feminine face of God. It exalts and celebrates wisdom as the supreme gift of God.

It is this gift that we—the faculty, administration, and staff—wish for you on this, your long-awaited commencement day.

Having this gift, however, you are admonished by Paul to remember that God gives a variety of gifts "working in all sorts of different ways in different people" but always out of the same Spirit. The epistle is a transparent plea for tolerance and diversity. What Paul writes to the Corinthians is that it is the variousness of creation that displays the reality of God. Thus, you yourselves, 1991 graduates of Mundelein College, are part of this reality. With your splendid range of gifts and graces, of ages and angularities, you are the image of God. You give back beauty to God, "Beauty's self and Beauty's giver."

And, finally, Matthew encourages you to let your variousness, your beauty, your light "shine in the sight of all" so that "seeing your good works, they may give the praise to your God in heaven."

So, Mundelein graduates of 1991, let your light shine out before the world as confident, self-assured, active women that people may marvel and ask, "Who lit this candle? Wherefore burns it so brightly?"

As none who went before you in the sixty years of Mundelein's brief history—there are some six thousand of us, you know—you will bear the special responsibility of telling our story: how once there was a white and shining college on the shores of Chicago's Lake Michigan where everything came together for you as women students. It was a place where you discovered your special gifts and learned not to be afraid to share your special charisma; where you gained knowledge and skills and learned to delight in history, in philosophy, in the arts, sciences, and mathematics; but most of all, where you learned how to live, how to create, how to celebrate. It was a place where you forged friendships with hoops of steel, where you worked and grew and readied yourself to let your special light shine out.

For this commencement at Mundelein is different from all other commencements in our history. It is at once, for all of us—women and men, students, staff, administrators—a beginning and an end. Indeed, all beginnings have their endings. Though few of us are privileged to see both edges of the spectrum! Nor do we ordinarily wish to. As Woody Allen put it, "I'm not afraid of death. I just don't want to be there when it happens!"

We today don't have that choice. We're all in at the end—a word resonant with sadness. Yet it is fringed with gladness, too. As it is clouded with mystery.

In one of his last poems, "East Coker" (named for the village where his family had its origins in England), T. S. Eliot wrote poignantly of the sense of an ending. The *Four Quartets* philosophizes about perennial human themes—about time and the past and about how both are perhaps present in time future. And time future contained in time past.

"If all time is eternally present," Eliot wrote,

All time is irredeemable
What might have been is an abstraction
Remaining a perpetual possibility
Only in a world of speculation.
What might have been and what has been
Point to one end, which is always present.

Footfalls echo in the memory
Down the passage which we did not take
Toward the door we never opened
Into the rose garden. My words echo
Thus, in your mind.

— FROM "BURNT NORTON"

In my beginning is my end. In succession
Houses rise and fall, crumble, are extended,
Are removed, destroyed, restored, or in their place
Is an open field, or a factory, or a bypass.
Old stone to new building, old timber to new fires,
Old fires to ashes, and ashes to the earth . . .
The houses are all gone under the sea.
The dancers are all gone under the hill.

—FROM "EAST COKER"

And yet—

What we call the beginning is often the end
And to make an end is to make a beginning.
The end is where we start from.

—FROM "LITTLE GIDDING"

In my end is my beginning.

So with you, graduates of Mundelein College of 1991. Today, we make an end of this college and its traditions as we have known and helped to shape them. We look back over the sixty years of our history and call to memory those who built the college, those who taught here, those who learned and grew here. And in their shadowy ranks we discover many a familiar, many a loved countenance.

I think of the base communities I visited in Nicaragua and how vividly they brought their absent members into their midst with a communal ritual in which each name of a fallen hero or heroine is read aloud and the congregation calls out, "Presenté!"—"Be present!" And one feels the company spiritually enlarge as each absent one responds to that call.

So, today, let us call out:

Sister Mary Justitia Coffey and the first little band of B.V.M.'s—"Presenté!"

Class of 1931—"Presenté!"
Students of the 1930s and 1940s—"Presenté!"
Students of the 1950s—"Presenté!"
Students of the 1960s—"Presenté!"
Students of the 1970s—"Presenté!"
Students of the 1980s and the 1990s—"Presenté!"

All past and present presidents, deans, faculty, staff, board members, and benefactors—"PRESENTÉ"!

Now, in this vastly enlarged spiritual assembly, together let us ponder the true gift of wisdom we have all received—to know that the past is but prologue to the future, that "the end is where we start from"!

Mundelein College will not cease to be. With all of its rich history and traditions it will but undergo a sea change—emerging as Mundelein College of Loyola University Chicago. It will continue to have a special concern for women—their needs, their hopes, their magnificent possibilities. It will bring to its mission new energies, new resources, and the backing of a major university. And to that university it will bring new talents, new perspectives, and a transforming vitality! Who knows—this affiliation of Mundelein and Loyola may prove to be a marriage made in Heaven!

Loyola may have thought it was acquiring a splendid piece of lakeside property along with a clutch of distinguished professors and scores of avid students. What it is really taking on is a vast spiritual assemblage with a dangerous memory. The memory of a college where women know what it is to be equal. And those of us affiliating with Loyola aren't likely to settle for less! Part of your job—graduates of 1991—is to keep alive that dangerous memory.

As we contemplate this hope-filled future, then, let us once more call to mind what we heard in Proverbs this morning and hear it again for the first time.

Wisdom is the distillation of experience.
Wisdom is a blueprint for the good life.
Wisdom is an enviable cultural achievement.
Wisdom is a reflection of the feminine face of God.

May you—may Mundelein College of Loyola University Chicago—be blessed with wisdom as together we make an end—and a new beginning. May it be a bright, bright future filled with promise! May it be yours!

Afterword

Ann Harrington asked whether I might suggest an editor to give a final review to this collection of Mundelein essays. A former professor of mine at Mundelein, Ann and I are now colleagues at Loyola University Chicago. Rather than offer a referral, I volunteered as editor, telling Ann that I knew I'd want to read the book anyway, and this assignment would give me a head start. A few days later, a large, heavy envelope arrived at my office at Loyola, where I am executive director of marketing communications and university publications. The irony wasn't lost on me—here I am at Loyola, which more than twenty years ago I dismissed as "just a neighbor" to my college. Today, it's my employer as well as the home to a "new" Mundelein College for adult learning. In any case, after reading the essays, I sent back to Ann my written comments and suggestions, along with the following brief reflection. More than the chance to share my small memory of making my way to Mundelein, may it represent a tribute from a grateful alumna to the inspiring and thoughtful words of every author.

By happenstance, my kitchen table became project central, mostly because, during our recent spell of summerlike weather this March, it served as a prime location to enjoy some splendid reading, along with warm breezes coming in through my back door. I picked this spot only because on the Friday I lugged home your bulky envelope of essays, the table was a convenient spot to drop it, along with the day's mail and newspapers. I had finished a long week and was relieved to be at home—and away from all things related to higher education. Starting on the essays, I figured, could safely wait until Saturday or Sunday. But I confess I was more than a little curious, so I opened the envelope round about 10:00 P.M. just to scan the essays and get a feel for the work ahead. The next thing I knew it was 1:00 A.M., and it was tired eyes, certainly not disinterest, that made me stop.

Over the following days, I read how Mundelein not only started and grew and changed, but also how it dared, defied, and dominated, and how much it was valued, passionately albeit differently, by each writer, decade after decade. I thought I knew quite a bit about Mundelein but quickly learned so much more, especially just how extraordinary my luck had been to have found myself part of that uncommon experience.

My luck in finding Mundelein went like this. The mandate issued by my parents (who agreed to foot a good deal of my college costs) was that

I attend a Catholic women's college, preferably in the Midwest. It didn't matter where, though secretly they hoped one just might be found a block or two from our home. I was told to "just pick the one you want," so long as it met the all-women, all-Catholic parameters that fulfilled my mother's once-fixed-never-to-be-budged notion of what was a "suitable" environment for me. Bound by that dictum, I wrote away to what seemed to be a hundred or so women's colleges of the St. Mary of Somewhere variety. *Go to South Bend? Where was Terre Haute? Actually live in rural nowhere, surrounded by trees—and miles from civilization? I'd be across the road from Notre Dame—that was a plus?* I had been living for the day I went off to college, and now it seemed that all my so-called options pointed to some rural charm school/cloister.

Things looked bleak until my mother and I went to a college fair at my high school. Up one aisle, down another, until we neared a table and the recruiter literally leapt around it to pump my hand: "Hi, I'm Dot Franklin! I'd like to tell you about Mundelein College in Chicago." Well, Dot had me right that moment—she was dynamic and enthusiastic, and she *just knew* I belonged at Mundelein. I not only liked her, I wanted to *be* like her, and I figured that just might happen if I went to that school. And you can just bet that hearing about a campus on the lake *in the city*—with nary a mention of trees or woods—was the clincher. I believe all the Mary Somewhere applications got chucked that very evening. And from that day til now, I've never had a moment's doubt nor regret about choosing Mundelein—or, thanks to Dot, having it choose me.

With all that in mind, it should be no surprise that I was thrilled to read these essays. And I'm dead certain that every other alum of what we Loyolans now call "classic" Mundelein will feel the same extraordinary pride. Thank you to the editors and to every author for making this happen—and for re-creating, around my kitchen table, the exceptional world and remarkable legacy that I was so privileged to experience. Along with affirming what so many of us knew and loved firsthand, I hope many, many others will read this book and be introduced to what was a singular and all-too-brief phenomenon. And I'm glad that by seizing the chance to review this rich and thoughtful collection, I had the chance to be part of it all again.

Mary Nowesnick
April 2000

CONTRIBUTORS

Nancy Bartels. B.A., English and history, Augustana College, Rock Island, IL.; MLS, Mundelein College, 1990. Current position: managing editor, *Software Strategies* magazine, Putman Publishing Co., Itasca, IL. Nancy is addicted to reading, especially mystery fiction and occasional history, biography, and theology. On the days when she believes in reincarnation, she wants to come back as either Dorothy L. Sayers, Annie Dillard, or Irene Adler.

David Block. B.A., liberal arts, Mundelein College, 1990, through the Weekend College. Dave was flattered to be able to participate in this project and he is grateful to Mundelein for staying open on weekends. Currently, he is president of Nu-Dell Manufacturing, Inc.

Gloria Callaci. B.A., psychology, Mundelein College, 1961. Assistant to the academic dean, 1961–64; president of the Alumnae Association 1989–93. Gloria has received two Emmy Awards and the American Medical Association's highest award for television documentaries on death and dying (PBS) and breast cancer (CBS). Currently, she is a freelance media producer and writer.

Joan Frances Crowley, B.V.M. M.A., history, Marquette University. Faculty, European and Russian history, Mundelein College, 1962–91. Faculty, Loyola University Chicago 1991–98. She coauthored *Lenin to Gorbachev: Three Generations of Soviet Communists*. In 1988 she won the Sears Foundation and Associated Colleges of Illinois Award for Teaching Excellence and Campus Leadership. Her current position is senior professor of history, retired.

Mary DeCock, B.V.M. B.A., sociology, Clarke College, 1944; M.A., English and journalism, Marquette University, 1955; M.A., social ethics, University of Chicago, 1971. Professor emerita at Loyola University Chicago. Some Mundelein alumnae will remember Mary as Sister Mary Donatus, teacher of English and journalism (1955–66), advisor to the *Skyscraper* staff (1955–64), or administrator in public relations (1957–66). On leave from 1967–74, she doubled as a graduate student and as a regional representative for the Chicago-area B.V.M.'s. In 1974 she joined the faculty of the Graduate Program in Religious Studies, became one of the "founding mothers" and faculty of the Weekend College, the Women's Studies program, and the Master of Liberal Studies Program. In 1991 she was affiliated with Loyola University's Department of Theology for which she is still a senior professor in religious and women's studies.

Carolyn Farrell, B.V.M. B.A., history, Clarke College, 1966; M.S.E., education administration, University of Western Illinois, 1971. She also did postgraduate work in higher education administration at the University of Iowa, 1976, and completed the leadership program at the Hubert Humphrey Institute for Public Affairs, 1988–89. Among her many experiences, she served as director of continuing education at Clarke College from 1974 to 1988, and as mayor of Dubuque in 1980. From February to June 1991, Carolyn served as interim president of Mundelein College. After the affiliation with Loyola

University Chicago, she became an associate vice president at Loyola and monitored the five-year implementation of the memorandum of agreement signed between the two institutions. Since 1996, she has also served as director of the Ann Ida Gannon, B.V.M., Center for Women and Leadership at Loyola, while functioning as the liaison with the Mundelein College Alumnae Association.

Michael Fortune. B.S., University of Wisconsin; M.A., University of Minnesota; Ph.D., University of Wisconsin. Former professor of English and religious studies at Mundelein College, he is presently writing and teaching part-time. He is involved in the Emeritus Connection, through Mundelein College of Loyola University Chicago, as a professor emeritus.

Elizabeth Fraterrigo. B.A., history, University of Illinois at Urbana-Champaign, 1993; M.A. public history, Loyola University Chicago, 1999. Elizabeth's interview with David Orr originated from a Loyola University Chicago graduate oral-history class project to collect the oral histories of former Mundelein faculty and administrators. Currently, Elizabeth is a Loyola University Chicago teaching fellow and is working on her dissertation in American history.

Blanche Marie Gallagher, B.V.M. B.A., art, Mundelein College, 1944; M.F.A., Catholic University of America. She returned to Mundelein College in 1955 and served as teacher and chairperson (for fourteen years) in the art department and as a professor in both the Master of Arts in Religious Studies and the Master of Arts in Liberal Studies degree programs. When Mundelein affiliated with Loyola University Chicago, she joined the faculty of the Institute of Pastoral Studies. As a professor emerita at IPS, she paints, writes about art and spirituality, and is currently teaching graduate courses. In addition to lecturing, serving as a spiritual mentor, and publishing a book on Teilhard de Chardin (*Meditations with Teilhard de Chardin*, Bear, 1988), she has traveled in North America, Asia, and Europe, studying the relationship between spirituality and art.

Jane Malkemus Goodnow. B.A., English and theater, Mundelein College, 1937. After receiving a *Diplome de Langue* from L'Alliance Francaise in Paris in 1963, she was qualified to teach French as well as English at the secondary level. She taught in Milwaukee and in Austin, Texas. After retirement she has continued teaching French with the Lifetime Learning Institute.

Mary Griffin (aka Agnes Griffin, class of '39; Sister Mary Ignatia, B.V.M., 1940–66). B.M.E., music education, Mundelein College 1939; B.A., English literature, 1947, and M.A., English literature, 1950, Catholic University of America; Ph.D. English literature, Fordham University, 1961. Assistant professor of English, 1954–57; academic dean, 1961–68; professor of English, 1969–70, 1973–91. In 1986 the American Association for Higher Education recognized Mary Griffin's long and distinctive academic career by naming her one of the top twenty educational leaders among college and university faculty. She initiated and/or supported a series of academic innovations at Mundelein: Basic Studies and The Early Bird Program (1960s); Weekend College and the Women's Studies Program (1970s); Master of Liberal Studies (1980s). Mary's retirement career as senior professor at Loyola University Chicago and member of the steering committee for this Mundelein College History Project was interrupted by her sudden death in 1998. "Reinventing Mundelein: Birthing the Weekend College" is the unfinished first draft of Mary's memoir that was written for this volume.

Ann M. Harrington, B.V.M. B.A., French, Mundelein College, 1962; M.A., Asian studies, Washington University, 1967; Ph.D., modern Japanese and Chinese history, Claremont Graduate University, 1977; M.A., French, University of Illinois-Chicago, 1986. After teaching high school in Wichita, Kansas, and St. Louis, Missouri, she returned to Mundelein College in 1969 to teach French and, eventually, Japanese and Chinese history. She served as chair of the history department from 1980–90. The author of *Japan's Hidden Christians* (1993), her current research explores the work of the first Roman Catholic women religious missionaries in Japan, who were of French origin. Currently, she is an associate professor of history at Loyola University Chicago.

Norbert Hruby. Ph.B., M.A., Ph.D., English, Loyola University Chicago. Honorary doctorates from Aquinas College (MI); Hope College; and Kendall College.Vice president, Mundelein College, 1962–69. Since retirement in 1986 he has written twenty-six plays, five of which have been performed, the most recent entitled *Peggy: The Life and Times of Mrs. Benedict Arnold* at the Gerald R. Ford Museum, Grand Rapids, Michigan, in March . 2000. He serves on the boards of the Catholic Human Development Outreach (Grand Rapids diocese) and Grand Rapids Area Council on the Humanities. Currently president emeritus, Aquinas College, Grand Rapids, Michigan.

Carol Frances Jegen, B.V.M. B.S., history, St. Louis University; M.A., theology, Marquette University; Ph.D., religious studies, Marquette University. Faculty and administration, Mundelein College, 1957–91. Administrative services included chairperson of the theology department; director of the Graduate Program in Religious Studies; chairperson of peace studies; initiator of the Hispanic Institute and of the Mundelein Center for Religious Education, currently housed in the Archdiocesan Office of Catechesis as the Jegen Center for Catechetical Media and Research. Current position: senior professor emerita at the Institute of Pastoral Studies at Loyola University Chicago.

Marianne Littau. B.S., mathematics, Mundelein College, 1964. M.S.; Illinois Institute of Technology, 1972. MBA, with a concentration in finance, 1985, University of Chicago. At Mundelein, Marianne taught mathematics and served as director of the continuing education program. After leaving the B.V.M.'s, Marianne worked in various finance positions at Ameritech, retiring in 1999 as vice president of operations, Ameritech Capital Services. She counts Mundelein as one of her most significant and constant life forces. She is grateful for all she learned from the hundreds of Mundelein continuing education students— in particular an eagerness to accept new challenges and an openness to new experiences, regardless of age.

Mercedes McCambridge. B.A., theatre, Mundelein College, 1937. Though popularly known for receiving an Oscar in her Hollywood debut (*All the Kings Men,* 1949), her professional career embraces radio, moving pictures, and theater. Radio performances include, among others, *I Love a Mystery, Studio One, Inner Sanctum,* and membership in Orson Welles' Mercury Players. She has made twenty moving pictures, including *Giant* (Oscar nomination), *A Touch of Evil, Johnny Guitar,* and *The Exorcist.* Theater performances include *The Glass Menagerie, Who's Afraid of Virginia Woolf, Agnes of God,* and *Lost in Yonkers.* Recipient of a number of honorary degrees, including one from Mundelein College in 1984, she also penned an autobiography, *The Quality of Mercy* (1981), and has lectured extensively on college campuses.

Prudence A. Moylan. B.A., Mundelein College, 1963; M.A., history, Stanford University, 1966; Ph.D., modern British history, University of Illinois at Urbana-Champaign, 1975. A Mundelein College faculty member from 1964, she is a professor of history at Loyola University Chicago. Currently, she is developing a new course on peace history and researching the relationship between gender and peace in modern Britain. Her research on the Skyscraper building for this book ignited her interest in studying the gendered uses of space.

Mary Nowesnick. B.A., English literature, Mundelein College, 1974. As a Rotary Scholar, she also earned a graduate certificate in linguistics in 1977 from Cambridge University, England. Among her many activities before joining Loyola University Chicago, Mary was vice president and editor-in-chief of the *Savings Institutions Magazine,* the national publication for the former U.S. League of Savings Institutions, now America's Community Bankers. She is also a past national president of the Society of National Association Publications (SNAP), and currently serves as an editorial adviser to *Psychiatric News*, published by the American Psychiatric Association. At Loyola University Chicago since November 1993, Mary is executive director of marketing communications and university publications. In addition, Mary created and continues to manage the university's first in-house advertising agency, as well as Loyola's first internal unit dedicated to marketing communications.

David Orr. B.A., history, Simpson College, 1966; M.A., American studies, Case Western Reserve, 1968; doctoral courses, University of Illinois at Chicago. Associate professor of history, Mundelein College, 1969–79. Former alderman, Forty-ninth Ward, Chicago, Illinois. Currently he is clerk of Cook County, Illinois. David still enjoys the "good fight" for progressive politics in Cook County and relishes being a dad with four children ranging in age from fifteen to four. He likes to hear from faculty friends and students from the Mundelein days.

Stephen A. Schmidt. Ed.D., Columbia-Union Seminary, New York, N.Y. Professor religious studies, 1976–91, Mundelein College; professor of pastoral studies, Institute of Pastoral Studies, Loyola University Chicago. His teaching areas include religious education, practical theology and theologies of suffering, and pastoral care. Currently, he is professor emeritus, pastoral studies.

Tomi Shimojima. B.A., philosophy, Loyola University Chicago, 1994. Mundelein College gave her the opportunity to fulfill a lifelong goal when, at age sixty-seven, she enrolled as an undergraduate student in its Weekend College. Receiving her degree at age seventy-four was a dream come true, but the real gift came in the excitement of learning. She is currently retired.

Mary Alma Sullivan, B.V.M. B.A., English, Mundelein College, 1951; M.A., English, Loyola University Chicago, 1965; M.A., speech (radio, film, and television), Northwestern University, 1971. Following her entrance into the Sisters of Charity of the Blessed Virgin Mary in 1953, she was assigned to teach English and journalism in secondary schools staffed by the B.V.M. congregation. In 1972 she joined the Mundelein College faculty in the Department of English (later English-communication) and served as chairperson of the Department of Communications. She joined the faculty of the Department of Communication at Loyola University Chicago in 1991 when Mundelein affiliated with the university. She retired and was appointed professor emerita in 1995. Currently she maintains a modest desktop-publishing business, researches family history, paints, and tends a garden.

MUNDELEIN COLLEGE TIMELINE

1929 November 1. Ground breaking on Skyscraper on ninety-sixth anniversary of founding of Sisters of Charity of the Blessed Virgin Mary (B.V.M.'s)

1930 September 29. First academic year begins with 378 students

1931 June 3. College dedication ceremony, Cardinal George Mundelein, presiding

1932 June 13. First commencement

1934 Laetare players, the drama club, begins weekly radio broadcasts

1936 Kappa Gamma Pi chapter of National Honor Society of Catholic Women established; National Broadcasting Company (NBC) buys broadcast rights to Mundelein verse speaking choir

1937 Home-economics program for Rogers Park women begun

1938 College becomes member of Association of American Colleges

1939 College fully accredited by North Central Association of Colleges

1940 *Skyscraper* and *Mundelein College Review* student publications receive All-American ratings by Catholic Press Association; Virginia Woods, class of '35, first graduate to earn Ph.D.

1941 College hosts Midwest unit of Catholic Association for International Peace, chaired by historian Augustina Morris, B.V.M.

1942 College offers its facilities to Admiral John Downes, Great Lakes Commander; Honore O'Brien, class of '37, cited for war effort, perfecting inexpensive food preservation; Justitia Coffey, B.V.M., appointed to Educators Division, Illinois State Council of War

1943 Mary Agnes Tynan Schroeder, class of '35, publishes *Catholics Meet the Mike,* first book by a Mundelein graduate; survey shows 56 percent of students involved in war work

1944 B.V.M. faculty hold planning session on "Immediate and future problems of Liberal Arts Colleges as they exist at Mundelein"; Student Council formed

1945 Loyola University withdraws faculty from service at Mundelein due to postwar enrollment growth at Loyola

1946 College is first to sponsor a five-day Institute for the Study of the United Nations Charter, which is broadcast on NBC

1947 First tuition increase from $75 to $100 per semester; Magnificat medal created to honor women leaders; first Magnificat medal awarded to Mrs. Henry Mannix, president of the National Council of Catholic Women

1949 Magnificat medal awarded to Mary Blake Finan

1950   Mary Blake Finan Award created for senior most distinguished for loyalty and service to the college; Mercedes McCambridge, class of '37, wins Oscar for best female supporting role

1952   Speech Clinic opens with twenty-five children enrolled; college joins twenty-eight private colleges in a cooperative venture to seek financial support from industry; Fathers Club formed to launch $100,000 fund drive

1954   College offers extension courses in Des Moines, Iowa, and Glendale, California

1955   College Silver Jubilee: Cardinal Stritch pays tribute to B.V.M.'s; Ford Foundation grant for $171,701 allocated for faculty salary increases

1956   College introduces Saturday courses for teachers

1957   College chosen by National Science Foundation as one of eighteen colleges to give in-service institutes for secondary school science teachers

1958   President's Council formed by Ann Ida Gannon, B.V.M.; plans announced for a new dormitory to be named Coffey Hall; night classes introduced

1962   Norbert Hruby plans and directs the Institutional Analysis for development of the college

1964   Degree Completion Program for women returning to college established; students and faculty participate in Selma march for civil rights

1967   Lay board of trustees established

1968   Graduate Program in Religious Studies introduced, first in Chicago area

1969   Learning Resource Center opens; students organize teach-ins on the Vietnam War; HICA program established to prepare students for inner-city teaching

1970   Mundelein Center for Religious Education (MCRE) established to provide catechetical resources for parishes; Con-Cur (Conference on Curriculum) includes administrators, faculty, students, alumnae, and trustees

1972   Laboratory kindergarten and preschool opened

1974   Lilly Grant for faculty development awarded; Weekend College in Residence created; Women's Management Program introduced

1975   Bilingual, Bicultural Studies Program established with government grants; Susan Rink, B.V.M., appointed president of the college; under Susan Rink, B.V.M., as president (1975–83), college receives Title III grants

1976   Crown Learning Center established for learning assistance to students

1978   Faculty Association formed

1980   Golden Jubilee; Skyscraper listed on National Register of Historic Places

1983   Master of Arts in Liberal Studies introduced in Weekend College

1984   Women's Network formed by alumnae

1985   Chicago Jewish-Catholic celebration of *Nostsra in Aetate* (*Declaration on the Relationship of the Church to Non-Christian Religions*) at college; college listed as "a pacesetter in education" in *U.S. News and World Report* survey "America's Best Colleges"

1989   Peace studies minor introduced

1990   Center for Women and Peace established with John D. and Catherine T. MacArthur grant for $100,000; Black Studies Mentor Program established

1991   June 10, affiliation agreement with Loyola University Chicago completed

INDEX

Fury, Maureen Patrice, 111

Gaertner, Virginia, 61
Gallagher, Mary Blanche Marie, 77, *88,* 109, 264
"Life Flows through the Dream," 75–91
Gambonini, Bette, 134
Gannon, Mary Ann Ida, x, 85, 106, 107, 110, 122 n. 33, 137–138, 142 n. 8, 147, 154, 155, 172, 181, *181,* 182, 183, 199, 204, 209 n. 4, 224, 226, 227
Gannon Center for Women and Leadership, x, 38
Garcia, Maria de los Angeles, 114
Geary, Mary Ann Margaret, 16
Geisler, Mary Sylvester, 11, 12
Gender, 241–243, 266–267, 270–271, 280
    bias and, 230–232
    space and, 41–44
George, Francis, 112
Geraghty, Margaret, 140
Gianopoulos, Peter, 44
Gleason, Marian Dwyer, 95
Glee Club, 18
Gleeson, Theresa, 132
Goetemann, Gordon, 85
Goldstein, Jeanne Pennie, 95
Goodnow, Jane Malkemus, "Memories of Mundelein, 1933–1937," 55–67
Gould, Mary Francine, 11, 12, 17
Gourlay, Helen, 143 n. 23
Graduate religious studies program. *See* Religious studies department
Graham, Mary Anne Leone, 132
Gramza, Anthony, 121 n. 30, 256, 264
Griffin, Mary Ignatia (Mary Griffin), 37, 50 n. 28, 65, 66, 88, 122 n. 33, 136, 138, 144–152, 153–154, *181,* 188, 192, 196, 200, 209 n. 4, *217,* 226, 235, 255, 256, 259, 264
    "Mundelein College Baccalaureate Address, June 9, 1991," 282–285
    "Reinventing Mundelein: Birthing the Weekend College, 1974," 215–224
Griffith, Sally Holland, 143 n. 24
Grill, Joseph, 77

Habits, 83, 139
    secular dress and, 185
Haley, Mary Pat, 122 n. 33
Halsey Stuart Bond House, 9
Haring, Bernard, 108
Harrington, Ann M., 30, 214, 286
    "A Class Apart: B.V.M. Sister Students at Mundelein College, 1957–1971," 123–143
Hart, Mary Adorita, 126
Harvey, Mary Jane, 77
Haslwanter, Jane, 111–112
Hassenger, Robert, 183–184, 186